SIDELINES
Selected Prose

Michael Longley

SIDELINES
Selected Prose
1962–2015

ENITHARMON PRESS

Enitharmon Friends Patrons:
Colin Beer, Sean O'Connor, Masa Ohtake

First published in 2017
by Enitharmon Press
10 Bury Place
London WC1A 2JL
www.enitharmon.co.uk

Distributed in the UK by
Central Books
50 Freshwater Road
Chadwell Heath, RM8 1RX

Distributed in the USA and Canada
by Independent Publishers Group
814 North Franklin Street
Chicago, IL 60610
USA
www.ipgbooks.com

ISBN: 978-1-911253-29-7 (hardback)
ISBN: 978-1-911253-35-8 (signed limited edition of 35 copies)

Enitharmon Editions Ltd (incorporating Enitharmon Press) is grateful
for an award through the Small Grants Programme of the Arts Council
of Northern Ireland, which has facilitated publication of this title.

British Library Cataloguing-in-Publication Data.
A catalogue record for this book is available
from the British Library.

Designed in Albertina by Libanus Press
and printed in Wales by
Gomer Press

The lines of print are always sidelines
And all our games funeral games.

– Louis MacNeice, 'Sports Page'

For Fran Brearton

CONTENTS

ACKNOWLEDGEMENTS

I am deeply indebted to Stephen Stuart-Smith for suggesting that Enitharmon should publish *Sidelines*, and for all his work on the book. I am also deeply indebted to Fran Brearton and Edna Longley for their editorial help. The archival researches of Jody Allen Randolph and Richard Rankin Russell have been invaluable.

'W. R. Rodgers' was first published as the Introduction to W. R. Rodgers, *Selected Poems* (Gallery Press, 1993); 'Robert Graves' as the Introduction to Robert Graves, *Selected Poems* (Faber and Faber, 2013); 'Frank Ormsby' as the Introduction to Frank Ormsby, *Goat's Milk: New and Selected Poems* (Bloodaxe Books, 2015). 'A Jovial Hullabaloo' was published by Enitharmon Press (2008); and, together with 'One Wide Expanse' and 'The West', in *One Wide Expanse* (Ireland Chair of Poetry & University College Dublin Press, 2015).

I am grateful for permission to quote copyright material. Douglas Dunn's 'The Friendship of Young Poets', from *New Selected Poems* (2003), is reprinted by permission of Faber and Faber Ltd. Excerpts from poems by Seamus Heaney, from *Death of a Naturalist* (1966), are reprinted by permission of Faber and Faber Ltd and Farrar, Straus and Giroux, LLC. An excerpt from Paul Durcan's 'The Seal of Burrishoole', from *The Laughter of Mothers* (Harvill Secker, 2007), is reprinted by permission of Penguin Random House UK. An excerpt from Ted Hughes's 'The Bull Moses', from *Collected Poems* (2003), is reprinted by permission of Faber and Faber Ltd and Farrar, Straus and Giroux, LLC. Poems and excerpts from poems by Patrick Kavanagh, from *Collected Poems* edited by Antoinette Quinn (Allen Lane, 2004), are reprinted by permission of the Trustees of the Estate of the late Katherine B. Kavanagh, through the Jonathan Williams Literary Agency. The excerpt from Philip Larkin's 'Wedding-Wind', from *The Complete Poems* (2012), is reprinted by permission of Faber and Faber Ltd and Farrar, Straus and Giroux, LLC. Excerpts from poems by Louis MacNeice are reprinted by permission of David Higham Associates. Excerpts from poems by Derek Mahon are reprinted by permission of the author and of Gallery Press Ltd. 'A High-Toned Old Christian Woman' from *The Collected Poems of Wallace Stevens* (copyright © 1954 by Wallace Stevens and renewed 1982 by Holly Stevens) is reprinted by permission of Alfred A. Knopf, an imprint of the Knopf Doubleday Publishing Group, a division of Penguin Random House, LLC; and by permission of Faber and Faber Ltd. James Schuyler's 'Sleep', is reprinted from *Collected Poems* by James Schuyler (copyright © 1993 by the Estate of James Schuyler) by permission of Farrar, Straus and Giroux, LLC. Gary Snyder's 'How Poetry Comes to Me' is reprinted from *No Nature* (copyright © 1992) by permission of Pantheon Books, an imprint of the Knopf Doubleday Publishing Group, a division of Penguin Random House, LLC. Poems and excerpts from poems by Ruth Stone are reprinted from *What Love Comes To: New and Selected Poems* (copyright © 2008 by Ruth Stone) by permission of The Permissions Company, Inc. on behalf of Copper Canyon Press; and by permission of Bloodaxe Books.Poems and excerpts from poems by James Wright are reprinted from *Collected Poems* (copyright © Anne Wright) by permission of Farrar, Straus and Giroux, LLC and University Press of New England.

PREFACE

Over the years poetry has generated most of my prose – reviews, essays, introductions, interviews. Very occasionally I have tried to write about painting and music, partly because I relish the company of painters and visiting their studios, and partly because listening to music is central to my daily life. I begin this selection with 'Tuppenny Stung', a memoir which Mick Imlah commissioned in 1985 when he was an outstanding editor of *Poetry Review*. It explores the complications of being born in Belfast of English parents and growing up in a divided society. Autobiography is not necessarily self-centred or self-important: it is about other people. An element of memoir surfaces throughout *Sidelines*, especially in the three interviews I have placed at the end of the book.

There were some adventurous, big-hearted editors around when I first began to publish in the early 1960s: John Jordan of *Poetry Ireland* who wrote thoughtfully and at length on rejection slips; David Marcus who every week devoted a whole page of the now-defunct *Irish Press* to new writing; and Terence de Vere White, the patrician literary editor of the *Irish Times*, who, with only a single Saturday page at his disposal, found room for my often opinionated poetry column. Timothy Brownlow and Rivers Carew accommodated more leisurely undertakings in the resuscitated *Dublin Magazine*. Later, in the North, James Simmons challenged everyone to join him in the scruffy pages of the *Honest Ulsterman* which he billed as 'Handbook for a Revolution'.

Shortly after joining the Arts Council of Northern Ireland in 1970, I initiated the programme for literature. With the help of a well-informed committee I would now be dispensing a modest budget to local writers and literary organisations. It seemed right, therefore, that I should keep my opinions to myself and cease expatiating on the contemporary poetic scene. Nevertheless, my new job compelled me to think about poetry and the arts in relation to Northern Ireland and the worsening political situation. In 1971 I edited for the Council a survey of the arts in Ulster: *Causeway*. By then our tawdry little civil war was underway. We had begun talking about the 'Troubles'. I include here part of my Introduction to *Causeway*. I stand by what I wrote all those years ago. Even after decades of mayhem, I would not choose to modify my tone or judgements.

For *Causeway* I also contributed the chapter on 'Poetry'. It was exciting to discuss the early work of Seamus Heaney and Derek Mahon in light of the achievements of Louis MacNeice and John Hewitt. And I placed a bet on the very young Paul Muldoon. I include this chapter as a sort of prelude to my longer essays and forewords, written to advocate poets I admire. Some poets who appear in *Sidelines* I first read as an undergraduate in Dublin: MacNeice, Robert Graves, John Montague, Richard Murphy, Philip Larkin, Patrick Kavanagh. In the sixties I was also reading (and sometimes reviewing) American poets such as the great virtuoso Richard Wilbur. More recently, I discovered James Wright and Ruth Stone, who deserve to be much better known on this side of the Atlantic. From the Scottish *avant garde* I single out Ian Hamilton Finlay, whose experiments simply delight me. And I am proud to include in these pages reviews of two brilliant début collections: Heaney's *Death of a Naturalist* and Mahon's *Night-Crossing*.

I am neither an academic nor an academic critic. Nevertheless, as early as 1962, when still a student, I was tempted to jump into the deep end with a paper on the love elegies of Sextus Propertius, delivered to the Trinity College Classical Society. Its formal analyses anticipated life-long obsessions. In 2008, forty-six years later, I returned, as Ireland

Professor of Poetry, to the Classics with a lecture called 'One Wide Expanse'. I met up again with Propertius, but concentrated on Ovid's *Metamorphoses* and, most intensely, the *Iliad* and the *Odyssey*. I was searching for Greek and Latin perspectives on contemporary poetry, and assessing the enfeebling effect of their decline as academic subjects. The lecture also marked a return to Trinity, and that mattered to me. I gave two other lectures as Ireland Professor: one at Queen's University Belfast, 'A Jovial Hullabaloo', a celebration of poetry's enrichments; the other at University College Dublin, 'The West', in which I examined the huge influence of Ireland's western seaboard on my imagination.

Over a long career I have probably given too many interviews. (How many interviews did George Herbert give?) It's tempting to emerge from studious solitude to talk to a sympathetic listener about oneself. In the hope that they might add up to some kind of composite portrait, I have chosen three interviews – Robert Johnstone's in the *Honest Ulsterman* from 1985, Peter McDonald's in *Thumbscrew* from 1998, and Jody Allen Randolph's in the *Colby Quarterly* from 2003. Here, as throughout *Sidelines*, I have avoided making changes beyond rectifying small errors and cutting repetitions (except where a cut would damage the sense). I have tried to refrain from tinkering. I want to remain true to my earlier selves. For me the writing of prose and the writing of poetry have always been interwoven. They are difficult in different ways. In a letter to Dorothy Wellesley, Yeats writes: 'The correction of prose, because it has no fixed laws, is endless, a poem comes right with a click like a closing box.'

M. L.

PART 1

MEMOIR

TUPPENNY STUNG

I

I began by loving the wrong woman.

In 1936, when she was seventeen, Lena came from County Fermanagh to work for my parents as a maid. At approximately 4 p.m. on 27
July 1939 I was born, followed half an hour later by my twin, Peter.
My sister Wendy was nine when we arrived. According to her we were
cranky babies, victims of the now discredited Truby King method of
feeding by strict regime rather than demand. We did not get enough
milk and because we yelled day and night were kept in separate rooms
and prams – one at the back of the house, the other in the porch at the
front. My mother concentrated on Peter, the slightly more difficult
child. Lena looked after me and turned into my mother. She exchanged
the uniform of a maid for that of a nurse, but this was for her much
more than a promotion. She was a natural and devoted surrogate
mother: the two of us became inseparable.

The Second World War began in September. My father who had
survived the Trenches enlisted again and was posted to England where
he remained for two years. My mother, Lena and a succession of
wayward maids looked after Wendy and 'the Twins' (as we were called
until puberty, when we changed to 'the Boys'). The crying stopped as
soon as we had graduated to solids; and some photographs show us
peaceably sharing a large black pram. Because those years are mostly
beyond my recall, I have to borrow Wendy's memories of the air-raids
on Belfast, the search-lights, the hand-bells and whistles, the gas-
masks into which Peter and I were inserted, the perspex visors through

which we peered and tried to make sense of the huddle under the stairs. There survive in my mind the rough feel of khaki as I climbed over a soldier's knee, the coolness of brass buttons, the kitchen light reflected in the polished toecap of an army boot. Had the maid been bringing her soldier boyfriend home?

Just down the road from our house the King's Hall, a huge Art Deco concrete and glass barn, was converted into a barracks for the troops. One of them, Bill Hardy, married Lena, and they left Belfast for Nottingham in 1941. I was inconsolable and for weeks afterwards toddled to the front door when the bell rang, expecting Lena to be there. The marriage was not a success. With her daughter Paddy, Lena returned in 1945 to live with us for a few more years. The three of us accepted Paddy as a sister and I liked it when she called *our* father Daddy. As my love for Lena deepened, my relationship with my mother grew more tense and complicated.

I last met Lena in 1967 when, on her way to visit relations in Fermanagh, she called briefly to meet my wife and our first child. My arms melted around her in acceptance and surrender. She was (and, so far as I know, still is) working as a priest's housekeeper in New York. A few years ago Paul Muldoon and I gave a reading there in the Public Theatre. I had thought of contacting Lena, but was anxious that no audience would turn up and that she would be upset and embarrassed on our behalf. The evening turned out to be a considerable success. Lena should have been sitting in the middle of the front row.

II

My parents came from Clapham Common to live in Belfast in 1927. My father was a commercial traveller for an English firm of furniture manufacturers, Harris Lebus. Before the war his territory was the whole of Ireland, and the family album is full of his photographs – Antrim, Donegal, Kerry: he seems quickly to have fallen in love with the island. Business did not resume until well into the fifties; so on leaving the army my father for several years scraped a living as a professional fundraiser – for the Ulster Hospital for Women and Children and, when the introduction of the National Health Service rendered him redundant, for the War Memorial Rebuilding Fund. The inventiveness and panache of his schemes were a minor talking-point in the community. Photographs of him receiving cheques and smiling at Ulster's grandees appeared regularly in the local press. He was always referred to as Major R. C. Longley, M.C., a billing he disliked. The war was over, he used to insist. But Ulstermen adore military titles and my father's, with its aura of courage as well as authority, endured stubbornly. To this day when certain people hear my surname, which is unusual in Northern Ireland, they ask: 'Any relation to the Major?'

As a commercial traveller my father did as little travelling as possible. In no time at all he had sewn up the smaller territory of the Six Counties. Rising late and after a breakfast of tea and Woodbines, he would accumulate the day's orders over the telephone. 'I've got a lovely little number here, Mr Gillespie. Only £200. No, you won't be disappointed.' He was that rare thing, an Englishman accepted and trusted by Ulstermen. Handsome, charming, deft with people, he could have gone far in public life, I believe. He had enjoyed his charismatic fundraising days, but now preferred to stay at home, in retreat. I picture him chain-smoking in his dressing-gown and giving the fire a last poke before strolling to the telephone with his bundle of catalogues.

Having lived through so much by the time he was thirty, perhaps my father deserved his early partial retirement. At the age of seventeen he had enlisted in 1914, one of thousands queueing up at Buckingham Gate. He joined the London Scottish by mistake and went into battle wearing an unwarranted kilt. A 'Lady from Hell'. Like so many survivors he seldom talked about his experiences, reluctant to relive the nightmare. But not long before he died, we sat up late one night and he reminisced. He had won the Military Cross for knocking out single-handed a German machine-gun post and, later, The Royal Humane Society's medal for gallantry: he had saved two nurses from drowning. By the time he was twenty he had risen to the rank of Captain, in charge of a company known as Longley's Babies because many of them were not yet regular shavers. He recalled the lice, the rats, the mud, the tedium, the terror. Yes, he had bayoneted men and still dreamed about a tubby little German who 'couldn't run fast enough. He turned around to face me and burst into tears.' My father was nicknamed Squib in the Trenches. For the rest of his life no-one ever called him Richard.

After the war he travelled through Europe as part of an anti-German propaganda mission, which he found distasteful. ('Goebbels learnt a lot from us.') He also disliked the snobbery of the officers' mess where he was dismissed as a 'trench officer', his medals failing to outweigh the fact that he had not attended public school or Sandhurst. But for this he might have become a career soldier. Instead he vanished to West Africa and mined tin and gold there until he was thirty. In the photographs from Europe and Africa he is often accompanied by beautiful women. As I grew older, I noticed that he behaved most vitally in women's company, and most peacefully as well. For him a sense of unexpected bonus pervaded all the ordinary aspects of life: he could not take being alive for granted. He once showed me the gas-burns like birth-marks on his shoulder, the scars on his legs. Running away from a successful German offensive, he had been wounded by shrapnel without feeling any pain. Back in his dug-out he discovered he had been shot through his scrotum, that the top of his penis had been severed. His children owe their existence to skilled medical orderlies. We were three further bonuses whom he enjoyed deeply and with as little fuss as possible.

III

To use a geological metaphor, my father's personality was sedimentary, my mother's volcanic. She had been born with a congenital hip malformation and walked with a severe limp. My grandmother, a beautiful Jewess called Jessica Braham, died at the age of twenty when my mother was still a baby. My Grandpa George, a man of limited sensibility, then married his housekeeper Maud who was insanely jealous of her step-child. My mother's childhood was an unrelieved misery: daily humiliation, mental and physical cruelty. My heart goes out to the little girl cowering in a corner, sobbing at the top of the dark stairs. My father told me of the first time he visited his future in-laws. Maud rushed at the young couple sitting nervously on the sofa, scrabbed her nails down my mother's face and then ran out of the room screaming. When my parents departed for their honeymoon, Maud took the wedding guests up to my mother's bedroom to show them the mess she had left it in (after working overtime the night before at her job in a record shop). My father's mother, by all accounts a saintly woman, said to the embarrassed assembly, 'You know the trouble with Maud? She's jealous!' Every time I remember that story I savour the release of vengeance.

When they married, my mother was not yet twenty and my father thirty. She told me several times of their first meeting. 'He was just back from Nigeria, tanned, a bit overweight but terribly dashing. I stopped to admire his red setter and he invited me to meet him in a tearoom the following week. He was something of a local hero in Clapham. Could have had any girl he wanted. Why did he choose me with my dot-and-carry walk? I still wonder. In the tearoom he said, bold as brass, "We're going to have wallpaper like that when we get married."' Soon they were living in Belfast, and Clapham shrank to a yearly phone-call to Grandpa George on Christmas Day, birthday cards from Auntie Daisy. I visited Daisy and two of my father's brothers, Maurice and Charlie, when I was sixteen and on holiday in London. I never met Uncle Hugh, nor my paternal grandparents (he a journeyman carpenter, she the possessor of second sight). Because my mother's retarded brother had molested her, Grandpa George threw him out of the house. He was last heard of following the stretcher parties into No Man's Land with a sack into which he was putting bits and pieces of soldiers.

So there was no hinterland of aunts, uncles and cousins to which Wendy, Peter and I could escape and still feel at home. Perhaps because of my father's passivity, her children became the main outlet for my mother's emotions. Her moods changed unpredictably. It has taken me a long time to forgive her that atmosphere of uncertainty, its anxieties, even fears. I appreciate now that somewhere inside her intelligent humorous personality crouched the tormented child. Perhaps I was responding to this even as a boy when I would bring her sticky little bags of sweets as peace-offerings. My father sat quietly until the storm clouds passed. If this was taking too long, he would venture, 'A little gin and orange, Connie?' Out of sight in the kitchen he would take a long swig of neat gin before presenting the drinks with ostentatious ceremony. 'There we are, dear.' Occasionally, if he realised Peter and I had been really disturbed by the climatic changes, he would say, 'Your Mum may walk a little bit funny, but she's a marvellous woman all the same.' A well-meant but patronising simplification.

I remember her solving crosswords swiftly in ink. She was a first-class bridge player. My parents did not engage in any regular social intercourse except for bridge parties. Where were their close friends? My mother's good moods could be a firework display of wit and surreal invention. She would laugh for minutes at a time, her eyes watering, so that even when Peter and I were too young to understand the joke we would join in. Though her bad moods meant, perhaps, that the child in her was competing with us, her generosities as a mother could be bottomless. During the war she limped down many streets to buy us second-hand tricycles and other toys. Despite rationing, powdered eggs, Oxo cubes, parsnip disguised as banana, we looked forward to her carefully prepared meals. Like my father she was depressive, and the latter part of Peter's and my childhood probably coincided with her menopause. By that time she would have been well into her forties, my father in his mid-fifties. They withdrew into themselves still further, and Wendy, a maturing teenager who at sixteen had already fallen in love with her future husband, Ernie Clegg, started to fill in the emotional gaps. She became my second surrogate mother.

IV

Grandpa George was the only relative who crossed the water to visit us. He took the train to Stranraer, then the boat to Larne – an ordeal for a man in his eighties. On arrival he would claim that his journey had been 'in the lap of the gods', a phrase I pretended to understand. Grandpa had been a teacher of ballroom dancing in Clapham. Top hat and tails, sequins and swirling tulle. He liked to dress up and hold centre stage, a natural master of ceremonies. His chief ambition, to be Mayor of Battersea, was never realised, despite his masonic connections (he had risen as high as Worshipful Master). I realise now that he could be vulgar and pompous, but at the time I found his Cockney accent with its genteel adjustments, his taste for polysyllables and periphrases, really exotic. A good meal was always 'a highly satisfactory repast'. Inclined to choke at the dinner table, he would declare, 'A particle of food would appear to have lodged itself against my uvula.' Every morning he would give us a full account of his 'motions' (I guessed what that word meant). Laxatives, All-Bran, elastic stockings, Vick, Thermogene, long johns: these were among his obsessions. At the seaside he would roll up his trousers and rub seaweed on his white shins. 'Iodine, Michael. Good for the pores.' On a calm day he would lie down at the water's edge and siphon the sea through his long nose. Legs astride, bending over, he would then snort out a stream of snot. 'Salt water, Michael. Very good for the tubes.'

Grandpa taught me cribbage, a card game not much played in Ireland. I was happy to listen to his endless monologues and fantasies as we pegged up and down the board: he needed an audience. Rickets had left him with bow-legs. 'Got those riding horses. The cavalry. Tipperary, 1916.' Sometimes it was the Boer War (he was jealous of my father's military record). He never mentioned his retarded son, and found it impossible to accept that he had fathered a physically imperfect daughter. 'A nurse dropped little Connie on the floor after she was delivered.' He referred once or twice, tearfully to Jessica Braham and seemed after all those years to be in love with her still. He also passed on to me an interest in good food and drink about which he knew a great deal. I owe him my first taste of pheasant, hare, smoked salmon, tripe and onion, lambs' kidneys. He allowed me to sip his Guinness.

Towards the end of his life I visited Grandpa George and Maud in London. They had rented out the rest of their house and were living in the ballroom in a maze of screens and curtains. Grandpa wept then, partly because I could not stay, partly because of the pain a catheter was causing him. 'The waterworks, Michael. The waterworks.' Maud burst out laughing. She may have been embarrassed, but I still hate those giggles. When he died in 1958 I was the only member of our family able to attend the funeral. A few of his old cronies turned up and went to the house afterwards. 'I need a whiskey,' Maud said. 'I've a bottle in the cabinet over there, but I'm not giving any of it to you lot.' This saddened rather than shocked me, because at the crematorium her tears had made on the linoleum circles the size of half-crowns. And she had sighed again and again, 'Poor George. Poor George. Poor George.'

V

Being a twin meant that until I was sixteen I hardly ever slept alone. My father had painted our names in red on the cream bed-heads and covered one wall with Disney characters. The Boys' Room. We fought a lot, our differences so freely expressed that it is only recently that Peter and I have recognised how much we have in common as personalities. Beneath the tussles, tangles, power struggles an affection developed, natural, quotidian, inexpressible, so deep and lasting that to comprehend it would be a madness. I was a withdrawn watcher, Peter a rebel. If he was chastised, I would shed tears of sympathy. When he was ten Wendy and I visited Peter in hospital where he was recovering from an eye-operation. Bandages covered both his eyes, but I knew he was crying as we prepared to leave. No surge of passion or compassion in later life has quite equalled the wracking of my whole being that I experienced then. His eyes were still in bandages when he returned home. I remember reading to him at night from *The Water Babies* and *The Snow Queen* and feeling completely fulfilled – fraternal, paternal, maternal. Being a lover, a husband, a father has since enabled me to draw parallel lines only.

29

VI

Because of our reduced circumstances my parents could not afford to send Peter and me to one of the posher preparatory schools. (They were both old-fashioned Tories). We attended a local Public Elementary School where, out of a large class of nearly forty pupils, we were almost the only middle-class children. Most of the others lived on 'the wrong side' of the Lisburn Road. Their clothes were different from ours – woollen balaclavas, laced boots with studs in the soles. Alongside them Peter and I must have appeared chubby and well-scrubbed. I noticed at once the skinny knees and snotty noses, but most of all the accent, abrasive and raucous as a football rattle. This I soon acquired in order to make myself less unacceptable. 'Len' us a mey-ek' – 'Lend me a make' (a ha'penny). At home I would try to remember to ask for 'a slice of cake' and not 'a slice a cey-ek', to refer to the 'door' and the 'floor' rather than 'doo-er' and 'floo-er'. By the age of six or seven I was beginning to lead a double life, learning how to recreate myself twice daily.

I made friends with other pupils and started to explore the Lisburn Road. Belfast's more prosperous citizens have usually been careful to separate themselves safely from the ghettoes of the bellicose working classes. An odd exception is the Lisburn Road which runs south from the city centre. Intermittently for about three miles workers' tiny two-up-and-two-down houses squint across the road at the drawing rooms of dentists, doctors, solicitors: on the right, as you drive towards Lisburn, gardenless shadowy streets, on the left rhododendrons and rose bushes. Belfast laid bare, an exposed artery.

I spent much of my childhood drifting from one side to the other, visiting the homes of my new friends: the lavatory outside in the yard, stairs ascending steeply as you entered, low ceilings and no elbow-room at all. My first tea at Herbie Smith's was fried bread sprinkled with salt. Herbie came to our house and gasped when he saw the size of our back garden. For the first time I felt ashamed of our relative affluence. Our separate drawing and dining rooms, the hall with its wooden panelling, the lavatory upstairs were all novelties to Herbie. He seemed curious rather than envious. Every corner of the home I had taken for granted was illuminated by his gaze as by wintry sunlight.

Another pupil John McCluskey was often caned for being late. He delivered papers for Younger the newsagent. If the *Belfast Newsletter* was delayed, John without complaint or explanation would be standing at 9.30 in front of the class, his hand presented to the whistling cane and then hugged under his armpit as he stumbled over schoolbags to his desk. Should I have told the teacher that he delivered papers to our house? Sometimes, as though to drown his sorrows, John would swig the blue-grey sludge from one of the small white inkwells. Every December my father gave me a half-crown as a Christmas box for the paper boy, as he called him. I never told my father that the paper boy was in my class. On the doorstep John McCluskey and I behaved like strangers and avoided each other's eyes as the half-crown changed hands. Later in class the transaction would not be mentioned.

John and Herbie shared with me their mythology which was mostly concerned with Roman Catholics. Did I know why Taigs crossed themselves? What dark practices lurked behind confession and Mass? Didn't the nuns kidnap little girls and imprison them behind the suspiciously high walls of the big convent at the top of the Ormeau Road? The Orange Order and the 'B' Specials marched through our conversations. The son of English parents, I was, at nine, less politically aware than my classmates. A photograph at home of Grandpa George lording it in his Mason's apron prompted me once to speak with snooty disparagement of the less dignified Orangemen. I was sent to Coventry until I apologised. To secure the conversion two friends smuggled to me under the desks pamphlets which purported to describe Catholic atrocities from the twenties and thirties. Every page carried blurred photographs of victims who, it was claimed, had been tortured and mutilated, their brains or hearts cut out, their genitals chopped off. Forgeries? Adaptations of photographs of road accidents from forensic files? Or real victims? This vitriolic propaganda burned deep into my mind, and I perused those grim pages with the same obsessiveness that I was later to devote to *The Red Light* and nudist magazines. I craved the bond of shared fears and superstitions.

At primary school (and later at grammar school) there was little on the curriculum to suggest that we were living in Ireland: no Irish history except when it impinged on the grand parade of English monarchs; no Irish literature; no Irish art; no Irish music. When we sang in music classes we mouthed English songs. One inspector criticised our accents and forced us to sing, 'Each with his bonny lawss/ a-dawncing on the grawss.' Our teacher in Form Three, an affable man who coaxed us through the Three R's with care and skill, became tense when for one term we were joined by a boy from Dublin – a Protestant but still a focus of our suspicions. Having flirted for a while with the unfortunate nine-year old's political ignorance and his own paranoia, the teacher eventually decided to confront this embodiment of menace and treachery. It was a crude question.

'Niall, who owns Belfast?'

'Dublin, sir.'

'Who? Who?' This was much more than he had hoped for. 'To the front of the class, boy.'

'Who owns Belfast?'

'Dublin, sir.' A slap in the face.

'Who told you that?' Another slap. A spittly crescendo of hatred. 'My granny, sir.' More slaps. And Niall in tears.

We were invited to correct the error, to put down the rebellion. We did so and felt frightened and exhilarated.

With its dozens of little shops and the Regal Cinema where entrance to the front stalls cost threepence, the Lisburn Road became my hinterland. The cinema was demolished not so long ago, and many of the shops have now been transformed into Chinese restaurants and fast food take-aways. But the rows of back-to-back houses remain, the homes of Herbie Smith, John McCluskey, Norman Hamilton, Sally Patterson, John Boland, Alan Gray, Helen Ferguson, Norma Gamble.

VII

I went on to specialise in Classics at grammar school and university. Peter left home at sixteen to take up an apprenticeship. He is now Chief Engineer on a Shell tanker and lives near Newcastle-upon-Tyne. Wendy and her family live in Toronto. My father died in 1960 when I was twenty and too young to appreciate his strengths or understand his weaknesses. My mother died in April 1979. For about a year beforehand we both knew that she was going to die. I wanted to feel free to embrace her as I had embraced Lena, and agreed to call with her every day for five minutes to five hours – for as long as both of us could stand it. Over several tumultuous months we lived out her childhood and mine. She gave me X-ray pictures in which the shadowy shapes of Peter and me curl up and tangle about five months after conception. ('Tuppenny stung for a penny bung,' my father had joked.) She confessed that in the early days of the pregnancy she had attempted in an amateurish way to abort us – or 'it' as we then were. I registered neither shock nor pain. Somehow this knowledge made it easier for me to hug her dying lopsided body. It was like a courtship, and I accompanied her on my arm to death's door.

VIII

Since April 1979 I have been promising myself that some day I shall phone New York and talk across the Atlantic with Lena.

Poetry Review, 74, 4 (1984)

PART 2

POETRY:
REVIEWS AND
SHORTER PIECES

DAY LEWIS'S VIRGIL

The Eclogues of Virgil, translated by C. Day Lewis

There are three main kinds of translation of poetry – the literal prose translation, the literary rendering into verse which keeps as close to the original as possible, and free translation. Anyone who has resorted to Loeb or Bohn will appreciate the pedestrian excellences of the first kind: the second is the most selfless, and the third the most selfish where the translator (almost always a poet himself) allows his own personality great freedom. He can be justified if we think of the reading of a poem as an experience and a translation as a reaction to that experience just as every poem is a reaction to an experience.

C. Day Lewis has already given us excellent translations of the *Aeneid* and *Georgics*. The *Eclogues* are perhaps his most difficult task to date because the originals are such peculiar hybrid poems – artificial copies of an artificial Greek form. Mr Day Lewis opts for the second kind of translation and renders the Virgilian hexameter for the most part into a line of six stresses which 'enables me to translate line for line with a minimum of padding and omission'. This makes slow reading and the rhythms are too different from those of Virgil. The hexameter is the most natural line in Latin and the best medium for translation would surely be the iambic pentameter, the most natural line in English.

The tone of the *Eclogues* is ambiguous, their artificiality concealing the stance of the poet. This gives them their excitement and charm, qualities held in a delicate balance which is destroyed by the added artificiality of too strict a translation. This tone could only be captured by another poet's free reaction to it. In spite of frequent felicities, Mr Lewis's line-by-line restatement of what Virgil says seems untrue to the originals. He has reacted as translator and not as poet. If he had kept his own personality in a less rigid and respectful subjection to Virgil's we might have been blessed with the kind of translation which is the final criticism, the appreciation of one poet by another carried to its logical conclusion – free translation at its best, the only *real* translation.

Irish Times, 30 March 1963

FURNISHING THE IVORY TOWER

F. T. Prince, *The Doors of Stone: Poems 1938–1962*; *Five American Poets*, edited by Ted Hughes and Thom Gunn

F. T. Prince is a poet primarily interested in his own perceptions. Poets of this kind thoroughly explore a small territory – as thoroughly as their talents allow. Consideration of their work is seldom in terms that are not literary. One thinks of, say, Vernon Watkins, whose writing, like Prince's demands the awkward phrase 'pure poetry'. The muse of such poets is individual and exacting, their poetry usually considered 'minor', their efforts to establish an intensely personal aesthetic liable to charges of being Ivory Tower and Art for Art's Sake. But their retreats are *into* rather than *from* reality – they need to stand at a distance before they can focus clearly. If their poetry seems almost deliberately minor, we have only to turn to a greater, though similar, poet like Wallace Stevens to be shown how much can be achieved within the narrowest and most personal limits of subject matter providing the talent is large enough.

Early in his career, Prince was cursed with having written a famous poem. One has only to mention his name and the cognoscenti will exclaim 'Oh yes, "Soldiers Bathing"!' And that's as far as it goes. This poem appears in most anthologies, and deservedly. Noble and restrained, it is probably the finest poem produced by the Second World War:

> Though every human deed concerns our blood,
> And even we must know, what nobody has understood,
> That some great love is over all we do.

Prince has a fine sense of the line, either spilling the words out mellifluously from margin to margin, or working within the tight limits of the short line and a simplified vocabulary. Word, image and emotion are intimately related, and the tension, which is discreetly present in most of the poems, mounts as one reads on. His is a quiet talent, as they say, but then there is a great difference between a whisper and a muted shout.

I don't quite understand the duumvirate of Ted Hughes and Thom Gunn, but here they are again with an interesting selection from the work of the American poets – Edgar Bowers, Howard Nemerov, Hyam Plutzik, Louis Simpson and William Stafford. This is not a general anthology but a group of substantial collections which give plenty of room in which to study the poets represented – very useful since none of them has yet been published this side of the Atlantic. There is no preface and the introductions to each poet are ruthlessly brief and factual. It would be pleasant to know why the editors admire these poets, but perhaps this is the way to present poetry – without fuss.

Each one of these writers is employed by a university – a usual and not altogether satisfactory practice in America. There is a sameness of rhythm and diction to their work – the iambic pentameter must cover about three-quarters of the pages. There are no Beat high jinks here. The subject matter is often informed by history and legend, and sallies beyond the campus usually take the form of highly sophisticated descriptive or contemplative poems. I sense the influence of that most consummate of artists, Richard Wilbur. These poets all belong to the school of American Academics which, for all its limitations, I admire very much – it is producing the bulk of the good poetry written today. In this volume pleas for the world of imagination (where 'everything is perfect, calm and clear' – Simpson) are prevalent, and occasionally a gentle dissatisfaction with the order of things – although most of the attempts at a world-view are rather strained, giving the impression that these poets are not really as worried as they would have us believe. If they lack passion and if they seem at times mere visitors in the world at large, it is nonetheless reassuring to find words used with such respect and affection. Here are two typically striking lines from Bowers and Simpson, respectively:

> The Alps ride massive to their full extreme

and

> The buzzard's black umbrella and collapse.

Extract from review, *Irish Times*, 1 June 1963

THE NUN OF AMHERST

Charles R. Anderson, *Emily Dickinson: Stairway of Surprise;*
C. B. Cox and A. E. Dyson, *Modern Poetry: Studies in Practical Criticism*

Emily Dickinson was a great poet. Her stature and extraordinary originality have only gradually been recognised. She was born in Amherst,
Massachusetts, in 1830, but the modernity of her language and imagery is perpetually astonishing – with Hopkins and Whitman she is one
of the great early innovators.

She spent the last twenty-five years of her life in isolation, seeing
no one outside her family. Whatever the reasons for this may have
been, it accentuated and accelerated the usual 'division' between man
and artist, and she made of it a practised objectivity, devoting herself
to the worlds of the imagination and of words. Perhaps (and I say this
tentatively) because she was a woman Emily Dickinson needed withdrawal to make the outside world available for art. Her objectivity is
unique in the nineteenth century, with its prevailing romantic climate.
She is a prototype of the twentieth century's idea of the outsider. But
this idea has been devalued, and when Mr Anderson in his excellent
study says that 'she mastered the outer world by renouncing it', the
emphasis is too negative. Emily Dickinson lived always in the neighbourhood of the universe: her life as a recluse was a continually
prepared reception for its wonders, a devotional quieting of herself
before its loud variety. Mr Anderson is right in as much as we often
understand best those things we have abdicated from.

In Emily Dickinson's earliest letters and poems a cool, detached,
witty personality is evident. The perfect satire of her early work was

turned against the standard nineteenth-century praise of material progress and the prim religiousness of a Puritan society. But all the time wit was being used to sharpen the poetic tools and perceptions of a developing major artist. In her solitude she forged her own religion and her own poetry. She employed the simple rhythms of nursery rhymes and Protestant hymns as vehicles for her advanced experiments with a highly individual vocabulary and her bold and always surprising dislocations of syntax. She describes bees as

> Jugs – a Universe's fracture
> Could not jar or spill.

Her ironies might be misconstrued as whimsy, did not one of her most potent devices – the sudden change of tone – ensure against this. A penetrating vision informs both witty and serious moods. In one of her most moving poems a bird

> . . . unrolled his feathers
> And rowed him softer home
> Than oars divide the ocean,
> Too silver for a seam.

She was using pararhyme over fifty years before Wilfred Owen, to whom its first use is often attributed. Indeed, the efforts of Eliot and Pound to achieve semantic rejuvenation are summarised in the poetic techniques of Emily Dickinson.

Charles R. Anderson deals with all this in great detail. He traces the growth of a complex artist step by step, quoting at length to make his study, amongst other things, a generous and valuable anthology. Completely aware at every instance of what the poetry is doing both technically and emotionally, he writes with affection, respect and great insight. Analytical criticism can be most tiresome, but I found this book a complete and rich experience.

Messrs. Cox's and Dyson's book is perhaps the most valuable for its succinct introduction on the history of criticism. There follows a series of essays on single poems, starting well with Hardy and fizzling out with that most drab of non-poets, John Wain. D. H. Lawrence and Michael Roberts are interesting inclusions. And there is a good study of Thom Gunn's splendid 'Considering the Snail', which asks

What is a snail's fury?

– a question worthy of the great Emily Dickinson.

Irish Times, 15 June 1963

POET IN A LANDSCAPE

Charles Tomlinson, *A Peopled Landscape*; John Lehmann, *Collected Poems*; Bernard Spencer, *With Luck Lasting*

Charles Tomlinson's poetry is formidable, impressive and, I find, difficult. His interest is landscape which he mines for meaning –

> Nakedly muscular, the beech no longer regrets
> Its lost canopy, nor is shamed
> By its disorder. The tatters lie
> At the great foot. It moves
> And what it moves is itself.

In the early poems his search often took the form of a series of reactions to an object, the object inhabiting several moods which illuminated it from different angles. He had learnt from the Wallace Stevens of 'Thirteen Ways of Looking at a Blackbird'. The trouble with this sort of aesthetic exploration is that it *could* go on for ever. Why not Twenty-six Ways of Looking at a Blackbird? Or One Hundred and Twenty-six? One longs for a proper full stop. In his later work Tomlinson has dropped this oblique approach and now views his objects (or, more exactly, his images) face on: he is less meditative because he is seeing more quickly, and he knows when to stop looking.

Tomlinson's previous book was called *Seeing is Believing*. The emphasis was obviously aesthetic and his poetic world was condemned by some as stark, uninhabited, inhuman. The title of his new book has clearly been chosen with great care. The poet (and this may always

45

have been so) intends his to be a moral landscape –

> A just geography
> completes itself
> with such relations, where
> beauty and stability can be
> each other's equal.

But a comparison with, say, Auden's 'In Praise of Limestone', where the intent is almost exclusively moral, shows that in Tomlinson's poetry the aesthetic bias is still prevalent.

Apart from great intelligence and insight and the remarkable gift of revealing to us our surroundings with a complete freshness, Tomlinson has large technical powers. He must be the first English poet to have absorbed fully the American achievement. His verse is an assured and felicitous escape from the rigours of iambic metre which still dominates British poetry. He follows those American poets – William Carlos Williams, Marianne Moore and many others – who have allowed their line to be shaped by the rhythms of speech. Tomlinson's lines, though some of the shorter ones seem footling, aching prosaically for the far margin, are swift and direct, worthy servants of his penetrating vision. All this plus a rich, controlled vocabulary and a great command of syntax (an aspect of technique often neglected nowadays), make his new book a fine achievement.

As the editor of the renowned *Penguin New Writing* and, later, of the *London Magazine*, John Lehmann has served literature well. His poetry, however, is unexciting, bloodless – the work of a literate, intelligent, sensitive man but not of a poet. His sincerity is not the ally of his imagination, and the pervading sobriety seldom deepens into a real seriousness. Mr. Lehmann's talent is revealed most honestly in his mildly interesting sallies into the prose poem, a form which most English poets, thankfully, have not been attracted by.

Bernard Spencer has a keen eye for scenery which, never merely describing, he comments on or rather interprets. He writes straight-forward free verse the looseness of which usually accommodates but sometimes confuses the unpredictable directions of his thoughts. The almost enjoyable untidiness is studded with startling ideas.

> Between these noises the little teeth
> of a London silence.

Unlike John Lehmann, Mr Spencer is sure of his feelings and many of his poems are, in their eccentric way, very moving – 'By a Breakwater' in particular, which describes a middle-aged couple on holiday at Dover – 'with his right hand he was emptying// A hypodermic syringe in her bare arm' – not quite poetry perhaps, but it continues:

> It is to be remarked
> this scene can be told for a laugh: at the hopelessness
> of a summer; at the fantasy
> of such an act and its setting; or at Medicine masked as
> Passion . . .

and ends beautifully –

> So clutched to each other, sitting nowhere
> and hiding from the wind.

Irish Times, 31 August 1963

POETRY: REVIEWS AND SHORTER PIECES

DEATH OF A POET

Louis MacNeice, *The Burning Perch*

Louis MacNeice was one of the first writers to open for me the
doors of modern poetry. The back of my mind is full of his lines – the
words of another man which, unsummoned, sail into the best
moments:

> The same tunes hang on pegs in the cloakrooms of the mind
> That fitted us ten or twenty or thirty years ago . . .

This is from 'Off the Peg', a poem in his last book which, by a sad
coincidence, came through the post on the day he died. It is a humbling
task to review it now. There are a few, dazzling, cheeky pieces, like
'Château Jackson' –

> Where is the Jack that built the house
> That housed the folk that tilled the field
> That filled the bags that brimmed the mill
> That ground the flour that browned the bread . . .

And so on for forty lines – enough to remind us of the brilliant impro-
visor who wrote 'Bagpipe Music' and 'Prayer before Birth', but, mainly,
this is a self-engrossed, unhappy book. MacNeice, preoccupied with
time and death, is pessimistic and disenchanted, but writing with
powerful sadness –

The lines of print are always sidelines
And all our games funeral games.

He is the would-be gay dog exiled in middle age, not yet acclimatised, raging against and lamenting his years, making his solstice a stormy one, and these last poems *his* Letters from Pontus. Death is an enemy, but one to be dealt with, for the time being, dealt with gaily, bravely –

Your health, Master Yew. My bones are few
And I fully admit my rent is due,
But do not be vexed, I will postdate a cheque for you

and the arch enemy is, in fact, not death, but growing-old, completely old –
Age became middle: the habits
Made themselves at home . . .

The car-crash victim 'knew in the dead, dead calm/ It was too late to die'. Nostalgia for childhood (and MacNeice was outstanding on this subject) has become a desperate escape route –

A second childhood remembering only
Childhood seems better than a blank posterity . . .

The predicament is of course the poet's as well as the man's and these poems seem to be an escape not only from time's siege but also from an achievement he was dissatisfied with: the desire to begin again, simply to retread the old ground more efficiently, seems stronger than any envy for youth. He writes about childhood but not about children.

Indeed, there is scarcely any appreciation of other people here, ground upon which MacNeice was surest and richest, producing most of his finest poems – especially the love poems which are about the best of the century.

MacNeice was a very interesting human being and this self-engrossment at least allows the poems here to be interesting and often very good. They are after all a real artist's honest and unashamed responses to emotional events or, almost, to just one such event and that a prolonged one – middle age. There is about them a sense of marking time as though MacNeice had been waiting impatiently to pass the point of no return, to be able at last to stop looking back and proceed to bigger things. They are like the tunes in 'Off the Peg' – 'And off the peg means made to measure now'.

Earlier volumes like *Ten Burnt Offerings, Autumn Journal* and *Autumn Sequel* – all of them technically brilliant – indicated a keen interest in extended forms and a desire to reach toward what we must call the major statement. The most recent of these, *Ten Burnt Offerings*, didn't quite come off, and there followed *Visitations, Solstices*, and, now, *The Burning Perch* – all volumes of short poems. Perhaps the efforts of *Ten Burnt Offerings* were premature: at fifty-five it must have seemed that MacNeice had plenty of time in which to await the proper moment for renewing such efforts and so crown his achievement.

He was the best poet Ireland has produced since Yeats. And he wrote the most truthful poems about Ireland that I have ever read. He was, I believe, a brilliant classicist too: certainly his verse translation of the *Agamemnon* is a perfect exercise – a deeply imaginative response to the thoughts and words of Aeschylus. As a sideline he was a sparkling natural journalist – especially good on Rugby. In fact, as somebody has said about the Welsh, he had a gift for practically everything except being middle-aged.

Louis MacNeice's chief qualities as a writer were intelligence and compassion; we should be very grateful for them. His poem, 'Death of an Actress', ends like this:

> Let the wren and robin
> Gently with leaves cover the Babes in the Wood.

Irish Times, 14 September 1963

ANATOMY OF LANGUAGE

e. e. cummings, *73 Poems*; Philip Larkin, *The Whitsun Weddings*

E. E. Cummings liked to be known as e. e. cummings. He died in the summer of 1962 and left us a large collections of exquisite lyrics. The beauty of his love poems is approached only by those of Robert Graves. He was a tireless experimenter whose typographical innovations unfortunately alienated many readers. Too much has already been made of these eccentricities, which are but one aspect of his work. Indeed, it is remarkable that such a bold experimenter could have avoided so consistently aesthetic mistakes: behind the strange shapes which so often cover his pages lie a profound tact, a reckless honesty, and a cool intelligence. The following example is a complete poem:

> "nothing" the unjust man complained
> "is just" ("or un-") the just rejoined

and it works miraculously: a carefully manipulated miracle.

This is a beautifully produced volume – a perfect final tribute to a great poet who cared so much how his work was printed – and it contains poems written since 1958. They are as fine as anything he wrote. Along with W. H. Auden, cummings gave the sonnet a new life, a twentieth-century vigour. Most of the poems in this book are in sonnet form. He violently dislocates the shape and line but the poems remain completely sonnets in pace, tone and texture and, although the rhymes are often unorthodox, recognisable rhyme schemes are adhered to:

> the trick of finding what you didn't lose
> (existing's tricky: but to live's a gift)
> the teachable imposture of always
> arriving at the place you never left

Another sonnet ends like this:

> – when all fears hopes beliefs doubts disappear,
> Everywhere and joy's perfect wholeness we're

Such a passionate curiosity about the anatomy of language led cummings to use (as he does in the above examples) English syntax with a flexibility usually confined to inflected languages. He uses words differently to make us look at life differently. Every poet has (owns?) privately numinous words, which allow us the deepest insights into his sensibility. Those of cummings are such words as *april, love, flower, spring, bird*. His poetry is one long hymn to the joys of being alive and it reaches its most beautiful crescendos in his love poems where he handles erotic material with a perfection and delicacy that are unequalled:

> wild (at our first) beasts uttered human words
> – our second coming made stones sing like birds –
> but o the starhushed silence which our third's

e. e. cummings split the infinitive with as much purpose as other men split the atom – and to richer ends.

Philip Larkin's first important collection, *The Less Deceived*, is easily the best book of poems to come out of England since the war. It was published in 1955 and we have waited a long time for *The Whitsun*

Weddings, which is just as remarkable a volume as its predecessor. Not all the poems here are as rich and significant as those in *The Less Deceived*. There are two dry little stutters, 'As Bad as a Mile' and 'Days', which is a poor man's e. e. cummings. In 'The Large Cool Store' and 'Here' the motivations of the poems stick out much more obviously than Larkin usually permits. And only a very fine poet could have rescued 'Water' from its rather twee beginning, to make it the beautiful and moving poem it undoubtedly is. But these are small failings which would go unnoticed in most other collections. I would have liked to quote in its entirety 'Home is so Sad' to illustrate how perfect a poem can be and how complete Larkin's talent is.

Larkin sometimes employs a gruffer voice – a voice to accommodate words like *blort* and lines like 'Get stewed: Books are a load of crap.' (Shades of Amis?) This is great fun but much less rewarding than his gentler compassionate approach. The tough guy pose seems to be his tenderness protecting itself – with the wrong weapons, possibly. Or perhaps the pose is meant to be as transparent as this. And there *are* poems which combine the two voices perfectly – 'Sunny Prestatyn', for instance, and 'For Sidney Bechet', his marvellous alto sax

> Scattering long-haired grief and scored pity.

But compare this line with the closing of 'Broadcast', where the poet hears on the wireless a performance at which his girl is present; the cut-off final chords

> Leaving me desperate to pick out
> Your hands tiny in all that air, applauding.

Such lines are worth so much, and this book is rich with them.

'MCMXIV' is an emotionally huge poem which conveys perfectly the terrible nostalgia of those old photographs of recruits and the unbearable sadness we must experience when looking at them. 'An Arundel Tomb', 'Ambulances' and many other poems here are written at the same pitch. These beautiful poems – in Larkin's own words – prove

> Our almost-instinct almost true:
> What will survive of us is love.

Irish Times, 29 February 1964

ELDER POET

William Carlos Williams *Pictures from Brueghel, and Other Poems*;
Ted Hughes, *The Earth Owl*; Jeremy Robson, *Thirty-Three Poems*;
Adrian Mitchell, *Poems*

William Carlos Williams, who died in 1963, belonged to that great generation of American poets which includes Eliot, Pound, Stevens, Marianne Moore and Cummings – all born within a decade. Of these he is the least well-known on this side of the Atlantic, and the least appreciated. This excellent introductory volume comprises three books of Williams's later work which energetically maintains the lifelong reactions which inform all his work: reaction against traditional cadence, prosody, rhyme, etc. and against what he considered Eliot's betrayal of poetry to the academics. His poetry is a self-consciously homespun American affair which demands that we forget all our cisatlantic aesthetic prejudices.

Most of the poems are celebrations of things – the celebration which lies simply in the naming (an earlier poem begins 'So much depends on/ a red wheelbarrow') has to fight continually against slipping into flat statement. This is not helped (nor, to Williams's credit, disguised even) by the conversational rhythms he employs in preference to recognisable metrics. These poems were written with great care and delicacy but, if it is too obvious to say that many of them sound like prose, it is a pity all the same that it should be so obvious.

There has been much speculation as to whether Ted Hughes's verses about imaginary moon animals are meant for children or not. If your child's cradle is a psychiatrist's couch this is the book for him:

if not, he will be bored stiff, for these poems read like elephantine Ogden Nash with a touch of the Edgar Allan Poes. Edward Lear never wore his neuroses on his sleeve quite like this, probably because he had not heard of such things – which doesn't say much for the spontaneity or authenticity of Hughes's subconscious excursions through his lunar menagerie.

Jeremy Robson and Adrian Mitchell have both tried poetry and jazz. Of the two Mitchell is easily the better poet. He specialises in brilliant satire of the Establishment, and, in 'For my Son', has achieved poetry of a less ephemeral nature. The antecedents of his fine comic verse are the Auden of the ballads and the MacNeice of 'Bagpipe Music'. A must.

Extract from review, *Irish Times*, 4 April 1964

MASTER CRAFTSMAN

Molière's *Tartuffe*, translated by Richard Wilbur;
Selected Poems of Keith Douglas, edited by Ted Hughes

Richard Wilbur's last collection of poems, *Advice to a Prophet*, received, most undeservedly, cool and even hostile reviews. A consummately professional poet, he *does* have the unhappy knack of making most other practitioners look like amateurs. In these islands amateurism (or amateurishness?) is for some reason sacred: the professional is to be suspected. With Philip Larkin and Robert Lowell, Wilbur is one of the most accomplished of the middle generation of poets. For sheer technical dazzle there is no one writing today who can touch him. He is the perfect antidote to the screeds of sincere incompetence which comprise the bulk of the output of poetry at any time.

In the best of his work technical skill is only the vehicle for a highly refined and subtle sensibility and a huge intelligence. The urge to perfect being, surely, a prerequisite of artistic activity, Wilbur, even during in-between periods, extends almost impossibly the frontiers of perfection by keeping his eye in with translation. His version of Molière's *Misanthrope* sparkled with epigrammatic wit, and now he gives us *Tartuffe* in equally faultless rhyming couplets. It reads through so beautifully it is hard to believe it is a translation:

> Some glory clings to all that Heaven has made:
> In you, all Heaven's marvels are displayed.
> On that fair face, such beauties have been lavished.
> The eyes are dazzled and the heart is ravished:

How could I look on you, O flawless creature,
And not adore the Author of all Nature.
Feeling a love both passionate and pure,
For you his triumph of self-portraiture?

Nobody interested in poetry can afford to ignore any of Richard Wilbur's work. He is an artist of rare brilliance.

Not the least attractive of Ted Hughes's activities is his promotion of other poets. Last year he and Thom Gunn presented *Five American Poets*, a very useful collection. Now he edits a selection of Keith Douglas's poetry. Douglas was killed in 1944 at the age of twenty-four. Hughes makes no great claims for him, but writes in the introduction appreciatively and with keen critical insight into 'an achievement for which we can be grateful'. Almost all the poems here are striking, and in the best there is a remarkable tact and a subtle movement. In 'Mersa', one of several poems about the North African campaign, Douglas describes paddling in the sea near a ruined town:

I see my feet like stones
underwater. The logical little fish
converge and nip the flesh . . .

Irish Times, 13 April 1964

Donald Davie, *Events and Wisdoms*; Sheila Wingfield, *The Leaves Darken*; Laurence Durrell, *Selected Poems*. Northern House Pamphlets: Geoffrey Hill *Preghiere*; Jon Silkin, *Flower Poems*; Ken Smith, *Eleven Poems*

Donald Davie, whom Dublin was unlucky to lose, is generally accepted as one of the three or four best poets to have emerged since the war. He belongs to the cover-up rather than the lay-your-heart-bare school, and his work has enjoyed less attention than that of, say, Hughes and Gunn which is superficially more spectacular though considerably less accomplished. This situation is paralleled in the States where Lowell, wearing his neuroses on his sleeve very deftly indeed, has shouted down the perfect (for psychology-minded America, all too perfect) genius of Richard Wilbur.

In this new collection Davie, as the blurb suggests, flirts with the lay-your-heart-bare school, and experiments with unrhymed, unmetrical forms. But like Wilbur he is, I think, one of those poets whose gifts function best when both stimulated and constrained by rhyme and metre – two pleasing methods of shortening the harrowing search for the *mot juste*. 'Across the Bay', one of the best of the new experiments, ends like this –

> But this was the setting for one of our murderous scenes.
> This hurt, and goes on hurting:
> The venomous soft jelly, the undersides.
> We could stand the world if it were hard all over –

Beautifully poised free verse whose perfect movement, one thinks, could only have been managed by a poet with a long series of mellifluous iambics behind him. Perhaps, indeed, the new rawness, the urge 'to be naked, vulnerable and defenceless before experience' is a little obvious, occasionally glib: one is or one isn't – these things cannot be planned. And, ironically, Davie's 'naked' efforts strike me as his most theoretical. Throughout this volume, however, he displays, in his old and new manners alike, his sense of place and occasion, his fine ear for the falling cadence and what it can achieve, and the true poet's knowledge of what will make a poem. But his skill with rhyme and metre is, as always, so convincing I am tempted to quote Wilbur's remark that the powers of the genie depend on its living in a bottle.

Like most good women poets (excuse the term), Sheila Wingfield's talent is highly idiosyncratic – one thinks at once of Emily Dickinson and Marianne Moore. Like them she prefers to inhabit an enchanted lake rather than risk the river of the mainstream of poetry. Her poems are precise and colourful: their original insights and rhythms work best in free verse, and those poems which present a regular pattern seem least satisfactory – irrelevantly regular and, paradoxically, less formal than the looser constructions. Miss Wingfield's poems are quite unlike anything else I have read: a delightful book.

Durrell fans will welcome this paperback selection of his poems. There was so much ballyhoo over his inflated, unreadable *Alexandria Quartet* that I was prejudiced against these poems before I began them. But they soon won me over with their charm and elegance, rich vocabulary and easy rhythms. They deal mostly with the Mediterranean landscape, evoking the spirit of places with an effortlessness and honesty seldom achieved in the novels.

The Northern House Pamphlet Poets is a very worthwhile enterprise. I am sorry Geoffrey Hill has disowned his earlier poems, which are among the best written in the last decade. His new staccato style

61

is intriguing but mainly because it is so impenetrable. Jon Silkin also goes for the staccato utterance, affecting a modish violence – ineptly here: how he reads so much menace into flowers I do not know. One of Ken Smith's poems, 'Grass', strikes me as poetically more sincere and botanically more accurate than any of Silkin's herbaceous stutters. Indeed, Smith's collection is the most enjoyable and rewarding of the three.

Extract from review of 'Recent Poetry', *Irish Times*, 27 June 1964

A YOUNG ULSTER POET

Seamus Heaney, *Death of a Naturalist*

This is the first collection by an impressive young Ulster poet. Seamus Heaney's subject matter derives mainly from memories of his childhood on a farm in County Derry. A first reading reveals great density and richness which embody precise observations of the people and landscape of that early experience:

> My father worked with a horse-plough,
> His shoulders globed like a full sail strung
> Between the shafts and the furrow.
> The horses strained at his clicking tongue.

But if one of his main qualities is descriptive power, Heaney's poems are much more than merely descriptive. The considerable imaginative effort he has put into the meaningful arrangement of facts and observations which seem so uncompromising, make his local descriptions the focus and illumination of a much broader human context. 'Death of a Naturalist', the title poem, which on the narrative level remembers gathering frogspawn, also hints at the loss of innocence. (In 'Blackberry Picking' Heaney repeats this process much less effectively). 'The Barn' is an unfaltering exploration of terror and nightmare. The water diviner, in one of the finest poems, might represent the artist and define his role in the community. The artist emerges with complete certainty and self-awareness in 'Personal Helicon':

Now, to pry into roots, to finger slime,
To stare, big-eyed Narcissus, into some spring
Is beneath all adult dignity. I rhyme
To see myself, to set the darkness echoing.

It is not a question of the poet having made a certain area of experience his own – he has made it everybody's. In other words his childhood landscape has acquired the validity of myth. Many of the poems seem like attempts at exorcism. The vividness of Heaney's obsessions (memories of death and decay especially, fear and repulsion) accounts for not only his poetry's strengths, but also its weaknesses. His imagination tends towards simile rather than metaphor, which results sometimes in a frantic, last-minute gear-change, a rather forced expanding of precept into concept. And occasionally, as in 'Ancestral Photograph' and 'Churning Day', he lets concrete description stand in for rhythm, the only concreteness which poetry cannot do without.

Generally, however, it is Heaney's rhythms which declare him a true poet of considerable importance. And in such poems as 'Lovers on Aran', 'Waterfall' and 'The Diviner' there are extensions of vocabulary and sound-excursions into the fields of metaphor and symbol, which add expectation to my gratitude. Heaney's progress implies that he will be rhyming less 'to see himself' and more 'to set the darkness echoing'.

Irish Times, 23 May 1966

Eavan Boland, *New Territory*

Admirable and obvious qualities in this collection are ambition, verve, nerve, devotion to the craft and a high percentage of successes. The best poems usually take the form of three, four or five well-orchestrated stanzas through which the argument is carried carefully. Miss Boland can sustain a clear intellectual movement whilst embodying some of the most remarkable images I have read in contemporary poetry for some time.

> He was released,
> But how do these perennial stones
> Endure the prospect of a living feast?
> No one can hear their groans
> Nor offer them a respite – we can at most
> Find in the granite eyes a fierce request.

And in one of several fine poems about art, poets' spirits

> . . . like a pride
> Of lions circulate,
> Are desperate, just as the jewelled beast,
> That lion constellate
> Whose scenery is Betelgeuse and Mars,
> Hunts without respite among fixed stars.

As should be obvious from the lines already quoted, Miss Boland's rhythms are swift and exciting. She enjoys experimenting with stanzas comprised of lines of differing length; she releases the potential of the iambic pentameter in which resides, surely, the genius of the English language, and she works deftly within the shorter octosyllabic metre, a difficult form to keep moving, although Coleridge once confessed that he wished he had imposed its economy and discipline on everything he'd written.

This leads me to some criticisms. In some lines there are too many words: 'Starved, wasted, worn, lost' – this is simple addition rather than multiplication – and occasionally that precision of observed detail which is one of the main warrants of a poet's love for their subject is absent. 'Massive', for instance, is too vague an adjective for a chestnut tree; 'coloured' is an inaccurate description of a swift and hardly illuminating at any other level; the spruce tree is evergreen and not deciduous, as Miss Boland implies; 'Her thighs like stems of flowers' is inexact in two directions.

This last quotation is from the long poem which ends the collection, 'The Winning of Etain'. I am not completely happy about it. Though some of the lines are impressive –

> . . . Etain, sick with long patience,
> Saw a figure like a far bird
> Enlarge at last and block the summer distance,
> And saw a horseman in a rich dress
> Drumming across the drawbridge of the palace . . .

the poem is too often, in form, language and notion, Keats pastiche. Nevertheless, it is a fantastic effort and certainly a useful guide to Miss Boland's shorter and more successful poems and their themes of rebirth and communication.

Despite the above quibbles, words are usually employed with a delicate sense of their personalities:

> . . . in their fast
> Ethereal way, mirages are
> This daylight world in summary and forecast.

Poems of the standard of 'The Poets', 'Mirages', 'Migration', 'Requiem for a Personal Friend', 'From the Painting "Back from Market" by Chardin', 'After the Irish of Egan O'Rahilly' and 'Athene's Song' make this a very remarkable first collection.

Dublin Magazine, 6, 3-4 (Autumn / Winter 1967)

John Montague, *A Chosen Light*

This is an impressive book, and with it John Montague steps quietly into the front rank of contemporary poets. His clear purpose is to create poems whose statement and movement are uncluttered, poems which combine a discreet suggestiveness with maximum verbal efficiency: as a result his poems often exhibit that finality of form, that feeling of inevitability which marks a first-rate talent; and sometimes as in his poems about love and friendship his work is, quite simply, very beautiful.

Indeed, the love poems of the first section please me the most. Here – and this is not always the case later in the book – the reticence of Montague's poetic personality has something to shape and make recognisable, to be truly tactful about. The aesthetic control and the quietness of the tone of the voice are the symptoms and the fruits of real tensions whereas elsewhere they occasionally seem little more than the products of accomplishment and a fine professionalism. Perhaps even in 'All Legendary Obstacles', one of the loveliest pieces in the whole collection and a poem which in itself may suggest possible new directions for Irish poetry, the enjambment ('All legendary obstacles lay between/ Us . . .') and the untypical heavy stresses of 'great flanged wheels' betray an obtrusive knowingness. These minor flaws, which seem to me the products of a rhythmical literal-mindedness, might well have been carried by the iambic measure and the English language's rhetorical tendencies which Montague has chosen to jettison: but these same flaws might then have blossomed into damaging dishonesties at deeper imaginative levels.

This is why we should salute the new rhythms and the experiments of this book. In the best poems they are brave and honest. Montague has learned from and developed the short line and the cadenced near-prose of the Black Mountain poets. Their methods are ideal for mapping a tone of voice; but very little can be encompassed by tone of voice alone, and Black Mountain poetry lacks stamina, staying power. These poets – to a considerable extent Montague's models – may offer one charm and occasional mild wisdoms but they have substituted the limits of personality for the scope of imagination.

How does this affect Montague's work? His new methods work perfectly in the more occasional poems, but in the set pieces they inhibit resolution, deny climax. To transcend and to affirm one must raise one's voice, and this is what Montague at the moment cannot do. Impressive as this book often is, I can't help feeling that, except for the finest pieces, it marks an interim stage, the main failings of which are an aesthetic rootlessness and a lack of affirmation, real pressure, that *joy* Yeats said was essential:

> This low-pitched style seeks exactness,
> Daring only to name the event.

Proud perhaps, but also a sad thing for a poet to admit. I'm certain Montague will soon grant his undoubted talents full scope and contradict himself.

Dublin Magazine 7, 1 (Spring 1968)

PATRICK KAVANAGH

I first encountered Patrick Kavanagh's poetry about ten years ago in *The Oxford Book of Irish Verse* – a wild rose blossoming in that dreariest of graveyards. I was then recovering from a late-adolescent Dylan binge, unable to see the word for the D.T.s, and ready to enjoy, though not yet to learn from, the unusual rhythms of Kavanagh's best lyrics. They seemed rough and tough, awkward even, but it was impossible then – and still is – to see how the words and rhythms could have been arranged otherwise.

His subject matter and landscape could not in themselves mean a great deal to me, but he captured Monaghan so unerringly, in his images and rhythms, that his poems gave it to my imagination in a way that visits there could not. Myth works in this way, and Kavanagh was a mythologist of ordinary things – as he implied himself, a Homer of the fields.

Myth tries to preserve and perpetuate, but it also seeks and offers answers: its roots are in fear and doubt as well as in love. And so much of Kavanagh's poetry seems to be both an attempt at exorcism and a frantic last-minute inventory made before the remembered pictures fade. His best work grew from the richest of disenchantments – that is to say, he knew exactly what he was writing about.

Passionate and precise detail is a token of Kavanagh's sincerity – this, his very definite tone of voice and his irregular but always unfaltering rhythms. Almost too many details must have presented themselves to this poet, and his remarkable achievement is to have conjured from them shape and pattern. The non-metropolitan or, as Kavanagh himself would have said, the 'parochial' poet inherits no aesthetic example and hears no urbane rumours of how things might be done. He makes his own painful way from childhood to manhood, from field to street, from village to city, enacting in miniature and often with awkwardness the development of man's imagination. Kavanagh, one of the noblest of such travellers, called this journey *The Great Hunger*. He turned his back on Monaghan in order to make it immortal and to give to those other writers who are born to a more varied, though less rich, heritage an imaginative hinterland.

At the centre of poetry like Kavanagh's shines a kind of innocence. Faced with this most writers, locked away as they are for much of the time in a spiritual McDaids, feel a profound nostalgia and even guilt. Du Bellay in a famous sonnet sums this up perfectly. Here is Anthony Hecht's translation of four relevant lines:

> And when shall I, being migrant, bring my heart
> Home to its plots of parsley, its proper earth,
> Pot hooks, cow dung, black chimney bricks whose worth
> I have not skill to honour in my art.

When young writers hear the voice of authority they should stay quiet but near: most contemporaries of my acquaintance have done just this with Kavanagh's work. One has to struggle very hard to come to terms, otherwise a part of oneself stops growing up. The struggle – a cross between a half-nelson and a love-embrace – usually occurs in solitude and with the master's book. It may sometimes take the form of arguing bitterly with a friend on behalf of a poet who would probably curse one to hell for doing so. Lastly, it entails attending the funeral of a person one didn't know. This is the irresistible pull of great poets and great men.

Contribution to 'Patrick Kavanagh: A Tribute in Poetry and Prose',
Dublin Magazine 7, 1 (Spring 1968)

A POET OF POWER

Derek Mahon, *Night-Crossing*

Derek Mahon's work began to be known when he published several years ago in the Trinity College literary magazine, *Icarus*. Even when he was only nineteen or twenty, it was obvious that we had amongst us a poet of remarkable power and originality. With the possible exception of Keith Douglas I can think of hardly any undergraduate verse since Auden's to compare with it. I was there at the time and I can say now that to be buffeted by so much creative force was a disquieting as well as an exciting experience. One could have asked then, I suppose, if Mahon was going to become a fixed star or burn himself out like Dylan Thomas or Hart Crane, two meteoric poets whom he greatly admires. Well, the answer is this book, its depth and strength of feeling, its warmth and coherence. As someone who benefited from the extraordinary fireworks display of his juvenilia, I don't think that my being one of the dedicatees of this volume should prevent me from saluting after so many years its arrival.

Even after a first reading of Mahon's poetry one is struck by the vigour and the swiftness of his rhythms, by the bold but appropriate wit and rhetoric, by the marvellous liveliness of it all. He re-engraves the worn, faceless coinage of cliché – an unborn child in one of his finest poems speaks of, and from, the womb:

> Its fabric fits me almost like a glove
> While leaving latitude for a free hand . . .

He takes shocking risks with puns – addressing Louis MacNeice at his graveside he says:

> This plot is consecrated, for your sake,
> To what lies in the future tense. You lie
> Past tension now . . .

And in 'An Unborn Child' a kitten lies 'sunning itself/ Under the bare bulb', while a line later, goldfish are 'mooning around upon the shelf'. But the risks come off because of the inner convictions, real tensions and concerns. Indeed, Mahon is often most profound when he is writing at his wittiest. His throw-away tone differs, however, from the self-defensive ironies of Larkin, say, and much English poetry; rather, it is the product of an exposure of self to experience, of emotional generosity and, at times, prodigality.

It is this generosity which brings me back again and again to Mahon's poetry – the unfailing charity of his vision. Though in his poems the most celebrated times of day and season are early morning and spring, his high spirits reach out somehow to include the misbegotten and the dispossessed – Van Gogh, Marilyn Monroe, the poetic failures of the late nineteenth century, an old crone in Brittany, Beckett's Molloy, the early Irish emigrants. 'Caught in a pose of infinite striptease', Marilyn Monroe becomes

> Cinders swept to the palace from her shack
> By some fairy godmother, in a flash
> Spirited to the front row from the back . . .

The last stanza of 'In Belfast' is heartbreaking in its embrace:

> One part of my mind must learn to know its place –
> The things that happen in the kitchen-houses
> And echoing back-streets of this desperate city
> Should engage more than my casual interest,
> Exact more interest than my casual pity.

The bleak complexities of Belfast have had to wait all this time for their laureate. What Seamus Heaney has done for the rural hinterland of Ulster, Mahon does for the shipyards and back-streets. In other words, he extends the imaginative estate of *all* Irishmen – and of all poets:

> The unreconciled, in their metaphysical pain,
> Strangle on lamp-posts in the dawn rain.

Though his subject matter derives mainly from 'the untransfigured scene', 'the ordinary universe', he is able to unlock the mysteries which lie beneath such surfaces and to rise imaginatively above those levels, like the 'light/ Refracted in a glass of beer/ As if through a church window' in his 'Van Gogh among the Miners'.

This ability to incorporate and at the same time transcend the everyday world can only have been born, surely, of an honest and rigorous exploration – to the depths of his craft – of the inner adventure of poetry, and the painful stretching of emotional capacities in order to come to terms with extreme experience. Mahon's poetry contains many true and valuable insights into the nature of art, which seem closely related to his courageous excursions into chaos and nightmare. The last two stanzas of 'Day Trip to Donegal' are among the best definitions of nightmare I know. Here are four lines:

That night the slow sea washed against my head,
Performing its immeasurable erosions –
Spilling into the skull, marbling the stones
That spine the very harbour wall . . .

This is poetry rejoicing in all its attributes, the aesthetic and the humane – unembarrassed by its richness and invention. *Night-Crossing* is a brilliant and moving collection, and I have no doubts at all that Derek Mahon is among the finest poets now writing anywhere.

Irish Times, 30 September 1968

D. M. Thomas, *Two Voices*; Andre Voznesensky, *Antiworlds* and *The Fifth Ace*

When D. M. Thomas's Science Fiction poems first appeared in one of the Penguin Modern Poets trios, I thought that they were interesting experiments, but ultimately less effective than straightforward Science Fiction. I still find them heavy going – confusing, sometimes boring; but some passages have a marvellous density, a strange kind of radiance, a terrifying logic of their own. Basically, so far as I can judge, Thomas resorts to Science Fiction as a treasure-trove of hitherto unexploited metaphor with which he illuminates sex, mainly the male-female confrontation. This device admits remarkable combinations of the humdrum and the cosmic – the sort of thing Elizabethan love poets took in their stride, but which the average modern poet, perhaps unnecessarily, is embarrassed by. In many ways Thomas could lay claim to being the first New Elizabethan: at the very least, these often baffling exercises deserve our close attention.

His book ends with a brave but disastrous attempt to commemorate Aberfan. This is far more than even Hopkins bit off when he tackled 'The Wreck of the Deutschland'. The italicised documentary material, which is printed in the margin as a commentary on the poems, is invariably more moving then the poetry itself. We salute the honesty of such a juxtaposition whilst recognising that the poet has of necessity admitted defeat from the word go. *Two Voices* includes one of the most beautiful poems I've read for years. It's a despairing love poem called 'Leif the Lucky' which echoes Donne in its voyage-of-discovery metaphor:

Did not the gods say other ships will round
Cape Cod, track marvelling up Nantucket Sound,
Deny the ignorant map I made of you.
Every Columbus had an Erikson,
And Martha's Vineyard shall be found again.

When Andrei Voznesensky's *Antiworlds* first appeared here, it was justly praised. He must be one of the finest poets writing anywhere – an altogether richer and more complex talent than Yevtushenko, who preceded him in reputation, like a John the Baptist. This makes even more exciting the fact that in Russia football stadiums are required to accommodate his poetry-reading audiences. In the West, it can only be the false simplicities of the Liverpool poets or the Beats that command an equivalent attention. The versions by various hands are selfless (as they should be) without being anonymous. The pieces translated by Auden and Richard Wilbur read most satisfyingly, probably because these two poets are the most accomplished of the group and not necessarily because these poems are the best. 'New York Airport at Night', for instance, although it is treated by William Jay Smith in a rather opportunistic fashion, is obviously a great poem. Russian experts are bound to welcome this bilingual edition which incorporates *The Fifth Ace*. And even non-experts like myself must relish the justice and dignity of such a publishing venture.

Extract from review of 'Recent Poetry', *Irish Times*, 28 December 1968

THE WOUNDED BADGER

Brendan Kennelly, *Dream of a Black Fox*; James Simmons,
In the Wilderness

Brendan Kennelly's latest collection is full of powerful and disturbing images. The pivotal point in many of these poems is a confrontation between irreconcilables, a drama which plays itself out in confusion, violence, pain and nightmare. A hawk kills itself attacking the cage of a singing bird. The fierce jaws of a badger grip the hound, which in turn clamps cruelly on the badger. Because of its 'simple savage style' the hunted badger triumphs. Such grim images emerge, in part at least, from Kennelly's growing preoccupation with the nature of the artist's role, or, more particularly, Kennelly's own personal role as a poet in the Irish (i.e. Dublin) literary context.

Thus the poet is the badger, wounded but victorious, or the inviolable but trapped singing bird. Nelly Mulcahy, a local version of the bogey man, represents, perhaps, the imagination. When she turns up in person, old and harmless, the children, frightened by hearsay, stone her. A similar figure is the strong man, who leaves 'the pub's comfortable light/ To be broken and remembered on the roadside grass' – the artist exposed (or the poet published?). The less successful, more direct pieces attacking Dublin could be taken as a commentary or gloss on these alarming poems. All that troubles the poet is summed up in the fine, ambiguous image of the black fox of the title poem, 'whimsical executioner', at one level an enemy of light and love, at another a possible but inevitably rejected tutor for the imagination.

The total effect of these poems is very moving indeed. In their particulars, however, they are sometimes slapdash, cheerfully careless, stubbornly unpolished. Kennelly can't quite decide between a cursive ballad-style utterance where the reader automatically accepts the occasional stock epithet or superfluous adverb, and the poised lyric where every word must do more than it says. This stylistic indecision echoes a certain moral evasiveness ('Only gestures remain/ To tell me the truth of things'), which I put down to Kennelly's desire to explain to us quite unnecessarily his own complexities, artistic and personal. He should wait for the complexities to bear their own fruit, in his verse as well as in public response, and abandon the running commentary. There is, after all, at the core of this book a voice and a vision, at once committed and insouciant, wild and afraid – unique in contemporary poetry ('I had a lot to spend; I spent it:/ Men's eyes opened in wonder/ At my extravagance'). The imperfections are, I suppose, part of the vision, a strategy almost, and its essence is to remain uncertain in itself of 'the bleak injury of its cry'.

James Simmons's *In the Wilderness* has the vitality, warmth and wit which were the main features of his fine first collection. Although this is poetry which anyone could understand, it hardly ever descends to the facile or the shallow. The poems spring from the desire to communicate clearly and readily, and not from any lack of richness and complexity in the subject-matter or in the original impulse. Simmons uses the simple ballad quatrain as though he had invented it –

> From twenty yards I saw my old love
> Locking up her car.
> She smiled and waved, as lovely still
> As girls of twenty are.

The reservations and ambiguities which grow naturally out of Simmons's warm, earthy humanity, correct or delay the immediate, rollicking solutions suggested by the traditional metre. The tensions of true poetry result. Even at its most straightforward, this poetry can convey subtleties of tone and emotional shifts.

Among the best poems is a group about married life. Their initially alarming candour is neither exhibitionistic nor callous, though clearly vulnerable to such charges. Nor can these poems, strictly speaking, be classed as 'confessional'. The confessional poet's centre is *I*: in Simmons's frank, intimate poems the centre is *you*. A vigorous tenderness cancels out any possible embarrassment. There are good poems in which the poet tries to define his Irishness; and an interesting but not entirely successful sequence (it needs a final polish) about *King Lear*. A very good collection which will enliven Irish poetry and place Simmons securely among the best of the younger Irish writers.

Irish Times, 8 February 1969

W. D. Snodgrass, *After Experience*; Elizabeth Jennings, *The Animals' Arrival*; D. J. Enright, *Selected Poems*

The sequence of poems about his divorce and separation from his daughter, *Heart's Needle*, which gave W. D. Snodgrass's fine first collection its title, contains some of the loveliest poetry to have come out of America. The pressures of painful experience shaped the tentative syllabic rhythms into complex stanzaic patterns which conveyed, with an appropriate fragility, the ebb and flow of regret and happy memories, of love and despair.

Worthy reputations claim that *After Experience* is a better book. This just is not so; hard-won poise has been reduced to attitude, a personal tragedy to a literary institution. Snodgrass in his second book has merely achieved the dubious distinction of doing for divorce what Robert Lowell has done for mental breakdown: Hell has become air-conditioned. The pat utterance of many of these poems seems incongruous beside the sad events they comment on. And in 'A Visitation', where Snodgrass tries to come to terms with his guilt by equating himself with Adolf Eichmann, his skill and needlessly ingenious stanzaic arrangement amount to an impertinence: the concentration camps are not the arena for literary dandyism. The collection ends boringly with a sequence on paintings and some tame translations. This is a book I have been looking forward to for years. My disappointment is not so overwhelming as to dampen completely my anticipation of Snodgrass's third.

A similar incongruity between subject matter and style would seem to be present in Elizabeth Jennings's work. She writes about mental breakdown and desolation with a plainness that becomes almost idiosyncratic. Her kind of integrity does not permit her to embroider or colour in. There is real tension in these poems. The frail, skeletal lines teeter on the verge of disintegration: their attitudes are the blankness of shock, the stunned repose of complete disenchantment, and they are expressed by a voice which convinces and moves.

Miss Jennings and D. J. Enright were contributors to Robert Conquest's *New Lines* anthology, an important milestone in the history of English poetry. This selection of Enright's work draws from five books and is welcome indeed. In its grumpy and sometimes too throwaway fashion, his poetry has wonderful warmth and humanity, alertness and accuracy. He has taught in the East for some years now, and many of his best poems record the misery and degradation there with a usually perfectly pitched irony which just manages to shape and control the shock.

Extract from review, *Irish Times*, 4 April 1969

Brian Jones, *Interior*; Douglas Dunn, *Terry Street*; Keith Bosley,
The Possibility of Angels

It is good to be able to recommend three books by young poets. Those
by Bosley and Dunn are first collections.

I underestimated Brian Jones's first book, *Poems*, and consequently
missed out on his second – a gap which the many excellences of *Interior* oblige me to fill. The title is beautifully apt, suggesting interiors
both domestic and mental. Jones's earlier work explored quietly what
it is like to be a suburban husband and father: although still home-
bound, he is now delving deeper and exploring the no man's land
between his imagination and his circumstances. This involves three
rewarding approaches. Firstly, he contemplates bravely his artistic
ruthlessness and the darker areas of his own mind which are uncovered as a result. Secondly, he tries to isolate and so render archetypal
and resonant the little ceremonies and rituals buried in the humdrum
daily round and at the same time be true to not only the frightening
biological simplicities they disguise, but also the merciful blurring
they effect. Thirdly, he maps with a disquieting blend of fear and
wonder feminine self-containment. Three short sequences, 'A Wife's
Tale', 'A Girl's Words', and 'Three Poems of a Frontier Guard', are the
highlights of a very satisfying collection.

I wonder if, in Douglas Dunn, Faber think they have enlisted a sort
of urban Seamus Heaney. Certainly he relates to Larkin as Heaney
does to Hughes. The first section of his impressive first collection
explores in often clogging detail, but always with compassion and
accuracy, the less salubrious areas of Hull. Catalogues abound; short
tightlipped sentences build up vivid pictures with a terseness which

too seldom deepens to become real tension; keen observation crowds out imagination so that the details work like simple addition rather than multiplication. Even so, Dunn's real worth is revealed in most of the endings of these otherwise top-heavy poems. He writes of the old men of Terry Street:

> Dying in their sleep, they lie undiscovered.
> The howling of their dogs brings the sniffing police,
> Their middle-aged children from the new estates.

The beauty of such lines anticipates a number of delicate and more stylish poems in the second section – 'Tribute of a Legs Lover', 'Love Poem', 'The Queen of the Belgians' and the remarkable 'A Dream of Judgement'. These, and isolated lines and stanzas throughout, are positive proof of a fine new talent.

Like Douglas Dunn, Keith Bosley hunts among the mundane for the redeeming feature, the glimpse, against all the odds, of human dignity, the individual face in the crowd – hence the title of his book. This preoccupation, which leads naturally to celebrations of the artist (a sequence of five poems about composers and a fine piece about Stanley Spencer) and of the eccentric (a deranged grandmother, Mad Meg, a Polish aunt), produces poems of great generosity about extremes of experience – birth, madness, growing old. Bosley's generosity can spill over into 'protest' poems which fail for the right reasons. By and large this book is unusual for its extremely attractive slant on life, of which 'Nuns on an Escalator' is a fair example. It ends:

> and I thought of their sister
> Thérèse in her cold castle
> wings clipt closer than her hair

scribbling against time how she
took the lift and spurned the stair ...

Irish Times, 11 October 1969

CECIL DAY LEWIS:
AN APPRECIATION

Why do the labels of literary journalism cling so adhesively? For nearly forty years now Auden, MacNeice, Spender and Day Lewis have been billed as 'thirties poets', as laureates of the pylon and the gasometer, long after changes of heart, stylistic adjustments, and despite the fact that each for many years went his own separate way. They must have had a tremendous impact on the reading public. Roy Campbell's Terrible Beastie, MacSpaunday, really added up to something worth noticing, and, obviously, worth remembering. It's too easy now to smile patronisingly at the innocently embraced Communism, the heady cocktails of Marx and Freud, the public schoolboys trying on cloth caps for size. The motives were, after all, generous and outward-looking: these writers remind us still of the public responsibilities of poetry.

Cecil Day Lewis accepted the mantle of committed poet with more enthusiasm, perhaps, and more youthful naivety than any of his contemporaries. Somewhat under the shadow of the great Auden, he mapped out a utopia shaped by Marxism, 'The Strange New Healer', and took many of his images from the language and ideas of modern science:

> Then life's pistons
> Pounding into their secret cylinder
> Begin to tickle the most anchorite ear
> With hints of mechanisms that include
> The man . . .

Some of his poems about the realities of life in the thirties – labour exchanges and means tests – have the raw vigour of successful propaganda:

> Thy mother is crying,
> Thy dad's on the dole:
> Two shillings a week is
> The price of a soul.

Later he was to resign from the Communist party and to evolve a speculative personal style, which suited him better, I think. He wrote well about love, places, travelling, the countryside, the pleasures of living. His long-felt sympathy for writers like Hardy, Edward Thomas, Wordsworth and Clare asserted itself, and in his best poems he continued that great English tradition which marries observation of the external world to private soul-searching: the lineaments of a place or the patterns of a situation are so described that the individual mind is revealed. Though he claimed to be an Anglo-Irish writer, I think he will be remembered as quintessentially English – despite his Irish connections, his love for this island, and the Irish subject-matter of some of his poems, especially some recent pieces.

> Those Himalayas of the mind
> Are not so easily possessed:
> There's more than precipice and storm
> Between you and your Everest.

But I don't really think of him as a maker of lines: he didn't have the epigrammatic flair of Auden or MacNeice. Rather, he could manage the long measure, the extended sentence nudged subtly towards the condition of poetry, rehearsing in its pace and rhythmic shifts the movements of his thought, dovetailing statement and qualification. This control of the verse paragraph made him one of the best verse translators Virgil has ever had. His versions of the *Aeneid* and the *Georgics* are substantial achievements. And I wonder if his translation of Paul Valéry's great and difficult poem, 'The Graveyard by the Sea', has ever been bettered.

Day Lewis was also a fine critic, probing deeply and intuitively. *The Poetic Image* is an important book. Some of his insights have a definitive ring about them: the hazardous mysteries and dark ambiguities of Edward Thomas's 'Old Man', for instance, found in Day Lewis their perfect commentator. And he always wrote revealingly about Hardy. I am grateful too for his immaculate edition of Wilfred Owen's collected poems – a wonderful book. Then there are his detective novels written under the pseudonym Nicholas Blake. Addicts tell me they're the real thing. From my school-teaching days I remember that, among successive Form Threes, Day Lewis's *The Otterbury Incident* was the favourite out of a wide range of 'readers', as we still called them.

So, he was a real professional, a man of letters – a natural writer in fact. Last summer, near Killadoon in County Mayo, I caught a glimpse of him driving a rather swish car past the stone walls and fuchsia hedges. I thought then about all those years devoted to words, all that work trailing behind him in the slipstream – the poems, the translations, the criticism, the detective novels, the autobiographical work, the children's books. And that's the way I think of him now.

Irish Times, 26 May 1972

The Collected Poems of John Hewitt, edited by Frank Ormsby

On most days of his long writing life John Hewitt must have produced what Derek Mahon calls 'the rows of words'. Versifying, which was his way of gathering his thoughts, pinning down impressions, easing his emotions, had become second nature, as was the case with John Clare. He found it convenient and useful. His attitude to language resembled that of the farmer to his land – utilitarian. He believed, or at least hoped, that we could *do* things with poetry. He was a word-farmer.

Although he revered good craftsmanship, Hewitt often expressed himself clumsily and with prolixity. ('We missed the last bus home and had to walk to Parkgate/ to catch a later bus by another route back to town.') We swallow a fair amount of verse in the process of getting to the poetry. His best work and his weakest share a strong family likeness: we can't have all of one without some of the other. The generous scale and copious apparatus of this *Collected Poems* are in the end justified.

'Strangers and Neighbours', a rather prosaic piece about 'the Jews of my childhood', begins by presenting the racial stereotypes without any saving irony. Even allowing for the fact that the poet is reliving the prejudices of his boyhood, the honesty seems inept, almost embarrassing. That's until the middle of the poem when Hewitt describes a museum showcase at Auschwitz. Here his pain ('my eyes burn dry beyond tears') inspires an astonishing image. He compares the 'swathes and billows of human hair' to a 'vast sombre sand-churning wave'. This is both boundless and precise, an immortal moment. The poem proceeds, or dwindles, for a further thirty lines to its low-key ending. It is typical of this volume. We have been obliged to follow Hewitt at his own pace, and to stay with him for fear of missing the sudden heart-stopping illumination that can arrive even as he contemplates history's worst nightmare.

In an early poem 'The Return' Hewitt dismisses – rather gruffly – his art as 'this uncouth compass' which is 'no more than a needle stuck in a straw,/ and floating in a shaking bowl of water' (a lovely figure). An insouciant drift does often correct his over-programmatic, even didactic tendencies, and allows space for those strange, upsetting insights which brighten his best poems. Many are well-known as anthology pieces, and rightly so: 'Once Alien Here', 'Turf-carrier on Aranmore', 'Because I Paced my Thought', 'The Ram's Horn', 'An Irishman in Coventry', 'The Scar'. These are refreshed rather than inundated by the voluminousness of their new context. And they lead us to other remarkable but less celebrated achievements: the confident speculations of 'Substance and Shadow', the harrowing 'Sonnets for Roberta', the perfection of 'The Man from Malabar', and 'A Local Poet' which may he his finest poem, the quintessential Hewitt utterance. In this apologia-cum-epitaph he sells himself short and yet manages to win our admiration:

> And so, with luck, for a decade
> down the widowed years ahead,
> the pension which crippled his courage
> will keep him in daily bread,
> while he mourns for his mannerly verses
> that had left so much unsaid.

There is something overpowering about such humility. We know that it is more than we deserve. The same might be said of Hewitt's return to our own grubby little corner, and his richly creative second sojourn among us. He gave us his last years, his well-stocked mind, and the benefit of the doubt.

As Europe painfully re-arranges herself, as Communism retreats discredited, as narrow nationalism and crude religion combine to release their toxins, so Hewitt's big-hearted open-faced versions of regionalism, socialism and atheism appear ever more relevant. Ulster's present brutalities should not blind us to the cultural complexity of our problems. This volume is a crucial hinge – albeit one that creaks occasionally – on a door that opens onto vistas of the past and the future, and through which we can study the programmes for redemption suggested by a many-faceted imagination. Its publication is of historical as well as artistic importance. Frank Ormsby, poet and scholar, has given of himself with a generosity the great man deserves. The job could not have been done any better by editor or publisher (Blackstaff Press).

1991

THE OLD MAN FROM DUNDEE

Some Thoughts on Rhyme

Too many people let off steam about Modern Poetry (with a capital *m* and a capital *p*) without ever reading it. Philistines in disguise and little more than ill-informed bigots, they have heard somewhere that 'Modern Poetry doesn't rhyme'. What nonsense. To draw up a random list of great modern poets is also to name some of the consummate exponents of rhyme: W. B. Yeats, W. H. Auden, Louis MacNeice, Robert Frost.

My own gifted contemporaries, Seamus Heaney and Derek Mahon, work with equal ease in free forms and in stricter conventional stanzas which use a rhyme-scheme. A younger Ulster poet, Paul Muldoon, has taken the art of rhyme to new heights of subtlety and sophistication. A virtuoso deployment of rhyme has been a feature of Northern Irish poetry for more than three decades.

So a lot of the best modern poetry does in fact rhyme. Is this what makes it poetry? No. Does poetry need to rhyme? No. Practically all Shakespeare's dramatic verse – poetry's Everest – does *not* rhyme. The poetry of Homer, Sophocles, Euripides, the epics and tragedies of Ancient Greece, do *not* rhyme; nor do the elegists and love poets of Rome, Catullus, Propertius, Horace; nor does John Milton's great English epic *Paradise Lost*.

Poetry's only essential attribute is *rhythm*. This is its heart-beat. This is what makes it memorable. If the rhythm falters, then the poem may die of heart-failure. Rhyme helps to promote the rhythm of a poem, but it is not essential. Good poetry takes advantage of all the things that words can do. One of these – but only one – is rhyme. Every line in my own first collection rhymes. I now rhyme only occasionally. Why? I'm not sure.

English is less rich in rhymes than other languages like French and Italian. Most of the full rhymes have already been used many thousands of times. Who wants to hear 'breath' rhyming with 'death' for the umpteenth weary time; 'womb' with 'tomb'; 'moon' with 'June'; 'book' with 'look' with 'cook' with 'shook' with 'nook'?

In order to convey the nightmare of trench warfare Wilfred Owen, the greatest of the First World War poets, unsettles us by rhyming 'hell' with 'hall': 'brambles' with 'rumbles'. Partial rhyme is nowadays common practice: 'fruit'/ 'afraid'; 'silence'/ 'nonchalance'. At the end of his wonderful poem 'The Thought Fox' Ted Hughes rhymes 'fox' with 'ticks' and 'head' with 'printed'.

When it is deployed effectively rhyme highlights meaning and rhythm. An obvious example is Shakespeare's use of the rhyming couplet at the end of his sonnets. The emphatic chime brings the rhythm and the argument to an obvious close.

Rhyme is a musical enrichment. But its presence does not prove that a piece of writing is poetry. Think of all that embarrassing doggerel, the sad jangle and mechanical *tee-tum-tee-tum* beat of obituary notices and birthday card verse. Here rhyme is lipstick on the corpse of dead language. The gap between *verse* and poetry is enormous, whereas the gap between good poetry and good prose is, relatively speaking, rather narrow. What good poetry and good prose have in common is vitality of rhythm.

I would sum up as follows: (1) Much modern poetry *does* rhyme; (2) much of the world's greatest poetry does *not* rhyme; (3) poetry does not *need* to rhyme; (4) the only essential is *rhythm*.

Those are my humble trade secrets. But I would prefer to end with a mystery and a joke. The mystery first. When asked where he got his ideas from, Yeats answered, 'Looking for the next rhyme.' Now for the joke:

> There was an old man from Dundee
> Who got stung on the neck by a wasp.
> When they asked did it hurt
> He replied, 'No it doesn't.
> In fact I'm very glad it wasn't a hornet.'

Poetry Ireland Review 40 (Winter 1993-4), first published in the *Belfast Newsletter*

The Faber Book of War Poetry, edited by Kenneth Baker

This is a finicky book about a huge subject. I'm not sure what its editor is driving at. Kenneth Baker has been Minister of Education and Home Secretary in the present alarming British administration. During his national service in the fifties he was a Lieutenant in the Artillery in North Africa and an Artillery Instructor to the Libyan Army. I presume that he was not unaware of the deliberations of Mrs Thatcher's war cabinet during the Falklands War. But the politician and the soldier cancel each other out. As a result, his introduction and the rubrics with which he prefaces each section read blandly. 'Wars are caused by the failure of politicians,' he suggests, 'and yet they are sustained by the participation of quite ordinary people.' You can say that again, Mr Baker. Is he being deadpan or glib?

The anthology is fussily divided into nearly seventy sections which include 'Spying', 'Climate and Circumstances', 'Useful Tips' and 'Old Ships' as well as the more pertinent topics such as 'Death in Action', 'Civilian Victims' and 'The Bereaved'. There is something disagreeable about this obsessive categorising, with many sections too daintily organised to do justice to their themes. The first poem in the first section is Swift's version of Horace's ode which contains the famous words 'Dulce et decorum est pro patria mori'. Wilfred Owen's denunciation of that sentiment as 'The Old Lie' follows only one page later. The arrangement leaves no space for reverberation, for echoes to chime and clash across the centuries. It might have made more sense to end the book with Owen's great poem, and allow him and Horace the first and the last say. Cheek by jowl they are hard to hear.

Baker's subdividing and labelling are the obverse of fine discrimination. Everything seems homogenised, as though the book had been compiled by a committee. Desk-bound poems about war are given as much weight as poems written at the extremes of suffering. Because they fit into the anthologist's artificial framework, precious space is taken up by Tennyson's schoolboyish 'Battle of Brunanburh' and Chesterton's chubby 'Lepanto', as well as yards of raucous verse by Kipling. The Holocaust, which Baker describes as 'the greatest crime against humanity the world has ever seen', gets only five pages.

The cataclysms of the twentieth century render already out of date Baker's historical perspective; render disproportionate his desire for a sense of proportion. The cavalry charges of earlier days and the infantry's muddy thumpings with broad swords can't have been much fun. But no one then could have imagined the carnage that would be caused by machine-guns, howitzers, poison gas, grenades, landmines, guided missiles, the atomic bomb in our own age of industrialised slaughter.

The miracle is that a Keatsian sensibility such as Owen's could, in the shambles of the trenches, harness the English lyric to a tragic vision. His Great War poems are matched only by Isaac Rosenberg's 'Dead Man's Dump' in which he cries out like a young Aeschylus staggering down the line to death. Surprisingly, Baker does not include this towering masterpiece. He does, though, represent with four marvellous poems the next great war poet in English, Keith Douglas who died on the Normandy beaches, nearly thirty years later, at the age of twenty-four. Douglas toughened the lyric in his own way and absorbed into it the horrors of tank battles and desert warfare. This anthology could more sensitively demonstrate how poetry's lyric impulse has adapted and metamorphosed in order to survive modern war.

Of course many wonderful poems do get in, among them the

stunning sonnet 'When you see millions of the mouthless dead' by Charles Sorley who was killed in October 1915 at the age of twenty. In a powerful anti-patriotic letter home he hoped that 'after the war all brave men will renounce their country and confess that they are strangers and pilgrims on the earth'. I have already mentioned 'Dulce et decorum est', Owen's evocation of a gas attack. Its terrible lines stain all our cenotaphs with blood 'gargling from the froth-corrupted lungs,/ Obscene as cancer . . .'. Brecht suggested that cenotaphs should be inscribed with the one word most soldiers utter at the moment of death: 'Shit'. In the Preface he drafted for a planned collection of his poems, Owen began by stating, 'This book is not about heroes. English Poetry is not yet fit to speak of them.' Kenneth Baker has not yet realised what Owen meant.

Irish Times, 12 October 1996

PAPER BOATS

Ian Hamilton Finlay

Catalogues which release the power of names by stringing them together to make rhythmic sense are at the heart of poetry and go all the way back to the catalogue of ships in Homer's *Iliad*. There are so many catalogues in my own work I sometimes feel I should ration them. But they continue to happen, especially at heightened moments, and I prefer to drift with what seems a natural tendency. Ian Hamilton Finlay's example makes me feel that I am right to do so. Each time a catalogue creeps into a poem I am reminded of his beautiful 'Green Waters' which consists solely of the names of trawlers. Since I first discovered it in the sixties, this poem has had a huge influence on me. I return to its twelve short lines again and again. I have not visited Homer's catalogue of ships nearly as often! 'Green Waters' taught me to scribble down lists of things before I could be sure of their relevance. Each of the four quatrains of my poem 'Trade Winds' consists of a short catalogue: the names of the locks on the River Lagan, of the apples from County Armagh, of clay pipes manufactured in Carrickfergus, and of fishing smacks in Portavogie harbour. The last of these allowed me to say as much about life and death in twenty-four words as I am ever likely to manage in so confined a space. The skippers who had so suggestively christened their boats offered me the poem, as it were, and Ian Hamilton Finlay showed me how to accept it:

Among the Portavogie prawn-fishermen
Which will be the ship of death: Trade Winds,
Guiding Starlight, Halcyon, Easter Morn,
Liberty, Faithful Promise, Sparkling Wave?

Some years ago when I was away from home looking for wild flowers
in the Burren in County Clare, the man who worked in our local ice-
cream shop in Belfast was murdered by paramilitaries. When I tried
to write an elegy for him, I opened the little green notebook into
which I had jotted down flower names. I worked hard to turn them
into a wreath of words, a prayer of sorts, and ended the elegy with a
catalogue of the wild flowers I had seen in the Burren in one day. Later,
the ice-cream man's mother wrote to thank me for the poem: 'The fact
that there were twenty-one flavours of ice-cream, and you wrote
twenty-one flowers was coincidental', she told me. But it was more
than a coincidence. My elegy and her heartbreaking letter would not
exist if I had not summoned up 'Green Waters', felt reverence for the
flower names and taken time to write them down.

Flower names. Boat names. When recently I discovered Finlay's
'Ovidian Flowers', I was overwhelmed by a feeling of kinship, which
was further intensified by our shared fixations on Ovid and the world
wars. Even without its gloss his poem is ravishing:

Veronica became *Temptress* –
Hibiscus became *Spry*
Arabis became *Saucy*
Periwinkle became *Restless*
Calendula became *Ready*
Begonia became *Impulse*
Larkspur became *Fury*

> Heartsease became *Courage*
> Candytuft became *Tenacity*

But the gloss takes us so much further and generates truly Ovidian transformations: 'Early in 1942 U-boat successes against American merchant shipping resulted in a number of Flower Class corvettes being transferred from the RN to the USN.' The poem and its gloss are printed on either side of a card that is smaller than a postcard. At first this seems an eccentric way to publish such remarkable work. But 'Ovidian Flowers' and all the other poem-cards and leaflets and posters modify our notions of how an *oeuvre* might accumulate. They also suggest that *sub specie aeternitatis* only a handful of poems will make it; that this could be one of them; that in any case every poem is a memorandum to posterity.

As though in recognition of the fact that our civilisation is paper-thin, Finlay throughout his career has remained loyal to paper, the flimsiest of materials. But he has also worked in wood and stone. Whatever the medium, he writes words down and gives them their place. Like Saint Colmcille, he has left his fingerprints in stone. The virtuoso of the confined space, he turns on a sixpence:

> Dove, dead in its snows

What more needs to be said? Finlay captures the moment of inspiration, and in a split second transports us from inkling to transfiguration. With its roots in the Latin *movere*, to move, 'momentous' which relates to 'moment' (a point of time, an instant) and means important, weighty, is the adjective I'm tempted to choose for Finlay's work. But 'momentous' doesn't really do justice to his quicksilver imagination, or the way he combines the witty with the devout. Such word-play and suggestiveness of image resist tidy epithets. It is easier for me to imagine Ian Hamilton Finlay folding paper boats for the boy Odysseus and launching them, happy-go-lucky, in the direction of Troy.

From *Green Waters: An Anthology of Boats and Voyages* (Stromness: Pier Arts Centre; Edinburgh: Polygon; Edinburgh: Morning Star; Lochmadd: Taigh Chearsabhagh, 1998)

THE WEAVER'S SKILL

Ted Hughes, *Tales from Ovid*

Metamorphoses, Ovid's longest work, his *chef d'oeuvre*, is an unrivalled treasure-trove of stories from Greek mythology and Latin folklore, all loosely connected, in fifteen books. The orchestrating theme is, for the most part, the miraculous transformation of men and women into animals and plants and natural objects such as rivers – the usual reason being love, passion, lust. A dazzling storyteller, Ovid organises his material with breathtaking architectonic control, and keeps the whole strange and wonderful show going in Latin hexameters that are limpid and fluent and, relatively speaking, easy to understand. This magician weaves a spell and at the same time keeps us in touch at unexpectedly profound levels with the mysteries of the heavens, the natural world, and our own bodies and psychologies.

In the farm section of his volume *Moortown*, in his beautiful book for children *Season Songs*, in classic poems such as 'Esther's Tomcat', 'Pike', 'The Bull Moses', 'To Paint a Water Lily', Ted Hughes has produced some of the finest writing about animals and plants in the English language. In addition, his ability to read the landscape and his sense of how elemental commotion can reflect human neurosis should make him a kindred spirit of the Roman poet. *Tales from Ovid* has its beginnings in the four much-praised passages Hughes contributed to Michael Hofmann's and James Lasdun's landmark collection of translations by contemporary poets, *After Ovid: New Metamorphoses*. So the appearance of a further twenty episodes raises our expectations.

This new book, however, is a bit of a bumpy ride. Although a poet of genius, Hughes has seldom shone as either a metrical or a stanzaic artist. Yet in these translations, as elsewhere, he seems to yearn for a form or, perhaps more precisely, a shape. 'Erisychthon' begins promisingly in quatrains but after a few pages these spill over into an uncomfortable compromise between stanza and free verse. In 'Callisto and Arcas' and 'The Rape of Proserpina' the same thing happens with three-liners and five-liners respectively. As a result the stanza's capacity to contain and thereby promote the action is diminished. In particular, the awkwardness of some bridge passages is the price a lyric poet pays for essaying narrative without a stanzaic or metrical framework. His improvisatory, even makeshift, line arrangements and word clusters can invigorate at first, but they are finally less sustaining than those passages where he achieves something like finality of form, as in these charming lines from 'Pyramus and Thisbe':

> This crack, this dusty crawl-space for a spider,
> Became the highway of their love-murmurs.
> Brows to the plaster, lips to the leak of air
>
> And cooking smells from the other interior,
> The lovers kneeled, confessing their passion,
> Sealing their two fates with a fracture.

Lovely stuff – although (or maybe because) most of it is an elaboration by Hughes himself. He makes of Ovid's thin chink ('tenui rima') what can only be called a window of opportunity:

> . . . primi vidistis amantes
> et vocis fecistis iter, tutaeque per illud
> murmure blanditiae minimo transire solebant.

The American poet Alan Mandelbaum translates this passage as follows:

> you were the first to find it, and you made
> that cleft a passageway which speech could take.
> For there the least of whispers was kept safe:
> it crossed that cleft with words of tenderness

I prefer Hughes's version, which is true to the spirit of the original and original in itself.

There are other remarkable moments. When men come to cremate Narcissus, they can find no body:

> But there, in the pressed grass where he had perished,
> A tall flower stood unbroken –
> Bowed, a ruff of white petals
> Round a dainty bugle centre
> Yellow as egg yolk.

The last three lines take off from 'foliis medium cingentibus albis' which means 'its (yellow) centre circled by white petals'. The word for yellow ('croceum') comes in the middle of the previous line. If Latin has an advantage over English so far as syntactical flexibility is concerned, English wins hands down when it comes to richness of vocabulary. Hughes presses home this advantage throughout these pages, often to excess; but here 'ruff' and 'dainty' 'bugle centre' and the 'egg yolk' simile really do pay their way. Much more than embellishments, they deepen the note of pathos. Sometimes Hughes gets it right simply by following the original quite closely. In the weaving competition between impertinent Arachne and the goddess Athene:

Neither was aware how hard she was working,
Feeding the cloth with colours
That glowed every gradation

Of tints in the rainbow
Where the sun shines through a shower
And each hue dissolves
Into its neighbour too subtly
For human eye to detect it.

There's a lovely sense here of both poets acknowledging as fellow-artists the weaver's skill, the swift movement of the shuttle. Perhaps Hughes resorts to the short line too readily, and misses the swell of the hexameter, sometimes even in those watery descriptions at which Ovid excels – in 'Arethusa', for instance, which he renders rather jerkily. Short lines, sudden enjambments are a poor substitute for emphases that exploit, rather than deny, a metrical pattern: 'The sole condition –/ Fixed by the Fates –/ is this:/ She can return to heaven/ On condition . . .' ('The Rape of Proserpina'). Or 'Let death come quickly –/ Carry me off/ Where this pain/ Can never follow' ('Echo and Narcissus'). These passages read like prose. The longer line unshackles Hughes – as in 'Creation; Four Ages; Flood' with which he impressively begins his book:

The unworked earth
Whitened beneath the bowed wealth of the corn.
Rivers of milk mingled with rivers of nectar.
And out of the black oak oozed amber honey.

These lines about the Golden Age do not sound all that far away from Dryden's glossy rhyming couplets:

> In following years, the bearded corn ensu'd
> From Earth unask'd, nor was that Earth renew'd.
> From veins of vallies, milk and nectar broke;
> And honey sweating through the pores of oak.

In the first great English translation of *Metamorphoses* (1567) Arthur Golding takes greater liberties than either Dryden or Hughes, and communicates earthy insouciance, rumbustious delight:

> No mucke nor tillage was bestowde on leane and barren land,
> To make the corne of better head, and ranker for to stand.
> Then streames ran milke, then streames ran wine, and yellow
>   honny flowde
> From each greene tree whereon the rayes of firie *Phebus* glowde.

Golding seems less overshadowed by his great Mediterranean forebear than any of the other translators I've been reading. His peasants speak with confident Somerset accents. In the story of Actaeon he gives the hounds the sort of names a sixteenth-century English huntsman might choose: Snatch, Rug, Royster, Fleetwood, Stalker, Blackfoot. Hughes, who exuberantly includes in his versions all sorts of anachronisms (such as spaghetti, popcorn, doughnut, photon, cockpit, vapour trail, methane, nuclear blast), for some reason sticks with Ovid's dog names. And they do sound odd: Melampus, Ichnobates, Poemenis, Harpyia, Dromas, Sicyon – thirty-six of them in all. I'm not sure of Ovid's intention, but Hughes's catalogue certainly does not race off the page.

More generally, Golding imbues his often straggling long lines with a richer sense of the English countryside than does Hughes. Which is surprising. Has this immensely gifted poet digested so much that he is now capable of practically anything – except re-invention, metamorphosis? Though full of riches and surprises *Tales from Ovid* can read monotonously at times, especially in the psychological sphere. Perhaps Hughes has yet to locate in Ovid that mystic pond he evokes in 'Pike' – 'Stilled legendary depth:/ It was as deep as England.' But there is plenty of scope for his exploration to continue. Although by contemporary standards this is a plump volume, it gives us only a sample from Ovid's compendium. I would not be surprised to learn that a volume called *More Tales from Ovid* waits on the slipway. I hope that this is the case. I would also put in an urgent plea for the long overdue re-issue of Arthur Golding's glorious masterwork, which Shakespeare once so fruitfully perused. In the wake of Lasdun and Hofmann's *New Metamorphoses* we are all queueing up to pick the capacious pockets of the supreme storyteller. Perhaps this endless re-creation is what the last word of the first *Metamorphoses* anticipates: 'vivam' – 'I shall live'.

Poetry Ireland Review 56 (Spring 1998)

JOHN MONTAGUE'S 'WINDHARP'

Windharp
for Patrick Collins

The sounds of Ireland,
that restless whispering
you never get away
from, seeping out of
low bushes and grass,
heatherbells and fern,
wrinkling bog pools,
scraping tree branches,
light hunting cloud,
sound hounding sight,
a hand ceaselessly
combing and stroking
the landscape, till
the valley gleams
like the pile upon
a mountain pony's coat.
            A Slow Dance (1975)

I have loved 'Windharp' for a long time. It was love at first sight. The narrow shape on the page helps to create this poem's strange efful-gence – as a single shaft of sunlight breaking through on an overcast day focuses our attention on features in the landscape – a searchlight. Many of John Montague's finest poems deploy short lines and need to be read aloud with a nano-second's pause at the end of each line. This applies even (or perhaps especially) when the lines end with apparently unimportant words such as 'of' and 'till'. For instance, in its fourth line ('from, seeping out of') the poem finds its balance precisely. Syllable and breathing-space interact with great refinement. We read these lines with bated breath and are drawn into an enraptured state of mind. Attentive, devout even, 'Windharp' is a halting prayer, a broken spell. We are carried away and then brought down to earth.

I look up to this celebrant of the Irish countryside, the precision of his descriptions. The spare music, cool as a breeze, lifts the 'heather-bells and fern' and the 'bog pools' well away from the stereotypical. Spaced in the single sentence like rosary-beads on their thread the participles – 'whispering', 'wrinkling', 'stroking' – generate an atmosphere of suspense. Adverbs can so often be superfluous but here the solitary adverb 'ceaselessly' is detonated brilliantly and in a way becomes the soul of the poem. Its sounds are what these sixteen lines are all about. The intensity of 'Windharp' lends its particulars an emblematic aura. One concise rural evocation comes to symbolize the whole island. Implicated in every detail, the poet's love of Ireland is most beautifully embodied in the heart-stopping final image of the mountain pony, an incarnation of the spirit of the countryside, the poet's Pegasus.

I am reminded of when I first met John Montague decades ago on the campus of Queen's University Belfast. He emerged out of the darkness of the quadrangle and into the dimly lit colonnade that led to the lecture theatre where he was going to read. This poet, whom I had been studying for years, all of a sudden took shape like one of his slim-lined poems. 'We meet at last', he said. He was nimble and wry, a commanding presence, and friendlier than he needed to be. He read very well, with the audience gradually growing accustomed to his unpredictable stammer. The literary conversation that followed was full of angles like a good game of squash. And so it continues. I want to wish this complicated man and superlative poet a happy eightieth birthday. It is high time I thanked him for his poems and for his devotion to the craft, 'a hand ceaselessly/ combing and stroking/ the landscape'.

From *Chosen Lights: Poets on Poems by John Montague* in honour
of his 80th birthday, edited by Peter Fallon
(Loughcrew: Gallery Press, 2009)

Richard Murphy, *The Pleasure Ground: Poems 1952–2012*

Way back in the 1960s, when we were just beginning to spread our wings, the poets of my generation looked for inspiration to the first collections of our immediate Irish predecessors, John Montague, Thomas Kinsella and Richard Murphy. We were eager to learn what makes a line and how a stanza is built; how far the iambic pentameter can be stretched. In Richard Murphy's milestone collection *Sailing to an Island* three narrative pieces in particular, 'The Last Galway Hooker', 'The Cleggan Disaster' and the title poem, released a new kind of music, melodious enough but also open to narrative wayward-ness and matter-of-fact detail:

> Down in the deep where the storm could not go
> The strong ebb-tide was drawing to windward
> Their cork-buoyed ninety-six fathom of nets
> With thousands of mackerel thickly meshed.

In a blink the documentary inflection can modulate into a surreal lyricism: 'What were those lights that seemed to blaze like red/ Fires in the pits of the waves?' The movement is risky and assured:

> In the dark before the moon rose, he could smell
> Fish-oil and blood oozing from the nets
> Where a shark was gorging on the tails of mackerel.

We hadn't heard a poetic noise quite like that before.

In Murphy's storytelling there is plenty of room for song. Intense lyrics sit side by side with the big narratives: 'Girl at the Seaside', 'The

Drowning of a Novice':

> Where was the pebbled cove
> and the famine cottage?
> His piano-playing fingers
> ached at the oars.

The verse can sometimes be overwrought. In 'Wittgenstein and the Birds' 'He clipped with February shears the dead/ Metaphysical foliage'. A whiff of insouciance is needed here.

The next major undertaking was *The Battle of Aughrim, 1691*, a sequence of thematically and musically linked short poems that explore the violent complexities of an historical moment, or, according to the poet's own gloss: 'A meditation on colonial war and its consequence in Ireland written in Connemara between 1962 and 1967.' Murphy's imagery is both down-to-earth and emblematic: 'A wolfhound sits under a wild ash/ Licking the wound in a dead ensign's neck.' Here, in its entirety, is 'Martial Law', one of many powerful lyrics:

> A country woman and a country man
> Come to a well with pitchers,
> The well that has given them water since they were children:
> And there they meet soldiers.
>
> Suspecting they've come to poison the spring
> The soldiers decide to deal
> Justly:
> So they hang them on a tree by the well.

The long and the short lines and the part-rhymes masterfully evoke the nightmare scene. I can think of no contemporary poet who has more tellingly transmuted the stuff of history into poetry.

Much of Richard Murphy's loveliest work is to be found, I think, in *High Island*, poems of the years 1967–1973, loose-limbed and open-throated. Is there a finer bird-poem than 'Stormpetrel'?

> Pulse of the rock
> You throb till daybreak on your cryptic nest
> A song older than fossils,
> Ephemeral as thrift.
> It ends with a gasp.

'Cryptic' is so daring there, and the last line in every sense breathtaking, simple and yet in no way straightforward. Murphy's celebrations of the western seaboard pulse with psalm-like intensity: 'Seals at High Island', for instance, exudes a vivid sexuality: 'When the great bull withdraws his rod, it glows/ Like a carnelian candle set in jade. 'Song for a Corncrake' ends with these heartbreaking lines:

> Quicken your tune, O improvise, before
> The combine and the digger come,
> Little bridegroom.

This poet also relishes turning on a sixpence. Several epigrammatic poems bejewel this collection. 'Double Negative' is a gnomic love poem for his friend Tony White:

> You were standing on the quay
> Wondering who was the stranger on the mailboat
> While I was on the mailboat
> Wondering who was the stranger on the quay.

113

These four lines compress swirling emotions and remind us that miniature is not the same as minor. This quatrain fills the page.

The Price of Stone is for me Murphy's least winning collection. Its dogged anthropomorphism is sustained over a suite of fifty sonnets in which various buildings associated with the poet's life soliloquise – from Nelson's Pillar to Letterfrack Industrial School, from a Waterkeeper's Bothy to Newgrange and a Beehive Cell. There's something too predetermined here, a lack of surprise, too few 'gasps'.

I much prefer the psychic desolation of the amorous, sometimes homoerotic poems in *High Island* (especially the exquisitely tender 'Sunup' and 'The Glass Dump Road' which faces into the darkness of child-abuse); the compassionate portraits of poverty and dispossession; the concentrated energy of the animal psalms; the delicate syncopations of 'Pat Cloherty's Version of *The Maisie*', a fugue-like masterpiece which brilliantly conceals its artfulness.

Murphy provides a preface that reverberates helpfully throughout this collection. There are several prose appendices explaining the provenance of some of the major poems and, at the end, a perceptive appreciation by Bernard O'Donoghue of 'Pat Cloherty's Version of *The Maisie*'. This critical apparatus bears further witness to Murphy's lifelong devotion to his craft. He is indeed one of our supreme makers. Oscillating from beginning to end and from page to page between narrative and lyric, public and private, love poem and elegy, *The Pleasure Ground* is a hugely significant achievement. Now well into his ninth decade Richard Murphy continues to be a poet of great fortitude and resource, one of the finest of our time.

Irish Times, 17 August 2013

JOURNEY OUT OF ESSEX

A Note on John Clare

The imagery of my poem 'Journey Out of Essex' is derived from John Clare's own desolate account of his escape from the asylum when he hobbled for many miles with a bad foot, soaked to the skin, eating grass and quids of tobacco. I wrote it in August 1968 after nearly two years in the creative wilderness. Whatever poetic skills I had acquired over the previous decade were no longer of use. From time to time during this barren period I tried to produce a poem about John Clare, who was already an obsession, already one of my patron saints. I accumulated a pile of notes, half-lines, phrases, bits and pieces, but my words continued to sound lifeless. I shelved the project for several months; then one evening in Dublin when I least expected it, and when I was without my notes and preliminary sketches, the poem I had laboured for so long to bring into being presented itself very quietly and with little effort. I wrote it out more or less as it stands now. It was as though John Clare's gentleness of spirit had corrected my ambition, dictated the pace of my imagination, and generously in the end given me a poem which, after forty-five years, I am still grateful for:

> I am lying with my head
> Over the edge of the world,
> Unpicking my whereabouts
> Like the asylum's name
> That they stitch on the sheets . . .

John Clare seemed to think and feel in sonnet form. His poems grow with what looks like an organic inevitability. But we should never consider him 'artless'. His finest lyrics – such as 'The Nightingale's Nest' and 'To the Snipe' – are among the glories of English poetry. He was also one of the first and greatest field naturalists – and probably the first human being ever to differentiate the constituents of wild birds' nests and consider the information worth publishing. He saw the natural world with such preternatural clarity that exultation and anguish often combine in his writing, even in his prose jottings: 'The flirt of the ground-lark's wing from the stubbles, how sweet such pictures on dewy mornings when the dew flashes from its brown feathers.' Under his devout gaze humdrum objects are transfigured, astonishment is always near at hand: 'And this old gate that claps against the tree/ The entrance of spring's paradise should be.' He wrote one of his last poems 'To be Placed at the Back of his Portrait' in Northampton General Lunatic Asylum. The closing lines of this self-elegy might express my love and reverence for Clare's pure genius:

> Bard o' the mossy shed,
> Live on for ages:
> Daisies bloom by thy bed
> And live in thy pages.

Catalogue, Clement McAleer, *The Open Field: The John Clare Series*, 2014

'AND IS THERE HONEY STILL FOR TEA?'

A Pageant of English Verse

First published by Longmans, Green in 1949, *A Pageant of English Verse* was edited by E. W. Parker, M.C., his military honour proudly printed on the title page as though to insist that it is perfectly normal and manly to enjoy poetry. A chunky brick of a book, with strong green boards and red lettering, thick pages that lay open easily, clear print, and a sense of abundance that was in no way suffocating, this was the first anthology that tempted me to explore poetry. It became a part of everyday life: the only poetry book in our household, a bright light among the Mathematics and Science, Latin and Greek and French primers. Crushed in my rucksack with other schoolbooks and muddy rugby gear, the words of the great poets survived being lugged around Inst's scattered playing fields.

In Fourth or Fifth Form a charming teacher from England, Keith Stevens, chatted about James Joyce's *Ulysses* and *Finnegans Wake*. He grew flushed with excitement when he steered his class of eager adolescents away from the curriculum and exposed us to Modern Poetry in the shape of Eliot's 'The Hollow Men', unlikely stowaways in *A Pageant of English Verse*. I for one was exhilarated by the strange sounds and rhythms: 'For thine is/ Life is/ For thine is'. I deluded myself that I was being tested at the cutting edge of Modernism. I now consider 'The Hollow Men' pretentious tosh. God knows how many dreadful undergraduate imitations it has engendered.

O the vagaries of fashion! By 1946 Siegfried Sassoon and Wilfred Owen, who are nowadays thought of as Great War poets, were still playing second fiddle to Rupert Brooke ('. . . oh! yet/ Stands the Church clock at ten to three?/ And is there honey still for tea?'). Isaac Rosenberg and Ivor Gurney are not represented at all. The most up-to-date section of the anthology is crowded with poets nobody reads any more: Edward Shanks, Martyn Skinner, Victoria Sackville-West, Osbert Sitwell and Alex Comfort, who much later found fame and fortune as the author of *The Joy of Sex*, a well-illustrated international best-seller. Parker gives Comfort three pages, Louis MacNeice only half a page.

But Rupert Brooke's 'The Soldier' is a fine poem – and here it is in the same company as Lawrence's 'Snake', Edward Thomas's 'If I should ever by chance', Yeats's 'Aedh wishes for the Cloths of Heaven', and unexpected poems by de la Mare and Masefield. (Oddly, neither 'The Listeners' nor 'Cargoes' gets in, two miracle poems.) Nowhere else would I have discovered John Drinkwater's lovely 'Moonlit Apples' ('. . . and the moon again/ Dapples the apples with deep-sea light') or the extraordinary closing lines of 'The Goat Paths' by James Stephens: 'I would think until I found/ Something I can never find,/ Something lying on the ground,/ In the bottom of my mind.' Enjoying these poems and learning some of them by heart partly prepared me, as a sixth-former, for *A Pageant*'s breathtaking hinterland: the Romantics, the Augustans, the Metaphysicals. And, thanks to this tough little anthology, I am still making discoveries about the tug-of-war between sincerity and artifice in 'Lycidas', or the understated brilliance of Wordworth's blank verse, or Keats's supernatural ear.

Yellow Nib 10, Seamus Heaney Centre, Queen's University Belfast
(Spring 2015)

PART 3

ESSAYS & FOREWORDS

SEXTUS PROPERTIUS

The main justification for this evening's gathering is the relationship between the poetry of Propertius, and us. Relationships are a tense series of attractions and fascinations: and tonight I want to deal with the facets of Propertius's writing which fascinate and attract me personally – his vocabulary, mythology, sincerity, drama and other points. I am dealing with a strange and fragile thing – another man's imagination; and, if it were possible to do so without monotony, would end each sentence of my paper with a question-mark. But even questions, I suppose, are statements of a kind.*

A poet's first duty is to words. This fact cannot be stressed enough, especially in these days of commitment when we are inundated with politics and sociology and philosophy masquerading as poetry. A poet must look after words. And he must not use them as a mere tool, but rather *make* with them, or just *work* with them. By making he will renew, by working revive, but by using he will exhaust. A poet usually works with words, and occasionally he is blessed with the chance to make with them. In his first elegy Propertius contrasts his own frustrating courtship with the more fruitful exertions of Milanion. And we find the following couplet:

> Nam modo Partheniis amens errabat in antris,
> ibat et hirsutas ille videre feras

The hexameter is a satisfactory working with words. In the pentameter, however, two quiet words, 'ibat' and 'videre', are placed beside two loud words, 'hirsutas' and 'feras', and draw from them a whole range of colour and meaning. 'Videre', in particular, borrows force to become the most powerful word in the line. The two quiet words are made into something more than themselves. They sing beyond themselves. In the hexameter we see an arrangement, in the pentameter a process. My second example is from the second book of elegies, the twelfth elegy where Propertius asks the cruel God of Love: 'if you destroy me utterly, whom will you find to sing such songs as these' and

> qui caput et digitos et lumina nigra puellae,
> et canat ut soleant molliter ire pedes?

Here we see the process reversed – two quiet words, 'soleant' and 'ire' play a strangely active role. They fuse into 'molliter' and explore for us its very essence, its personality. The meaning of lightness is enhanced by lightness of tone, and the word is given room to take flight. Propertius has given us a good portrait of 'molliter'.

These are just two examples of Propertius making through, and within, poetry. The words are not merely doing but becoming something. Syntax would seem to hold the secret, but it lies beyond even this, I think. Let us look at two more examples:

> ... in magnis et voluisse sat est
> quin et erat magnae pars imitanda domus ...

'Et' releases the potential of the whole line. Unfortunately, in English we have to translate it as 'even', which deadens the original mystery completely. And it *is* a mystery, an aesthetic mystery. In the Latin 'et' is both precise and ambiguous, forcing us to choose and surprising us that there is a choice. 'Pars' plays a similar role to those quiet words I discussed in the first two examples; it owes a great deal to its position, to the syntax of the sentence: but the tensions it produces are of itself, not only of its position – it is like the dramatic pregnant pause, which is exciting because of its context and because it is silent. And to heighten the tension, 'pars' has a meaning. It is difficult to say what the magic is, and dangerous, no doubt, to venture an explanation. I think of counterpoint in music. Though a highly intellectual construction, counterpoint has a profoundly emotional effect on the listener. It is more than two fine themes, more than two fine themes played together. The mystery lies in the relationship between the themes, or at the very least in the attraction between them. The magic is more than the effect the two themes make together. Perhaps it is the light they cast over the no man's land which lies somewhere between them. And so with love and poetry.

What is love but a strange light falling between two individuals? In high poetry the words have relationships with each other, and on various planes: there are counterpoints of meaning, sound, cadence, pace and tone. The chemistry, the relationship, the magic, the mystery – call it what you will – is there and it is inexplicable. From this confusion, let us say that in high poetry the words love each other.

Usually in Ovid and Tibullus the unit is the line. L. P. Wilkinson compares this to Hebrew parallelism, and the effect is one of antiphony. In Propertius the unit is the couplet, and the effect is harmony: his pentameters modify the hexameter, those of Ovid and Tibullus mirror it. What is the relationship between the hexameter and the pentameter? It seems that something happens in the hexameter which is commented upon by the movement and meaning of the pentameter – especially the movement. The pentameter gives direction to the action of the hexameter. Propertius achieves this in many ways, but usually by syntax or arrangements of sound. He places a strong main verb in the hexameter, whose force branches off into a subsidiary verb, mood or movement in the pentameter. In the second elegy of Book I we find the following:

> See what colours the lovely earth puts out,
> And how ivy grows better when it comes spontaneously . . .

An imperative starts the hexameter – 'aspice' – and goes directly and forcefully to an object – 'See what colours'. The pentameter, however, stands back and views a situation. It explains the tendency of the hexameter and traces its movement. This pattern occurs frequently in Propertius. My next example is from the eighteenth elegy of Book III:

> Go now, be filled with confidence and imagine your glory,
> And may the whole theatre stand up to applaud and delight you.

Here in the hexameter we have three imperatives, in the pentameter one subjunctive which explains and fulfils the imperatives.

'And' is one of the most poetic words in any language. It dominates and it insinuates, separates and joins. Its cousin is the word 'of'. Let us look at a few examples from English poetry. First from Robert Frost:

> The woods are lovely, dark and deep,
> But I have promises to keep,
> *And* miles to go before I sleep,
> *And* miles to go before I sleep.

And two more examples, this time from 'Thirteen Ways of Looking at a Blackbird' by Wallace Stevens:

A man and a woman
Are one.
A man and a woman *and* a blackbird
Are one . . .

It was evening all afternoon.
It was snowing
And it was going to snow.

And lastly a quotation from 'Pure Death' by Robert Graves:

We looked, we loved *and* therewith instantly
Death became terrible to you and me.

Because the unit in Propertius is the couplet, 'et' is of considerable importance. He always uses it in a particular and subtle way to weld, and not merely link, his pentameters and hexameters together. In the first couplet quoted above ('Nam modo Partheniis') 'et' is an indicator, carrying the emphasis 'moreover' as well as 'also': 'he wandered distraught in the Parthenon caverns, and moreover went to face . . . [etc.]' The two verbs are welded together, depending completely on each other: 'ibat' modifies and draws colour from 'errabat'. In the seventeenth elegy of Book I Propertius begins his poem with 'et':

Et merito, quoniam potui fugisse puellam,
nunc ego desertas alloquor alcyonas . . .

How right it is that I am calling out to the desolate halcyon birds
Since I have had the heart to fly from my mistress . . .

'Et' announces a result and its consequences. It places the whole couplet and implies more than a plunging 'in medias res'. In translating this into English, I have had to make the whole couplet depend on the phrase 'et merito' – 'How right it is'. An invisible pentameter makes itself felt at the very beginning of the poem. The hexameter and the pentameter do two things, but not exclusively. It is, incidentally, brilliant to begin a poem with 'et'. An uncompromising poetic decision is implied. In the second couplet quoted above ('qui caput et digitos') 'et', which goes with 'ut', welcomes 'canat' into the pentameter and reminds us of the hexameter where perhaps 'canat' would have been more at home. The importance and force of 'et' at the beginning of the pentameter is underlined by the presence of two very quiet 'ets' in the hexameter. The character of the hexameter and the pentameter are always distinct, but mingle, as in these examples, in the personality of the Propertian couplet. They are a partnership and an organism.

Propertius also employs alliteration and assonance to create tensions within a line and between lines. He achieves a complex pattern in these lines, which flows throughout with R sounds and N sounds:

> Quid iuvat ornato procedere, vita, capillo
> > et tenues Coa veste, movere sinus?
> aut quid Orontea crines profundere murra,
> > teque peregrinis vendere muneribus . . . ?

And we have '-undere' followed by 'murra' in the hexameter echoed in the pentameter by '-endere', which in turn is followed by 'muneribus'. 'Crines' is echoed in '-grinis', and 'per-' occurs in both lines. However, this kind of examination can be carried too far. Alliteration and assonance are qualities of poetry and not devices. A poet seldom works out such patterns consciously, but one word suggests others to him, and the range of vocabulary suitable for any given line becomes narrower and deeper. His ultimate choice will be, or seem to be, inevitable: if not inevitable, at least natural. Assonance and alliteration are best when unobtrusive, helping and not hindering the action of a line. We are defeating them when we draw attention to them.

Perhaps one way of exploring the personality of the couplet, is to consider how we should translate it into English. The rhyming couplet is, I think, too clear-cut a form to capture the interplay of light and shade between hexameter and pentameter. The half-rhymed couplet's tone of suggestion rather than definition, would be an improvement. But since Propertius conceives most of his ideas within the couplet, I venture to suggest that a fairly loose gathering into quatrains would make it possible for various rhyme-schemes and line-lengths to capture the mood of the original. Ideally, two couplets would form a quatrain, but with a clear rhyme-scheme to make each stanza an entity in itself, this would not be a strict rule: and the meaning of one quatrain could run into the next. In fact, as many lines as possible throughout the translation should run into the next lines following, in order that the rhyming be kept unobtrusive and subtle. I think the most suitable rhyme-scheme would be ABBA. The neighbouring rhymes BB would echo the force of the hexameter, and the separated rhymes A-A the more reserved mood of the pentameter; it would enclose the quatrain as gently as the pentameter finishes the couplet.

Perhaps the deepest part of a poet is vocabulary. Obviously ideas influence vocabulary but, as vocabulary develops, so do ideas. There are obvious differences between Propertius's language in Book I and in Book IV. The earlier books are linguistically richer, abounding in polysyllables and Graecisms and archaisms. He often uses words decoratively. There is no linguistic hierarchy – words are not chosen because they are 'poetic' or disregarded if they are not. The simple language of Virgil, say, implies such a hierarchy. Some modern American poets are similar to Propertius in this respect, approaching all words equally and freshly. Take this example from the American poet, Richard Wilbur:

> . . . the wind's exciting minors,
> The leaves' panic, and the degradation
> Of the heavy streams.

'The degradation of the heavy streams' has Propertian qualities. Words are used richly, but it is a careful richness as in Book I of the elegies: Book IV consists of careful choices. A sign of the developments and modifications in Propertius's language is the endings of the pentameter in the two books. In earlier books Propertius by no means limits himself to disyllabic endings, and we frequently find words of three, four, or five syllables. This lends power to his earlier pentameters, and they almost shout down their heroic neighbours. In the third and fourth books the disyllabic ending is used almost exclusively. And the later elegies of Propertius look forward to Ovid. The changes we observe in Book IV are due, I think, less to a decision about language than to the demands of form. He completely realises the true nature of the pentameter in his last book. To achieve this Propertius quietened and simplified his language throughout. Had he lived to write more, it is likely that he would have combined the richness of his early work with the deeper control and co-ordination of Book IV.

I want now to examine Propertius's structural methods. His poems often fall into parts. This is because the poet has taken up a hidden standpoint, to which all changes of thought, subject-matter and tone are related. He is not travelling from A to B, but rather standing at the point where he can best view everything that happens between A and B. We don't need to know the poet's standpoint, and we can only begin to guess when we have read the last line, which should decide the final poise of the poem. This constant striving towards equilibrium means that a poem is never static. The beginning of a poem is not necessarily the beginning of what a poem is about: its last line finishes but does not end a poem. In the third elegy of Book One a wealth of experience is given its tone and point by the attitude of Propertius on finding Cynthia asleep when he comes home drunk. To quote Louis MacNeice, 'Time was away and somewhere else' as this moment includes Ariadne, Andromeda, a Bacchante and the poet's own drunkenness:

> Like Ariadne who lay swooning on the deserted shore when Theseus sailed away; or like Andromeda unchained from the hard rocks at last, and sunk into her first sleep: or like a Thracian Bacchante exhausted by the unending dance who falls on the grassy banks of Apidanus, – so Cynthia lay, breathing softly and peacefully, her head propped on faltering hands, when I came dragging my tipsy feet, drunk with many draughts of wine . . .

This very tender moment holds great drama: Propertius is torn between passions excited by wine and gentle love:

> Although a double frenzy had hold of me, and the drastic gods of Love and wine were urging me to pass my arm around her gently where she lay, and with outstretched hand take passionate kisses; yet I lacked the courage to intrude upon my lover's rest (for I was afraid she would scold me with her usual anger). I stood transfixed with

fascinated eyes, as Argus gazed on the strange horned
brow of Io . . .

With painful intensity the poet focuses on Cynthia, as he takes the
chaplet from his head, places it on his lover's brow, arranges her hair
and gives her gifts of apples. There is a terrible and dangerous moment
of distraction when we look from Cynthia to the moon, 'the officious
moon with lingering light,' which awakens her. And the whole tense
drama is released when the furious Cynthia bitterly rebukes him for
his gay night away from her and pities herself left alone and miserable
until she falls asleep weary of her embroidery. Her speech gives a final
dramatic balance to the poem, and it also flows back to explain the
opening lines where Propertius finds her sleeping. Propertius seems to
stand at the centre of a poem's cosmos, viewing different aspects of it
in an order dictated by the poem itself, while he responds to them on
their own merits.

I quote now the opening lines of an elegy from Book II:

> Whoever he was who first painted Love as a boy, don't you
> think he had marvellous hands?

Propertius is immediately oblique and his standpoint is hidden –
'whoever he was' – but his response is direct: 'don't you think he had
marvellous hands?' and he goes on to describe the God of Love. The
obliqueness and direct response of the opening lines are explained
and given edge and force when Propertius, halfway through the poem,
tells us what dire effects love has had on *him*. The poem acquires
momentum and direction when Propertius turns to address Love
personally:

you have chosen a withered heart for your home: better far to assail those who have never felt your venomed arrows. And yet, if you destroy me utterly whom will you find to sing such songs as these: and who will sing of the face, fingers and dark eyes of my girl, and how soft her footsteps go? . . .

Cynthia is not mentioned until the last two lines, but in his descriptive approaches to love her presence is always implied, creating the main tension of the poem. With gentle surprise he finally mentions her and the tension is resolved: 'and who will sing of the face, fingers and dark eyes of my girl, and how soft her footsteps go?'

Abbreviated version of paper given to the Classical Society of Trinity College Dublin, 1962

*Note: all the translations from Propertius are my own.

A MISREPRESENTED POET: LOUIS MACNEICE

Louis MacNeice found his voice very early. This doesn't mean, of course, that he didn't develop: he moved forward through a series of minute adjustments – a progress which echoes that of the true tradition of English poetry to which he belongs. He was, like all the major poets of this century, more or less untouched by the Modernist movement. His poetry, like Yeats's or Auden's, was new without being novel. But a poetic personality which was so soon assured and recognisable meant that critics and anthologists found *their* voices very early when they came to deal with him. And critics and anthologists are seldom blessed with that capacity for change which marks the artist. MacNeice seems to me to be a severely misrepresented poet.

A number of damaging prejudices come to mind at once:

1. His first volume, *Blind Fireworks*, is best forgotten.
2. His finest book is the volume published posthumously, *The Burning Perch*.
3. His fatal Cleopatra was the long poem.
4. He was a thirties poet.
5. He is a poor man's Auden (or, to quote Cyril Connolly, 'The tortoise to Auden's hare').
6. He was a poet-cum-journalist.
7. His most anthologisable poems are 'Bagpipe Music', 'Prayer before Birth', 'Sunday Morning' (I don't need to name the rest!)
8. His poetry is the direct reflection of an ironic Northern Irish personality.

To publish is to acquiesce in an imperfection. One must flog one's wares in the market-place because that is where one's audience is. Being misrepresented, swindled, short-changed is the perpetual risk all poets have to take, but MacNeice came away from the critical bartering worse off than most.

The handsome *Collected Poems* (edited by MacNeice's friend, the Greek scholar E. R. Dodds) begins with *Juvenilia, 1925–1929*, a group of poems which came second in the earlier *Collected Poems 1925–1929* – no doubt because MacNeice sensed their weaknesses and vulnerability. But the collections of Keats and Wordsworth, say, contain far more trivia. This section does contain a fair number of feeble pieces, but a few house lines of an authority unusual for a poet in his early twenties: 'Trains in the Distance', for example –

> Trains came threading quietly through my dozing childhood,
> Gentle murmurs nosing through a summer quietude,
> Drawing in and out, in and out, their smoky ribbons,
> Parting now and then, and launching full-rigged galleons
> And scrolls of smoke that hung in a shifting epitaph.
> Then distantly the noise declined like a descending graph . . .

This is only the second poem in the book, but already we see MacNeice handling most skilfully the theme of childhood which was to preoccupy him right through his career and into his final volume. The lines and their rhythms are bold and efficient, the rhyming is effortless, and the poet's senses are as alert to the physical minutiae of his environment as his intellect is to their significance. Indeed, this little poem exhibits what were to remain MacNeice's major strengths as a poet. Another of his juvenilia, 'Mayfly', is a masterpiece, the first of a long series of wonderful love poems which established MacNeice as one of the finest love poets in the language. 'Mayfly' centres round a typical contrast between the delights of a moment and the knowledge that they cannot last. The poet addresses his lover and says that it is they:

> Who make the mayflies dance, the lapwings lift their crests,
> The show will soon shut down, its gay rags gone,
> But when this summer is over let us die together,
> I want always to be near your breasts.

From such tensions springs much of the vitality of MacNeice's verse. In 'Trilogy for X' (1938) he writes:

> O my love, if only I were able
> To protract this hour of quiet after passion,
> Not ration happiness but keep this door for ever
> Closed on the world, its own world closed within it.

In his love poems, MacNeice avoided that impatience, that refusal to let his ideas settle to a depth, which in his lesser poems results in surfaces made brilliant in order to cover up imaginative inconsistencies, and in verbal ingenuities which distract from what is being said. But all that is deepest and most flashing in MacNeice coheres unforgettably in his love poems:

> God or whatever means the good
> Be praised that time can stop like this,
> That what the heart has understood
> Can verify in the body's peace
> God or whatever means the Good. ('Meeting Point')

He was undoubtedly a great love poet, and with 'Mayfly' had already come into his own. The hub of his work is his love poetry, and from it branch out like spokes his poems on people, Ireland, friendship and childhood. MacNeice played his tunes round about Middle C, on the central octaves of human experience.

Auden in his elegy for MacNeice describes him as a 'lover of women and Donegal'. And MacNeice usually achieved a concentration comparable to that of his love poems when he was writing about Ireland. As we move from 'Mayfly' to 'Belfast', we come of age with the poet. The sudden change is like a cold shower:

> The hard cold fire of the northerner
> Frozen into his blood from the fire in his basalt
> Glares from behind the mica in his eyes.

MacNeice had a kind of love-hate relationship with Ireland. In *Autumn Journal* one of the cantos is a scorching attack on his native land – 'a bore and a bitch' who

> . . . gives her children neither sense nor money
> Who slouch around the world with a gesture and a brogue
> And a faggot of useless memories.

But Ireland also provided that pause in time, that fragile repose which MacNeice in his love poems found between four walls. During the war, understandably, there was more love than hate:

> Salmon in the Corrib
> Gently swaying
> And the water combed out

135

> Over the weir
> And a hundred swans
> Dreaming on the harbour:
> The war came down on us here.

Like many of his contemporaries, MacNeice wrote some of his best poems during the war. (He was a fire warden.) In that period of fear, farewells, excitement, bonhomie and nostalgia the concert halls were packed, the arts were *popular* – the common intense experience seemed to demand a higher level of life, and for the poets this meant a higher level of poetry:

> O delicate walker, babbler, dialectician Fire,
> O enemy and image of ourselves . . .

But not many of MacNeice's 1939–45 poems are directly about the war. Instead there came a more appreciative understanding of his fellow human beings: 'Ordinary people are peculiar too' ('Conversation'). The young poet and classics scholar from public school and Oxford found himself embracing in his poems the men in the streets, in the tube stations, in the shelters. He began, as it were, to 'interpolate/ Swear-words like roses in his talk'. MacNeice's poems about people are an extension of his love poetry. There is 'The Mixer' who

> . . . cannot away with silence but has grown
> Almost a cipher, like a Latin word
> That many languages have made their own
> Till it is worn and blunt and easy to construe
> And often spoken but no longer heard.

MacNeice sensed that the old order of things had changed for ever. In 'Death of an Actress' Florrie Forde 'stood for an older England'. The poem ends tenderly and very beautifully:

> Let the wren and the robin
> Gently with leaves cover the Babes in the Wood.

These poems, amongst his finest (and the best of them were written during the war), have not received the critical attention they deserve, nor credit for spawning in the fifties and sixties many poetic essays into imaginative biography. At least other poets have noted and learned.

After the war, MacNeice's poetry slackened – understandably: the intense lyrical phase had to broaden out so that the poet could salvage themes from the stunned silence and workable rhythms from emotional exhaustion. War or no war, there are, I think, these cycles in most poets' work – high tides and low tides, a tendency towards either density or sweep. MacNeice looked to the long poem for solutions. In 1943 he had combined both sweep and density in his fine elegy for a drowned friend, 'The Casualty' (one of my personal favourites):

> . . . if your pains
> Were lost the loss is ours as well: for you are out of
> This life and cannot start any more hares for ever.

But already by this time, in poems like 'Plurality', 'The Kingdom' and 'The Stygian Banks' it was evident that MacNeice would find it difficult to spread what amounted to a superb lyrical talent over extended forms – to repeat the success of *Autumn Journal* (1938), that magical, rambling and complete autobiography and account of the 1930s nightmare – one of the luckiest poems I know, in which everything some-how falls into place. But the best poets *are* the luckiest.

The crunch came with *Ten Burnt Offerings* (1950-51), ten long, sectioned poems some of which can be pretty turgid. But no one could have called the long poem his fatal Cleopatra, had MacNeice kept only the best of them, 'Day of Returning' and 'Flowers in the Interval', for example, as nostalgic companions for 'The Casualty' and *Autumn Journal* instead of using them as leaven for an artificially contrived sequence. MacNeice was always inclined to publish too much. So far as I know, these ten poems were commissioned by the BBC, and the weakest display the will-power of a poet mistakenly trying to write what he imagines to be 'major' poems. By and large, an uninteresting volume, though a few contain passages as good as anything MacNeice ever wrote. 'Day of Returning' is about Circe and, obviously, MacNeice's philosophy of friendship:

> Who would be loved by a goddess for long? Hours which
>   are golden
> But unreal hours, flowers which forget to fall,
> And wine too smooth, no wrinkles to match my own . . .
> Who would be loved by a goddess who cannot appreciate
> The joy of solving a problem, who never wept
> For friends that she used to laugh with?

And 'Flowers in the Interval' bubbles with MacNeice's unique gaiety:

> Because you intoxicate like all the drinks
> We have drunk together from Achill Island to Athens,
> Retsina or Nostrano, pops and clinks . . .

As though haunted by the ease and scope of *Autumn Journal*, in 1953 MacNeice published *Autumn Sequel*, a long meditative poem in 26 cantos which, typically, honours his friends, the momentum of his celebrations carrying the poet through an impressively wide range of concerns. MacNeice chose to compose this *magnum opus* in what is supposed to be the hardest metrical form in English, *terza rima* – a fool-hardy choice and, perhaps, to blame for those passages which echo the failings of *Ten Burnt Offerings*. A lot of *Autumn Sequel* can be heavy going, but even in this poem, which takes such hair-raising formal risks, MacNeice succeeds wonderfully when he writes about child-hood or his friends. Canto XX, an elegy for his friend Dylan Thomas, is one of the loveliest long poems in modern poetry:

> We close the door
> On Wales and backwards, eastwards, from the source
> Of such clear water, leave that altered shore
> Of gulls and psalms, of green and gold largesse,
> November the Twenty-fifth. We are back once more
> In London. And will he keep us waiting? . . . Yes.

Visitations (1952–56) marks MacNeice's return to the short lyric, but it is as though his gifts are still scattered. I find these poems loose and unfocused compared with his best pieces from the thirties and forties. MacNeice has stayed away too long from the lyric and the gestures of the intervening long poems intrude awkwardly here. Practically every one of these poems rhymes brilliantly and moves with flair, but their structures lack finality, their forms seem make-shift. MacNeice tried to plaster over the cracks with surface colours borrowed too easily from his friend and fellow-Ulsterman W. R. Rodgers, then a colleague on the Third Programme. 'The Other Wing', for instance, is pure Rodgers pastiche. New problems (of diction and structure especially) weren't really tackled until his last two volumes – *Solstices*, christened with a grim aptness, and *The Burning Perch*.

In these two books MacNeice was working towards a new kind of music – hard, stark and adaptable. Though most of the poems in *Solstices* are successes, they are mainly try-outs, old themes and familiar ideas testing the new lyricism. *The Burning Perch* looks more to the future. These are strange poems – disenchantment is played off against powerful rhythms, a spare vocabulary against a wide range of subjects, a down-to-earth utterance against weird settings and atmospheres. Charon

> looked at us coldly
> And his eyes were dead and his hands on the oar
> Were black with obols and varicose veins
> Marbled his calves and he said to us coldly:
> If you want to die you will have to pay for it.

This dark gloomy book does not form a climax. As I've said, it looks to the future, to 'green improbable fields'. MacNeice with new-found powers was halfway to reshaping the lyric, but he died just before his last book was published.

A posthumous *Collected Poems* should occasion nothing but gratitude. Many poets, on purpose or inadvertently, compose their own epitaphs. MacNeice, typically, did not. Derek Mahon has written a beautiful elegy for him called 'In Carrowdore Churchyard'. I think I should give Mahon the last word:

> This, you implied, is how we ought to live –
> The ironical, loving crush of roses against snow,

Each fragile, solving ambiguity. So
From the pneumonia of the ditch, from the ague
Of the blind poet and the bombed-out town you bring
The all-clear to the empty holes of spring,
Rinsing the choked mud, keeping the colours new.

Dublin Magazine 6, 1 (Spring 1967)

POETRY IN NORTHERN IRELAND

I

The progress of Ulster poetry this century has defined itself in a sequence of energetic spurts. The Muse has come and gone and come again: her sojourns here often prolonged, but never continuous. By 1921 the first indigenous literary movement in the North, the Ulster Literary Theatre, with its magazine, *Uladh*, had finished. Joseph Campbell had gone to London, James H. Cousins to India, Alice Milligan to Dublin, Moira O'Neill to Canada, Cathal O'Byrne to the United States. These represent neither the first nor the last group of debilitating emigrations – a sad and typically Irish haemorrhage. And by 1921 Florence Wilson and Padraic Gregory had ceased publication. Richard Rowley alone remained active, his books providing a single bridge to the next period, 1920 to 1930.

Locally this decade was represented by Rowley, Richard Hayward, Elizabeth Shane and W. F. and R. L. Marshall. Outside the province R. N. D. Wilson, who was born in Coleraine, and J. Lyle Donaghy took part in the Dublin literary scene, but hardly impinged on the North. From 1930 to 1940 the central figures were Louis MacNeice and W. R. Rodgers, both working in England, and, in Belfast, a group of poets who were closely associated with the magazine, *Lagan*: Maurice J. Craig, Roy McFadden, Robert Greacen and John Hewitt. McFadden and Greacen edited *Ulster Voices* in 1943. This was followed by *Rann*, edited by McFadden and Barbara Hunter. It ran to twenty numbers and takes us to the early fifties. By this time, one read here and there poems by John Montague, James Simmons, Padraic Fiacc and Richard Kell. But none of these was involved in the sort of local coterie or group which, whatever the originality of its individuals, can inspire its different members and help to extend the imaginative estate of the community to which it belongs. This applies all the more if that community is, like Ulster, small, defined and comparatively isolated. Out of such conditions, and not as a result of self-protective or self-regarding motives on the part of the artists, evolved the Ulster Literary Theatre and the *Lagan* group of poets.

The fifties and early sixties were fairly quiescent. It was not until 1965 that the *Festival Publications* series of pamphlets inaugurated a new phase. Promoted by Michael Emmerson, the Director of the Queen's University Festival, this series published between covers for the first time an impressive list of young poets which included Seamus Heaney, Derek Mahon, Joan Newmann, Stewart Parker, James Simmons and Seamus Deane. It also printed the work of an English poet, Philip Hobsbaum. While he was a lecturer in English at Queen's, Hobsbaum ran a weekly discussion group which several of the new generation of poets attended. At these sessions new work was analysed with Leavis-ite rigour: the atmosphere was electric. Various talents may certainly have been emerging on their own, but Hobsbaum's enthusiasm and energy did much to accelerate the process. Two other members of the 'Group', as it was called, were Arthur Terry, Professor of Spanish at the university, and Norman Dugdale, a senior civil servant who comes from England. Terry's excellent translations from the Spanish and Catalan were read at the Group and eventually published in two Festival pamphlets. Dugdale, who had been writing quietly on his own for years, was also encouraged by Hobsbaum, produced a Festival pamphlet and eventually a full hardback collection, *A Prospect of the West*.

The belated appearance in print of such hitherto convinced poetic solitaries is just as telling a symptom of the present healthy state of poetry in Ulster as the considerable list of younger talents. Indeed, although it may merely be a coincidence, it is surely significant that recent years have seen not only the publication of hardback collections by Seamus Heaney, Derek Mahon, James Simmons and others, but also the long-awaited arrival of John Hewitt's *Collected Poems*; Padraic Fiacc's *By The Black Stream*, his first book for many years, appeared in 1969; Roy McFadden, whose last important collection, *The Heart's Townland*, was published in 1947, has a new volume, *The Garryowen*, with the printers; and Oxford University Press are soon to produce the *Collected Poems* of W. R. Rodgers. Ulster poets seem at the moment willing to stay at home, to work and write here. And John Montague, whom my generation used to regard as something of a Dublin poet, linking him with Thomas Kinsella and Richard Murphy, has, in a metaphysical sense, 'come home'.

Harry Chambers was among the first to advertise in his magazine, *Phoenix*, the new poetic flowering. From his present base in Manchester he has subsequently published in pamphlet-form work by a number of Ulster poets. When James Simmons returned from Africa in 1967 he founded *The Honest Ulsterman* which under his editorship was often eccentric and outspoken, seldom dull. Simmons's two main achievements as an editor are to have brought out *The Honest Ulsterman* almost every month – a unique record in the annals of Irish literary magazines! – and to have discovered and encouraged many new talents, most of them under twenty-five. Indeed, he has inaugurated what might almost be termed The *Honest Ulsterman* School of Poets. These he published in small pamphlets which accompanied the magazine. Simmons has since handed on his editorship to two young poets, Michael Foley and Frank Ormsby, who maintain the abrasive, irreverent tradition. The first issue of *Threshold* came out in 1957. Edited by Mary and Pearse O'Malley of the Lyric Theatre, it has run to twenty-two issues. A forum for the young as well as the established writer, it has averaged one or occasionally two issues a year and provides what amount in effect to very useful anthologies of current Ulster writing.

Recognising this new vitality the Arts Council of Northern Ireland has increased its budget for literature. It granted a subvention to the Festival pamphlets series and continues to give subsidies to *Threshold* and *The Honest Ulsterman*. The Council has also promoted successful poetry reading tours – 'Room to Rhyme' in 1968 with Seamus Heaney, the folk-singer David Hammond, and myself; and in 1970 and 1971 'The Planter and the Gael' with John Hewitt and John Montague. In 1970 for the first time three bursaries were awarded to writers, two of them poets. Official recognition, although still small compared to what is enjoyed by the other arts, helps to ensure that the labours of solitude percolate through to the public, and encourages the Muse to prolong her stay.

II

Because he lived and worked for most of his life in England, it might be argued that Louis MacNeice does not really qualify as an Ulster poet. Apart from a few excuses which may appear too convenient – his Ulster voice and manner and their natural effect on the texture of his verse, and his frequent visits here – deeper considerations make him a touchstone of what an Ulster poet might be. MacNeice is still underestimated. Judgments would be more precise and just, I think, if the Northern Irish context were taken more into account. Many English critics are clearly not attuned to some of his qualities and procedures. He is too often billed as *l'homme moyen sensual*, a flashy juggler, slick and modish, a freewheeling epicurean, a poet too worldly to be really wise. The dizzy word-play and the riot of imagery might well tempt a casual reader to suspect that MacNeice lacks depth and penetration, that he is really not much more than a professional entertainer. A proper consideration of his background, however, should help us to understand that all the gaudy paraphernalia of his poetry is finally a reply to darkness, to 'the fear of becoming stone'. His games are 'funeral games': the bright patterns he conjures from the external world and the pleasures of being alive are not fairy light and bauble but searchlight and icon. And the seeds of darkness were sown during his childhood. Ulster was a place hard with basalt and iron, cacophonous with 'fog-horn, mill-horn, corncrake and church bell', 'the hooting of lost sirens and the clang of trams', 'the voodoo of the Orange bands', dark and oppressive with religion, 'devout and profane and hard'. Narrow religion and life-denying puritanism mark the point at which Ulster's darker attributes shade into the more personal aspects of MacNeice's childhood: 'Religion encroached upon us steadily'. He was afraid of his Father's 'conspiracy with God'. The autobiographical writing indicates that he was terrorised by a precocious sense of sin and feelings of guilt which were connected with early encounters with death and mental illness:

> When I was five the black dreams came;
> Nothing after was quite the same.

MacNeice is a poet of the solstice, of the uneven and unbalancing pull, at his best in his twenties and thirties, and again towards the end of his life. Indeed, a later book, published in 1956 is entitled *Solstices*: it promises recovery. In this book and in the posthumous volume, *The Burning Perch*, MacNeice was working towards a new kind of music. These are poems of the winter solstice. The nightmares of childhood have become the actual nightmares of old age and approaching death. MacNeice remains, I think, our most considerable poet. His early death is an immeasurable loss.

Ulster must be about the last area in the English-speaking world which is still likely to produce poets who write out of a response to religion. Louis MacNeice and W. R. Rodgers were such poets: motivated by strong anti-puritan feelings, the vividness they share was projected partly as an assault on religious narrowness and cultural restriction. The late W. R. Rodgers was Minister of Loughgall Presbyterian Church, Co. Armagh, from 1934 to 1946. In 1946 he became a scriptwriter and producer for the BBC in London. His first volume, *Awake! And Other Poems*, appeared in 1941. In an interesting prefatory note he describes his own position and at the same time pinpoints some of the problems which may face a provincial poet:

> That this volume contains all the poems I have so far written is not an accident; that none was written earlier than three years ago is not without meaning; for I was schooled in a backwater of literature out of sight of the running stream of contemporary verse. Some murmurs of course I heard, but I was singularly ignorant of its extent and character. It was in the late thirties that I came to contemporary poetry, and I no longer stood dumb in the tied shops of speech or felt stifled in the stale air of convention.

After this emotional thaw Rodgers's language flowed in headlong spate. He was taken over by 'the arriving winds of words' and remained 'their most astonished host'. One is immediately struck by the tumble of words and images, the puns, the risky deployment of colloquialism and cliché, the rich, idiosyncratic vocabulary, the alliterative music derived partly from Hopkins – in short, by one of the most unembar-

147

rassed and exuberant talents in the language. In his memorial poem
to Rodgers John Hewitt captures the man and the poet well:

> The slow low voice that wandered on and on,
> slipping or looping from outrageous pun
> to some split atom of semantic lore,
> where sparking opposites would generate
> a flash of wit or wisdom . . .

Though one sometimes feels that Rodgers is forcing the pace, trying
too hard to load every rift with ore, his best images combine the inevitability and surprise of high poetry: 'the marrow of water in the bone
of ice'; 'the bee's furred foot,/ The honeysuckle's hinge'; the fish rising
'through all their octaves of gloom'. These yoke disparates with a
Metaphysical ingenuity, and yet seem naturally and easily shaped by
the personality of the language, sensuously related to everyday realities. He puns with a Joycean abandon: the lovers in 'The Net' 'bed-
spread eagle'; in the title poem of his second volume, *Europa and the
Bull*, the bull comes 'tiptoadying' and the sea is 'grotesticled'. If some
of his effects do seem excessive, amounting to failures of tact, they
form part of a strategy so vigorous it usually sweeps us past them:

> . . . only
> By daring do we learn our manyness,
> Safety stints us, turns us to stone, to one.

Rodgers's philosophy is simple but not, as Kenneth Allott suggests,
commonplace. He opposes 'the heart's levelled drives/ Of habit', 'all
the lock-gates of class, caste and custom', 'the crates of government',
'exact dignity, calculated awe', authority, humbug, rank – anything

that precludes a generous and open-hearted response to life, that sieves 'the fancy/ From the fact'. It is usual to praise a poet for uncovering the mysteries concealed beneath appearances: one of Rodgers's central achievements is to have revealed, as under a magnifying glass, the wonder of life's surfaces, to have cajoled us out of 'our armoured rims' with his almost frenzied scrutiny. He views the world in such obsessive close-up because it is as a result of the distant stance and the objective view that

> . . . Earth's scene grows shallow, and we stand
> Only ankle-deep in its agony.

In order to solve 'the exquisite equation of self', he celebrates the external world in all its particulars, accepts the contradictions of the inner life, the fact that 'Goodness is foreskinned and frisked by Evil', and hymns existence with an extravagance which gathers up before it his disenchantments:

> . . . the music goes round and round
> In the old rings, new every morning,
> The spin of flesh on the spindle of bone
> Concentring all, with its brute ambitions,
> Its acute and terrible attritions.

Rodgers enlists 'all the bells and hullabalooes of joy', an archetypal bestiary of bulls, hares, hounds, hawks, classical mythology, and of course, the story of Christ. Among his finest work are the specifically Christian poems: the long and generally well-sustained 'Easter Sequence', 'Nativity', 'The Journey of the Magi', 'Carol', 'Christ Walking on the Water' and, perhaps finest of all, 'Lent', with its extraordi-

149

nary generosity, its deep understanding of the relationship between
Christ and Mary Magdalene:

> Over the balconies of these curved breasts
> I'll no more peep to see
> The light procession of my loves
> Surf-riding in to me
> Who now have eyes and alcove, Lord, for Thee.

In this poem, in 'The Net', one of the most passionate love lyrics in
English, and in many others Rodgers treats tenderly and with dignity
erotic feelings. He can sustain over many lines moments of ecstasy
and transform them into profound religious experience. In his best
poetry we are privileged to find 'The Word made flesh, melted into
motion'.

If MacNeice and Rodgers with their gestures and flourishes can be
seen as Cavaliers, then chief among the Roundheads is John Hewitt.
He deliberately avoids spectacular devices, colourful tones, verbal
pyrotechnics, preferring a plain utterance, the 'walking pace' of the
fairly regular iambic line. His poems are quietly orchestrated, organised with care. But the unobtrusive craftsmanship only temporarily
conceals an interest in language no less intense than that of his two
more flamboyant colleagues. In a poem like 'Once Alien Here', for
instance, the argument is promoted by very delicately chosen conso-
nantal rhymes: 'overtones/ downs', 'hills/ spells', 'rich/ hedge'. A good
poet christens the world exactly; and the precision with which Hewitt
names and describes is in itself the surest token of the love he feels for
his various subjects: 'life is man and place and these have names'
('Landscape').

Hewitt's understanding of the structures of rural life and his deliberate, painstaking delineation of these tempt one at first to describe him as a nature poet, a sort of Northern Irish neo-Georgian. But he is altogether a more complex figure than these terms suggest. Certainly, a fair number of good, straightforwardly descriptive rural pieces are scattered through his *Collected Poems* – 'The Owl', 'Hedgehog', 'The Stoat', 'The Watchers', and so on. But even some of these seem disturbed, uneasy beneath the calm surfaces: the unease is not psychological as in the nature poetry of Edward Thomas whom Hewitt admires, but social. As a city man drawn to the countryside, he finds there that he is both fulfilled and excluded, that the poet is defined by the landscape while to the people who live in it the man is an outsider. He realises sadly that, in the eyes of the countrymen he loves, no achievement of his will ever have the importance of

> even a phrase or a story which will come
> pat to the tongue, part of the tapestry
> of apt response, at the appropriate time,
> like a wise saw, a joke, an ancient rime
> used when the last stack's topped at the day's end,
> or when the last lint's carted round the bend.
> ('O Country People')

And yet, despite this loss Hewitt, typically, knows his own worth and asserts it, defending his knowledgability, his involvement and his detachment, as in *Conacre*:

> No tweed-bright poet drunk in pastoral
> or morris-dances in the Legion Hall,
> I know my farmer and my farmer's wife,
> the squalid focus of their huxter life,

151

> the grime-veined fists, the thick rheumatic legs,
> the cracked voice gloating on the price of eggs.

A discreet drama is enacted throughout his poetry as he argues with himself, tests his stance and position. Diffidence follows certainty, withdrawal follows assertion. His most generous embraces carry with them a hint of *noli me tangere*.

The city man's feelings of exclusion in the countryside modulate with some pain into the Protestant Planter's uneasy desire to be assimilated into Celtic Ireland and yet remain true to himself. This tension, which has produced some of his most impressive work – 'Once Alien Here', 'The Glens', 'The Colony' – has also encouraged Hewitt to pursue a philosophy of regionalism and to insist on his Ulster heritage. Reviewing *Collected Poems* in *Threshold*, Seamus Heaney wrote that Hewitt's 'lifelong concern to question and document the relationship between art and locality has provided all subsequent Northern writers with a hinterland of reference, should they require a tradition more intimate than the broad perspectives of the English literary achievement'. The poems born out of what Heaney calls 'those accurate, painful quests towards sell-knowledge' explore with uncomfortable honesty the fears and prejudices of the Planter stock. In *The Colony*, written prophetically more than twenty years ago, Ulster is thinly disguised as a Roman province:

> some of us think our leases have run out
> but dig square heels in, keep the roads repaired;
> and one or two loud voices would restore
> the rack, the yellow patch, the curfewed ghetto.

Only after such self-questioning can claims be staked. The poem ends in qualified optimism; the Roman mask dissolves completely, and Hewitt's confused love for his province shines through:

> for we have rights drawn from the soil and sky;
> the use, the pace, the patient years of labour,
> the rain against the lips, the changing light,
> the heavy clay-sucked stride, have altered us;
> we would be strangers in the Capitol;
> this is our country also, no-where else;
> we shall not be outcast on the world.

John Montague has written of Hewitt that he is 'the first (and probably the last) deliberately Ulster, Protestant poet'. In normal times I would insist that he is much more than this: in the present political situation, however, Montague's description reasonably suggests the importance of John Hewitt's poetry.

The long opening poem of Roy McFadden's third collection, *The Heart's Townland*, is addressed to John Hewitt:

> In all that's honest, native, relevant,
> You have an eye to greet the miracle.

Earlier in the poem, however, he claims that Hewitt used to be 'Philosopher of all the noisy blind/ Who flouted those who swore they saw the sun'. One senses a lively rivalry compounded, not always evenly, of irritation and respect, a controversy rooted in differing aesthetic philosophies, with McFadden's by far the more romantic and subjective.

McFadden was slower than Hewitt to find his own voice. The first two collections, *Swords and Ploughshares* and *Flowers for a Lady*, are influenced by the neo-Romanticism of the forties, by the quasi-surre-alist mode which at the time was christened The New Apocalypse. McFadden was later to refer to his youthful self as 'a sadmouthed boy'; this seems a fair and, I presume, self-critical description of a young poet morbidly obsessed with transience, death and the past. The tone is unremittingly elegiac – a *lacrimae rerum* lament sung against a back-cloth of falling leaves or twilit seashores, and expressed in rhetorical questions and imperative apostrophes. Pathetic fallacies, large abstrac-tions and interpolated 'O's' abound. But the energy and the ambition were there. Long sentences are stretched with skill across an often complex stanzaic grid; and the lambent utterance shapes the occa-sional delicate cadence: 'the slow funerals/ Of leaf and wing'; 'The north lies backward in a fold of time'.

At the beginning of 'The Heart's Townland' McFadden expresses his wish

> That I may stiffen into discipline
> And feel that pruned and certain self arise
> To carry frost into the heart of spring.

In 'Directions for a Journey', 'My Father Had a Clock', 'Virgin Country' and other poems he displays a concrete imagery and a solidity of expression which anticipate the achievements of his forthcoming book, *The Garryowen*. This is McFadden's first collection for twenty-four years. In it he has discarded most of the romantic properties of the earlier verse. A conversational tilt loosens a diction which was in danger of becoming cluttered. The reality of Ireland and her recent history are now preferred to the legendary past. The mythologising process is reserved for real people, the heroes of the poet's Belfast childhood, Clutey Gibson and Jackie Dugan:

154

At Kick-the-can, Relieve-i-o,
He was the master in the ring.
I turned away from bedtime kiss
Each night he yodelled in the street,
Assassin of my innocence.

Most impressive are the personal poems, the mysterious 'Contempla-
tions of Mary', in particular, and the sequence, 'Family Album'. Even
though it is undignified to describe the ending of a twenty-four-year-
old silence as a breakthrough, I do so because the term has an appropriately sporting ring to it. Here we have, after all,

The Garryowen, and the game set free.

John Montague lives in Paris and has taught in universities there and
in America. He brings to Irish poetry a welcome awareness of developments in the international scene. Of all the Ulster poets he is possibly the one most deliberately and consciously forging a style. With
each volume his work becomes more resolutely modern. He has three
hardback collections to his credit: *Poisoned Lands, A Chosen Light* and
Tides. The first volume displays a fluent and flexible talent: the range of
tones wide, the strategies various. The most notable feature is, perhaps,
the poet's profound involvement in this island's past and present, or,
more particularly, the pre-historic Ireland of standing stones and
horned cairns and the Ireland of his rural childhood in County Tyrone.
Out of a marriage of these come many of Montague's best poems:
'Like Dolmens Round my Childhood, The Old People', for instance,
where the vividly recalled derelicts and eccentrics who were his
childhood neighbours – Jamie MacCrystal, Maggie Owens, Wild Billy
Harbison – for years

>   . . . trespassed on my dreams
>   Until once, in a standing circle of stones,
>   I felt their shadows pass

>   Into that dark permanence of ancient forms.

Throughout his career Montague has been concerned both to capture with documentary exactitude and to release the mythic potential of such figures: the centenarian; the dying man making his will; the poor old woman – the *Sean Bhean Vocht* – 'eyes rheumy with racial memory'. The *Sean Bhean Vocht* reappears in his latest collection in a poem called 'The Wild Rose' and as 'The Hag of Beare', one of many translations he has made from the Irish. The fantastic and the factual cohere to disturbing effect in these poems: the attentively delineated details augment their strangeness and mystery.

   A Chosen Light is an altogether more introspective collection. An emotional crisis, which is not referred to explicitly, has bruised the poet into writing several love poems of a haunting and redemptive beauty. 'All Legendary Obstacles' allusively describes an uneasy and long-awaited reunion in a wintry American railway station:

>   You had been travelling for days
>   With an old lady, who marked
>   A neat circle on the glass
>   With her glove, to watch us
>   Move into the wet darkness
>   Kissing, still unable to speak.

This plangent note – 'the lost cry/ of the yellow bittern' – typifies Montague at his best, although he can also write with a nice humorous lift or with satirical edge, and can mimic uncannily the movements of country speech. The darkness which frames *A Chosen Light* is grimly relieved in *Tides* by 'the pallid lightning flash' and the moon's 'pressure of/ Underwater light'. In the poems at the beginning of the book violence and nightmare command the lovers' situation:

> Blood, like a scarlet curtain,
> Swinging across the brain
> Till the light switches off –
> And silence is darkness again.

Blood and flesh are the linking images. The poet scrutinises the degradations of the body so mercilessly that the obsessive sensuality of Section III can only offer a partial compensation. Here female sexuality is celebrated with a candour rare in Irish poetry, and is seen finally as

> luring us to forget,
> beget, a form of truth
> or (the last rhyme
> tolls its half tone)
> an answer to death.

John Montague has a fine ear but he usually eschews the singing line; he adopts a contemporary technique and format with which to explore Ireland's distant past; he relishes sensuous experience but expresses his pleasure in a deliberately hesitant and constrained metric, rather like the Irish dancer whose arms remain rigid by his side while his feet go wild; he has published lyrics shaped with an ivory-carver's precision and worked simultaneously for years on a massively long discursive poem about his native Ulster, *The Rough Field*, which will appear soon. His stance and procedure seem to be based on paradoxes. He tantalises while he rewards.

James Simmons is not an aesthetician like Montague: where Montague insists on tailoring the language to his requirements, Simmons will often accept the ready-made – the ballad quatrain, couplets, parody, the cadence of a blues or a popular song. He usually transforms the received mode into completely personal utterance. In particular he can deploy the ballad quatrain as though he had invented it, easily and with not a hint of the embarrassment one feels in Auden's attempt to popularise poetry in the thirties by using the same form. In many respects a didactic poet, Simmons believes that his main responsibility is to communicate; he chooses to address his audience directly and with simplicity: 'only a simple act/ Can be wholly successful', he writes; or

> The best – the good best – is a variation
> on a popular tune.

Two lines from Louis MacNeice's last volume may justify Simmons's approach, offer a deserved alibi:

> Each tune, each cloak, if matched to weather and mood,
> > wears well
> And off the peg means made to measure now.

Between Simmons's three books one can trace no startling stylistic developments. The last poem in his most recent collection, *Energy to Burn*, would not seem out of place in *Late but in Earnest*, his first book. His philosophy takes shape and clarifies itself within the lucidities of popular forms: he is most profoundly an artist when he chooses to entertain. Although in many poems he avoids them, it seems reason-

158

able to suggest that the dangers inherent in his plan of attack include prolixity, thinness of texture, casual rhyming, rhythmic repetitiveness. Simmons writes excellent songs: reading his poems one sometimes regrets the absence of his guitar, sensing that it might be needed to cement the relationships between the words. His strongest pieces bear a very strong family likeness to his weakest: this may explain in part why his work is still seriously underestimated.

A line from his first book provides a motto under which most of Simmons's themes and concerns can be grouped: 'the continual miracle of sun and dust'. He writes about the facts of life: birth; the end of youth – 'I/ Who loved Illona Massey at fourteen/ With a great love am now a has-been'; the rewards and disappointments of friendship; alcohol, 'that subtle alchemist'; mortality, whether his own, his wife's, or his children's; his family – 'I celebrate/ the equilibrist skill/ my granny had'. Primarily a love poet, he insists on 'The tenderness of passion,/ The innocence of lust', 'The common magic/ That fingers feel on skin'. His frankness cuts like a searchlight through the *arcanum* of sex:

> Be it car-crash or childbirth,
> Each line tells a story,
> Has a moral, my love,
> My memento mori.

In a review of his second book I wrote: 'Among the best poems is a group about married life. Their initially alarming candour is neither exhibitionistic nor callous, though clearly vulnerable to such charges. Nor can these poems, strictly speaking, be classed as 'confessional'. The confessional poet's centre is *I*: in Simmons's frank, intimate poems the centre is '*you*'.

Not all of his poems carry such a strong autobiographical flavour.

His finest achievement so far is a sequence of poems based on *King Lear*. Through the adopted *personae* of France, Gloucester and the Fool he explores very movingly and with resonance his themes of love, loyalty and family ties. Here Simmons has found a powerful setting in which to test his own peculiar brand of disenchanted optimism: 'But in the darkness each good thing/ Stayed good'. Another excellent Shakespearean poem, 'Stephano Remembers', summarises neatly how Simmons, I imagine, would like poets and poetry – his own in particular – to be judged:

> We were distracted by too many things . . .
> the wine, the jokes, the music, fancy gowns.
> We were no good as murderers, we were clowns.

I see Simmons as a sort of modern troubadour whose permissiveness, both in a literary and a moral sense, turns the old notion of courtly love inside out but not upside down. In his most convincing work compassion and warmth allow the seamier aspects of sexual love, life's underside – the dust – to dance in the sunlight.

More than most people, poets carry with them through life the experiences of the different stages of growing-up: childhood, adolescence, youth. The hurts and the happinesses of each earlier phase continue to cast their light and their shadows over present triumphs and crises. The younger self who is the *eminence grise* behind many of Simmons's poems would seem to be the adolescent. In Seamus Heaney's work it is the child. Most of the good poems in Heaney's first collection, *Death of a Naturalist*, have their roots deeply embedded in his rural childhood. This he evokes with an almost overpowering concretion of imagery and a slow, searching rhythm uniquely his own:

> . . . the warm thick slobber
> Of frogspawn that grew like clotted water
> In the shade of the banks.

Heaney immerses the reader in the experience, his most successful lines appealing to all the senses at once. The perfectly judged ebb and flow of their movements allow us to accompany him word by word on his journey back, to reach with him into the recesses of his mind. The processes of memory as we sense them working in Heaney's verse find a nice analogy in 'The Barn':

> A scythe's edge, a clean spade, a pitch-fork's prongs:
> Slowly bright objects formed when you went in.

If their justly celebrated descriptive powers account for his poems' immediate attractiveness, their subtle implications make them continuously satisfying. The title poem about collecting frogspawn and 'Blackberry-Picking' are parables of lost innocence; 'The Barn' defines nightmare; 'Follower' dramatises the poet's ambivalent attitude to his rural past; 'Personal Helicon' is both credo and manifesto; it hints at possible future developments:

> I rhyme
> To see myself, to set the darkness echoing.

In his first book Heaney rhymes more 'to see himself', in his second 'to set the darkness echoing'. *Door into the Dark* is in many respects a stronger collection. In it Heaney attempts ambitiously to extend his themes and vary his manoeuvres. His preoccupation with his own past shades into explorations of Ireland's history; he breaks out of the boundaries of his Derry locale to embrace the whole island; the mythologising process depends less and less on the pivotal 'I'; he adopts *personae* – the salmon fisher, 'Undine', a pregnant woman; he dramatises, as in the Frostian 'Wife's Tale'. The book's title suggests its variety and richness: it is a door into the dark of history, the prehistoric past, religious mystery, nightmare, memory, birth, sexuality. But this book is often, paradoxically, most reticent, oblique, even evasive, at these very points of growth. Sexuality, for instance, is broached most boldly not in the love poems but in descriptions of animals and things – a bull, a Victorian guitar, eels, the frozen pump in 'Rite of Spring', the land in 'Undine'. A somewhat periphrastic utterance indicates that in many of these poems Heaney is stalking rather than pouncing. Perhaps what he is circling with such profound carefulness is the disturbingly personal note more in evidence in *Death of a Naturalist*: the cry of guilt-ridden revulsion at the end of the title poem – 'I knew/ That if I dipped my hand the spawn would clutch it' – or the pained, vulnerable complaint in 'Blackberry-Picking' when the disillusioned child materialises and takes over the adult poet's voice:

> I always felt like crying. It wasn't fair
> That all the lovely canfuls smelt of rot.

Reviewers of the first book, who wondered patronisingly what Heaney would achieve once he had worked the earthy origins out of his system, were wrong.

Death of a Naturalist mapped a world and a mythology whose universality *Door into the Dark* confirms but does not exhaust. The second book ends with three very remarkable poems, 'Whinlands', 'The Plantation' and 'Bogland': they are assertive and confident beneath the mysterious, allusive surfaces of the later Heaney manner. They defiantly recall the old territories and promise a return there in poems which will delve still more deeply and bravely. The whin bush, like the poet himself one suspects, 'Persists on hills, near stone ditches/ Over flintbed and battlefield'. In 'The Plantation' – 'Its limits defined/ So they thought, from outside' – 'You had to come back/ To learn how to lose yourself'. And towards the end of 'Bogland' Heaney answers, in a moment of triumph, those critics who would have him desert his imaginative terrain or at least define its limits 'from outside':

> Our pioneers keep striking
> Inwards and downwards . . .

Heaney's talent complements interestingly that of Derek Mahon. Since both refer frequently in their work to the four elements, a comparison might be pursued by granting Heaney water and earth; Mahon, fire and air. Or, to crystallise the notion in a geological analogy, Heaney's poetry emerges from the sedimentary processes, Mahon's from the igneous. Again, one is Catholic and rural, the other Protestant and urban. Heaney, who recalls John Hewitt more than any other poet discussed in this essay, has a foot in the camp of the Roundheads, whereas Mahon is very much a Cavalier: the rigour and swiftness of his rhythms, the boldness of his wit and rhetoric, the general impression of brilliance and cheeky showmanship, are all reminiscent of Louis MacNeice. Mahon is a poet of considerable resource and panache, profoundest when he is most flashing. In his elegy for MacNeice, 'In Carrowdore Churchyard', for instance, he refuses to be sombre – rightly so, given his subject. He risks everything in pun and word-play:

> This plot is consecrated, for your sake,
> To what lies in the future tense. You lie
> Past tension now . . .

And of MacNeice's epitaph, 'a 'phrase from Euripides', Mahon says it 'suits you down to the ground'. A compassionate portrait of Marilyn Monroe switches suddenly from cosmic imagery to recall a popular song and end in an audacious enjambment:

> . . . when an immovable body meets an ir-
> Resistible force, something has got to give.

In 'An Unborn Child', a poem of great dignity and resonance and one of his finest achievements, the 'kitten that lies there *sunning* itself/ Under the bare bulb' leads us in our innocence to the surprise and humour of 'goldfish *mooning* around upon the shelf' (my italics).

Like MacNeice, Mahon admits unwillingly that his roots are in Ulster, among 'the/ dank churches, the empty streets,/ the shipyard silence, the tied-up swings' ('Ecclesiastes'). But he makes a bigger effort to embrace his origins: 'One part of my mind must learn to know its place'. An imagery of light and darkness pervades his poetry as it does MacNeice's. He may, within a rhetorical gesture, set the two side by side, simply, as facts of life:

> First there is darkness, then somehow light.
> We call this day and the other night . . .
> ('Early Morning')

Or, more disturbingly, he will venture down the dark tunnel which MacNeice, using all his fireworks, tried in vain to obliterate:

> Now we are running out of light and love,
> Having left far behind
> By-pass and fly-over.

> The moon is no longer there
> And matches go out in the wind . . .
>> ('Girls in their Seasons')

Ulster, 'the January rains when they/ darken the dark doors and sink hard/ into the Antrim hills, the bog meadows', all the constrictions Mahon diagnoses here, are indispensable imaginative properties. They give his rhetoric edge and focus his brilliance like the 'islands of dark ore' in 'Epitaph for Robert Flaherty', 'Where winter is so long/ Only a little light/ Gets through, and that perfect'.

More than just the opposite of darkness, light in Mahon's poetry also represents the imagination. In 'Van Gogh among the Miners' the painter says:

> Like a glow-worm I move among
> The caged Belgian miners,
> And the light on my forehead
> Is the dying light of truth . . .

And 'The Forger' has 'sheltered in my heart of hearts/ A light to transform the world'. Mahon's brave acceptance of 'the darkness of nightfall', of man's tragic situation makes his resolutions all the more decisive and inclusive when they come: when he forecasts for 'Dowson and Company' that 'the day/ Will be all sunlight, and the night/ A dutiful spectrum of stars'; when he claims for MacNeice in his fine elegy that 'you bring/ The all-clear to the empty holes of spring,/ Rinsing the choked mud, keeping the colours new'. A hushed, unobtrusive poem towards the end of his first book indicates how painfully the warmth and liveliness of his talent have been achieved. 'The Prisoner' describes emotional crisis:

> It is taking longer than almost anything –
> But I know, when it is over
> And back come friend and lover,
> I shall forget it like a childhood illness
> Or a sleepless night-crossing.

One willingly and gratefully allows Mahon 'The bright reception at the end of all'.

Stewart Parker has published two Festival Pamphlets. A versatile and prolific writer, he has turned his hand to plays, novels, short stories and radio features. One feels that his poems are smithereens generated by his other literary activities rather than the result of a consistently felt poetic vocation. But Parker, I suspect, would not choose to draw strict boundaries around the activities of verse and prose, preferring to claim that his best prose is poetry and willing to admit that his poorer verses are not much more than weak prose. His first pamphlet, *The Casualty's Meditation*, displays a raw, vigorous talent which forces resolutions rhetorically and only occasionally embodies them in appropriate rhythms. He achieves, however, moments of undeniable beauty:

> There is only the lifting of hands to shake hands
> And the lifting of arms to embrace.

Parker loosens up considerably in *Maw*, his second pamphlet. The earlier stridency has given way to the wry humour we recognise from his prose. These poems are sensitive evocations of America captured in an easily cadenced free verse:

I am pretending that this is the Rock Island Line
and that Poor Paddy, Railroad Bill and Casey Jones
are at my elbow;

and they are.

A number of poets still in their late teens or early twenties have in recent years started publishing in the Irish magazines and periodicals. It is no doubt premature to single out individuals at this stage, but Paul Muldoon, who is an undergraduate at Queen's University, and William Peskett, who has just left school, do seem particularly interesting. Already they have produced poetry which is poised and original, and both have deservedly been selected to appear in the forthcoming Faber anthology, *Introductions 2*. Frank Ormsby and Michael Foley, the co-editors of *The Honest Ulsterman*, Tom McGurk who was the youngest contributor to *The Penguin Book of Irish Verse*, Michael Stephens, Tom Matthews and Tom McLaughlin have all published promising work in pamphlet form. I hope this essay helps to show that these young poets and the dark horses among their contemporaries are the inheritors of a worthy tradition.

From *Causeway: The Arts in Ulster*, edited by Michael Longley
(Arts Council of Northern Ireland, 1971)

'WHITETHORN HEDGES':
PATRICK KAVANAGH

Patrick Kavanagh's poem 'Innocence' ends with these lines:

> I do not know what age I am,
> I am no mortal age.
> I know nothing of women,
> Nothing of cities,
> I cannot die
> Unless I walk outside these whitethorn hedges.

The whitethorn hedges appear again and again in the poems – and in the autobiographical fiction. In *Tarry Flynn*: 'The whitethorn hedges heavy with summer leaves could give Tarry's imagination the idea of a tropical jungle, but the mother did not like those hedges.' And later: 'With the whitethorn hedges in full leaf the road seemed no more to one looking across country than a particularly thick hedge. Tarry sat on the crown of the hill with his back to a bank of massed primroses and violets, and as he sat there the slumberous time and place made him forget the sting of the thorn of a dream in his heart. Why should a man want to climb out of this anonymous happiness in the conscious day?'

In the words of the novelist: 'That was Tarry: Eternity and Earth side by side.' In the words of the poet: 'I cannot die/ Unless I walk outside these whitethorn hedges.' There is, for me, at the heart of Patrick Kavanagh's finest writing a religious intensity, a celebratory excitement that ranges from the rapturous to the rapt. Like his fictional counterpart he was 'a man who had seen the ecstatic light of Life in stone, on the hills, in leaves of cabbages and weeds'. And again: 'He was able to see the wild and wonderful meaning in the commonest things of earth.' It is one of the paradoxes of art that mystery is best conveyed through precision. The details add up and suggest something beyond themselves. The details are in fact everything. As William Carlos Williams has it: 'No poetry but in things'. 'Spraying the Potatoes' begins:

> The barrels of blue potato-spray
> Stood on a headland of July
> Beside an orchard wall where roses
> Were young girls hanging from the sky.
>
> . . .
>
> And I was there with the knapsack sprayer
> On the barrel's edge poised. A wasp was floating
> Dead on a sunken briar leaf
> Over a copper-poisoned ocean.

Up until this point the poem – to use a musical metaphor – has proceeded straightforwardly in a major key. But in the next stanza the poet, with a bold but delicate modulation manoeuvres us into the disturbing zone of a more remote key-signature:

> The axle-roll of a rut-locked cart
> Broke the burnt stick of noon in two.
> An old man came through a cornfield
> Remembering his youth and some Ruth he knew.

There's an Homeric grandeur in these lines. An echo from the Bronze

Age breaks the silence. The poem is opened up to all sorts of possibilities and relationships. By its end the sprayer of potatoes has been subsumed in the persona of the poet. And yet the poet remains 'the dreamer that the land begets'. We do not forget that once and, in many ways, still – 'the field of potatoes in blossom was the full of his mind'. The poem concludes:

> And poet lost to potato-fields,
> Remembering the lime and copper smell
> Of the spraying barrels he is not lost
> Or till blossomed stalks cannot weave a spell.

In a discreet argument the word 'lost' is used twice in the closing stanza to suggest *loss* in the first instance, and then to declare imaginative independence. But in this poem, which is about the birth of the imagination, the most striking repetition is that of the word 'potato' in a series of utterly practical compounds – potato-spray, potato-stalks, potato-drills, and (twice) potato-fields. The elliptical syntax of the last line leaves the poem in a state of suspension and allows it to ripple outwards whither it will. This, like many of Kavanagh's finest poems, is about being in two places at the one time. It compensates in language for not being somewhere else in person. In the end it relies on 'fields that were part of no earthly estate'.

Was it Paul Muldoon who referred to this poem as the historic site where the knapsack sprayer made its first crucial appearance in Irish poetry? But here we have a knapsack sprayer transfigured. And it is indeed Kavanagh's transfiguring vision that makes him immortal. Early in his career, in a poem like 'To the Man After the Harrow', he is producing visionary, transcendental poetry out of his rural experience, its commonplaces and simplicities. In the 'low dishonest decade' of the thirties – indeed in a godless century like the twentieth – the freshness and courage of this work make it as indispensable as it is unprecedented. What other modern poet has negotiated more successfully the difficulties of writing good religious poetry? (And in the 1990s these difficulties still add up to a central challenge for the poet.) Because he keeps no distance between himself and life, there seems to be no great distance between Kavanagh and his god:

> Forget the worm's opinion too
> Of hooves and pointed harrow-pins,
> For you are driving your horses through
> The mist where Genesis begins.

The Welsh poet David Jones writes: 'The works of man, unless they are of "now" and of "this place", can have no "for ever".' Patrick Kavanagh's 'forever' is Inishkeen or it is nowhere. Like Wordsworth's skylark he remains 'True to the kindred points of heaven and home'. In poems such as 'Kerr's Ass' he sweeps clean for all of us 'the wet gutter reflecting the sky of truth'.

> The winkers that had no choke-band,
> The collar and the reins . . .
> In Ealing Broadway, London Town
> I name their several names . . .

In his sonnet 'The Hospital' Kavanagh remarks famously that 'nothing is by love debarred'. His poetry offers a second life to straggly barbed wire, rusty corrugated iron, rotten palings. old buckets, cow dung. His imagination burnishes the discarded just as it cherishes the useful and beautiful: wild flowers, birds, a tractor, milk in a pail, hay ricks, wheaten bread, a knapsack sprayer. And, in the 'Hospital' sonnet we are given:

> The main gate that was bent by a heavy lorry,
> The seat at the back of a shed that was a suntrap.
> Naming these things is the love-act and its pledge;
> For we must record love's mystery without claptrap,
> Snatch out of time the passionate transitory.

In his review of *Come Dance with Kitty Stobling* A. Alvarez praises 'that concentration which transforms outer and inner worlds into a single, compelling and fresh poetic whole'. So urgently and nakedly does the poet's mind interact with the external world that we seem to be eavesdropping on the actual moment of inspiration, the very moment of creation.

In 'Kerr's Ass' it is the love behind the description of the harness that gives this poem its powerful emotional charge. Once something has been stated or described with such natural authority, we are inclined to take its arrival and presence for granted, as though it has always been the property of generally shared experience. We become instant *aficionados*. We recognise what we do not know. Although his affections might at times embarrass him, in his love for such impoverished things Kavanagh takes us back to the Shakespeare of the Henry IV plays with their richly specialised vocabulary for the humble bits and pieces of concrete existence, to Chaucer, to the Virgil who wrote the *Georgics*, to the stables of the *Iliad*. And, because of the sheer depth of his expertise and witness, Kavanagh perhaps has the edge on all of them. On the way to Dundalk with Kerr's ass, does the poet pass 'The Long Garden'?

It was the garden of the golden apples,
A long garden between a railway and a road,
In the sow's rooting where the hen scratches
We dipped our fingers in the pockets of God.

What he calls 'spirit-shocking wonder' irradiates the penultimate stanza of this uneven but lovely demonstration of how simple things can be transfigured. He joins together the heavens and the Monaghan landscape and releases the sacred penumbra that, for a true artist like himself, or the Vincent van Gogh who painted kitchen furniture and old boots, surrounds each humdrum object:

And when the sun went down into Drumcatton
And the New Moon by its little finger swung
From the telegraph wires, we knew how God had happened
And what the blackbird in the whitethorn sang.

However far-reaching its implications, poetry like this works because it is earthed and free of pretence. It was born in a stable.

'A Christmas Childhood' is for many readers Kavanagh's most incandescent creation. By now there should be no need to draw attention to the innocence and purity of its vision. What we get is a miraculous sense of ordinary life going on, even at Christmas, especially at Christmas. This magic happens only intermittently in, say, Dylan Thomas's 'A Child's Christmas in Wales' – because Thomas seems to be trying too hard. Kavanagh lets the simple objects speak for themselves: the melodeon, the stable lamp, the bellows wheel, the penknife. We have to go to the boathouse in the opening chapters of *David Copperfield* to catch an equivalent symphony of *things*. 'The mute phenomena' – in Derek Mahon's phrase – find their own voices:

Outside in the cow-house my mother
Made the music of milking;
The light of her stable lamp was a star
And the frost of Bethlehem made it twinkle.

A water-hen screeched in the bog,
Mass-going feet
Crunched the wafer-ice on the pot-holes,
Somebody wistfully twisted the bellows wheel . . .

Seemingly 'simple' poets may be harder to grasp than poets who parade their difficulty. John Clare leaves me gasping in wonder in a way the Ezra Pound of the *Cantos* does not. One of my sacred texts is Kavanagh's five-line lyric, 'Consider the Grass Growing'. It is like a pool of rainwater, pellucid, sky-reflecting, bottomless:

Consider the grass growing
As it grew last year and the year before,
Cool above the ankles like summer rivers,
When we walked on a May evening through the meadows
To watch the mare that was going to foal.

Extracts from talk given at 'Kavanagh's Yearly' in the 1990s

W. R. RODGERS

In the graveyard of Cloveneden Church in Loughgall, County Armagh, W. R. Rodgers is commemorated on his headstone as Poet and Preacher. He was born in Belfast in 1909, the son of respectable Presbyterian parents. Intensely religious and, in the Ulster phrase, 'good living', they banned alcohol, tobacco, dancing, theatre-going and full-length mirrors: 'Sunday dinner was cooked on Saturday, and the Sunday boots were polished the night before, and profane books and music were put away till Monday, and nothing, absolutely nothing, was allowed to disturb "the Day of Dreadful Rest", as we restless children called it.' In his pioneering essay 'W. R. Rodgers: Romantic Calvinist' Terence Brown argues that 'the intense pressure suggested by Rodgers's verbal practices exist[s] ... because of, not in spite of, the repressive constrictions of his early experience'.

Though Rodgers came from a strict Calvinist family and suffered in childhood from Old Dissent puritanism, his cultural background was neither threadbare nor tongue-tied. In his radio feature *The Return Room*, which was first broadcast in 1955, he recreates his early childhood in Belfast:

There was a halo of hills round me from the start, and a hug-me-tight of holiness. All the pubs held their breath that day, and the bells of the city danced with their hands in their pockets, and the soothering river ran wild, and a decorated tramcar took over the hills and far way. My father, who had a fine sense of occasion – 'We may put a nick in the post today!' – my father got down the Good

Book and read from the roll of the generations of great men: '. . . Enos which was the son of Seth which was the son of Adam which was the son of God'.

In July the family would rent a holiday cottage in the countryside at Carryduff, not far from Belfast: 'The duck twirled like a stick on the stream, each gay cloud was off on its own, the very clod sang. Apart from my enemy, the nettle, there was only one flaw to it all.' He is referring to the Plymouth Brethren's gospel tents which descended 'on our fields like pentecostal tongues, and the reapers of souls cut swathes of hymns through the standing silence'. The boy longed to be back in Belfast for the more raucous celebrations of the Twelfth of July, 'to hear the dreadful thunder of the big Orange drums' and 'to see the Kingly-painted walls, and the wonderful rafts of rivering flags winding through the streets of the windfall city':

> There would be a bonfire in our back street that night. It would light up the roses on the wall-paper of the return room. It would flicker on the picture of Robbie Burns. It would glimmer on the tallboy with its deep drawers full of treasures – a black silk topper, a purple Edwardian waistcoat with lace on it, a copy of the Solemn League and Covenant, a Volunteer hat that looked like a cowboy's, a silver sovereign-case. The bonfire would redden it all; even the still little Georgian mirror would go wig-wag in the glare of it. How long would it be, I reflected, before my farthing face would grow to a crown? And would I ever be able to see myself, *all* of myself? For there was no full-length mirror in our Puritan house. Such a thing would have been an

abomination, a sin in excelsis, for it might get too enamoured of a person.

After receiving his B.A. with honours in English at Queen's University in 1931, Rodgers entered the Presbyterian Theological College to prepare for the ministry. The *Armagh Standard* reported his ordination on 18 January 1935. The sermon was preached by the Reverend R. G. Fry of Ahorey:

> You may take it that your minister, like every other minister, will be 'a man of sorrows and acquainted with grief'. He can only teach you what he has learned himself, and if on any Sabbath Day ... he seems to speak with unusual power, be sure that he paid a great price for that freedom. He got it through the furnace. The foundations are laid in tears and blood.

The *Armagh Standard* also recorded how later, at the manse, Rodgers introduced himself to his parishioners: 'There were one thousand and one influences working upon his life in bringing him to that day ... He was animated with a desire to do his part in the ingathering of Christ's Kingdom ... He could only pray that he might be worthy of his hopes and inspirations ... He came that day as their minister and teacher, and yet he had many things to learn from them.' He describes his ministry in an unpublished essay: 'A rural community is a close and intricate wickerwork of human relationships and functions ... The role I was called to fill was that of parson and, being young, I found it a formidable one. Old men, full of worldly experience, farmers who never hesitated to advise me on practical matters, would at once defer to me, as sons to a father, when it came to otherworldly matters and spiritual crises. Not that they were impressed by my personal authority; authority for them resided in the role and office which I happened to occupy ... I realised that I, as an individual, did not matter, and this in a way was a relief to me as well as an instruction.' In many respects an unorthodox clergyman, Rodgers is still remembered affectionately in Loughgall for reserving part of every sermon for the children; and for the broad sympathies which gained him the title 'the Catholic Presbyterian'.

In 1936 he married Marie Harden Waddell whom he had first met when he was studying for the ministry and she was a medical student at Queen's. In his monograph on Rodgers, Darcy O'Brien describes their relationship sympathetically. 'Her physical and intellectual vitality seemed complementary to his diffident and rather dreamy nature ... With her, he might learn to be more at home in the world. With him, her bright rationalism might soften under his lyrical sense of the mystery of things. A year after his ordination, he brought her to his parish ... She was to be the village physician. While he was ministering to the souls of his flock, she would look after their bodies.' The niece of Rutherford Mayne the playwright and of Helen Waddell, the scholar and translator of medieval Latin poetry, she was herself an unfulfilled writer. A son was stillborn; but in 1939 their first daughter Harden was born, and in 1941 Nini. The marriage did not prosper, and Marie became mentally ill, subject to fits of depression. In O'Brien's account 'each became the other's best enemy and, to retreat, they drank, so their rows became drunken ones'. He strove to carry on his ministry and to shield Marie and himself in a small community. In 'Paired Lives' husband and wife present, 'like swing doors, one smooth front/ Of summed resistance', but the reality is different:

Each singly yields to thrust,
Is hung on its own hinge
Of fear and hope, and in
Its own reticence rests.

As a poet Rodgers was a late starter. In 1938, three years after his ordination, his friend John Hewitt lent him books by contemporary poets,
of whom Auden made the biggest impact. Poems came steadily after
that. By 1940 the thirty-two lyrics he had written to that date were
collected in *Awake! and Other Poems*. The first printing was destroyed by
the blitz on Plymouth, but the publishers brought out a second printing in 1941, and an American edition appeared in 1942. In John Hewitt's
generous account 'the reviews were enthusiastic and the poet's reputation was made. Rooted in the landscape of Armagh and the Mournes
and given their mood by the European war, the volume presented a
new poet with an exuberant vocabulary and a subtle sensory awareness.' Rodgers's prefatory note to *Awake!* (quoted in full on p. 147
above) celebrates a release: 'It was in the late thirties that I came to
contemporary poetry, and I no longer stood dumb in the tied shops of
speech or felt stifled in the stale air of convention.'

Rodgers's view of poetry and inspiration became Pentecostal. His
verbal spate is often attributed to the influence of Gerard Manley
Hopkins, but John Hewitt puts us right: 'Superficial critics insist on his
derivation from Hopkins, whereas the fact is . . . that the greater body
of his book, *Awake! and Other Poems*, was written before he had read
that infectious Jesuit.' Hewitt directs to James Joyce 'those who wish
to detect the element of Irishry in him'. Rodgers shares with his
contemporaries Dylan Thomas and George Barker a linguistic and
rhythmic ebullience, a tendency towards excess. He himself suggests
that 'the faculty of standing words or ideas on their heads – by means

of pun, epigram, bull, or what-have-you – is a singularly Irish one . . .
To the English ear, which likes understatement, it is all rather excessive
and therefore not quite in good taste. But to the Irish mind, which likes
gesture, bravado, gallivanting, and rhetoric, it is an acceptable tradition.' But even to an Irish mind, surely, Rodgers throughout his career
often goes over the top: 'Nothing pleases me so much in writing as to
be able to sit on both sides of the sense, and if there were six sides I
would sit on them all.' In his essay 'The Dissidence of Dissent' John
Wilson Foster proposes that Rodgers's 'liberties, abandonments and
superfluous energies might be laid at the door of a transposed evan-
gelical fervour'. The preacher has not yet been subsumed in the poet
who, like a diminutive John Bunyan, allows personified abstractions
to clump through his lines. One such is 'Contempt the caretaker' who
rather spoils 'The Party'. In Kathleen Raine's opinion Rodgers 'is never
dull, never flat – except when he has something to say of a philosophic
nature, when he drops into bathos'.

Beneath the celebrations there sounds a grumbling ground bass,
'ratchets of agitation', as though the light of poetry is too bright for eyes
grown accustomed to 'the darkened house', the manse: 'It was always
afternoon in my parish, the full tide of sleep brimming the sky; the
shot bird hung in the air, the blown rose refused to fall, the clock stood
still.' Obsessive images of entrapment recur – nets, thongs, ropes,
webs, threads. The poet, 'listening for the fat click of the softly-shut
door', feels threatened in his private life and by external circumstance:

> I shouted and none answered, one by one
> My listening hopes crept back to me
> Out of that dead place; mine was a lighted face
> Looking into darkness, seen, but seeing nothing.

'These early poems are,' Terence Brown suggests, 'the work of a personality at war with itself, torn between the Calvinist's sense of duty
and responsibility, and a romantic's need for a rich diversity and
profusion of experience.' Claustrophobia shades into paranoia. In
'Beagles' Rodgers identifies with 'the little and elastic hare' pursued by
'the whole blind world'. The hunters' shouts turn into 'A tether that
held me to the hare/ Here, there and everywhere'. The first book tests
possibilities of change and escape. He refers again and again to boundaries, borders, edges, rims, the horizon. One of his poems about the
war is called 'Escape':

> ... You will be more free
> At the thoughtless centre of slaughter than you would be
> Standing chained to the telephone-end while the world cracks.

Also at the end of his tether, exhausted after writing and producing
seventy programmes in four years, Louis MacNeice escaped in 1945
from London to Ireland where he contacted Rodgers and suggested
that he might work for the BBC. It took Rodgers more than a year to
make up his mind. In 1946 he left his manse in County Armagh for the
BBC in London. Darcy O'Brien provides the details: 'It was to be a total
break. He would go to London alone, and not as a parson taking leave
but simply as a poet. Marie was to study in Edinburgh, the children
would stay behind with aunts. 'A seal,' he felt, 'had been put on the
past.' The neighbouring Catholic priest was his last visitor. And Rodgers preached his last sermon on the text: 'By faith Abraham, when he
was called to go out into a place which he should after receive as an
inheritance, obeyed; and he went out, not knowing whither he went.'

Poetry came more slowly after the first urgent burst. Another eighteen poems had been written by 1946, and ten more were completed

in England. These made up *Europa and the Bull and Other Poems* which was published in 1952. Richer, more various, more ambitious, this collection was not so well received as *Awake!* 'The poems were,' in John Hewitt's words, 'more difficult and unusual and farther away from the War Years and their literary conventions.' An unembarrassed paganism pervades three narrative poems based on Greek myths, 'Pan and Syrinx', 'Apollo and Daphne' and the title poem which takes up the first sixteen pages with a longwinded dramatisation of seduction, penetration, and orgasm. Weirdly epic in its sweep, the poem seems to teeter at the edge of cosmic revelation, to hold – like 'The Swan' – 'the heavens, shores, waters and all their brood'. But even this poet's verbal invention fails over such a distance; and his tirelessness becomes tiresome, perhaps even ridiculous, and, at an imaginative level, detumescent. The best poems in the book – those which can now be seen as the core of Rodgers's achievement – explore Christian themes, or express an open-faced and big-hearted randiness, or both. Rodgers has allowed his Grecian annex to obscure the church-door. But inside the church, 'Europa and the Bull' and its two companions seem little more than a prelude to the small group of great poems. This includes the erotic masterpiece, 'The Net', and that extraordinary reinterpretation, 'Lent', in which Jesus is reborn in the womb of Mary Magdalene once she has relented and allowed her Lenten mask of self-denial to thaw. In return for her warmth Christ returns to her the emblems of her sensuality:

> Dance, Mary Magdalene, dance, dance and sing,
> For unto you is born
> This day a King. 'Lady,' said He,
> 'To you who relent
> I bring back the petticoat and the bottle of scent.'

This magnificent poem gathers around itself several other original meditations and celebrations: 'The Trinity'; 'Carol', which is perfect; 'Resurrection', in which the voice of authority rings out over two hundred and sixty lines as Rodgers like a modern Saint Paul rethinks and feels afresh the Easter story; 'Nativity' and 'The Journey of the Magi', overlong and flawed, but, in their best moments, rich and generous:

> It was the child within themselves
> For which they'd sought, for which Age delves
> – Now Age and Innocence can meet,
> Now, now the circle is complete,
> The journey's done. Lord, Lord how sweet!

What other poet brings the reader closer to the Jesus who washed the feet of the disciples; who 'figured it forth/ In the breaking of bread'; who conceived 'The Lord's Prayer' and 'The Sermon on the Mount'? As in 'Nativity' ('His holly hair, his berry eyes are here,/ And his chrysanthemum wound,/ This Christmas day ...'), so in 'Christ Walking on the Water' Rodgers portrays Jesus the man, his doubt and despair, his naturalness, his earthiness, his sexuality, and thereby his greatness:

> ... he like a lover, caught up,
> Pushed past all wrigglings and remonstrances
> And entered the rolling belly of the boat
> That shuddered and lay still. And he lay there
> Emptied of his errand, oozing still ...

Christ is at once an omnipotent god – 'the hub,/ Both bone and flesh, finger and ring of all/ This clangorous sea' – and a bewildered man. At the end of the poem he slumps down in the boat, agitated and exhausted, 'His knees drawn up, his head dropped deep,/ Curled like a question mark asleep'. In his review of *Europa and the Bull* G. S. Fraser writes of Rodgers's 'sacramentalisation of sex'. At moments of great intensity religious and sexual experiences seem for this poet to be one and the same. The inspiration behind these remarkable pieces was his affair, lasting seven years, with Marianne Gilliam, whom he had first met in 1945. She was the wife of his immediate boss, Laurence Gilliam, Head of the Features Department in the BBC. 'The Net', one of the most passionate love poems in the language, is addressed to her. The anatomical hard facts have seldom been conveyed with such fierce precision and loving care:

> Quick, woman, in your net
> Catch the silver I fling!
> O I am deep in your debt,
> Draw tight, skin-tight, the string,
> And rake the silver in.
> No fisher ever yet
> Drew such a cunning ring.

Rodgers's wife, Marie, held a number of positions in Scottish hospitals, but she never completely regained her health. She died in Newcastle, County Down, in 1953. Rodgers crossed to Ireland for the funeral. In the same year he married Marianne. O'Brien quotes Laurence Gilliam as saying: 'She may make him happy, but he will not write any more poetry.' In 1956 their daughter Lucy was born. *Collected Poems* which was published in 1971, two years after his death in America, contains a further ten pieces (plus the never-to-be-completed 'Epilogue'), the rather disappointing harvest of sixteen years. At the BBC he invented a form of radio collage – known as 'the Rodgers method' – which is now taken for granted. By carefully editing and cross-cutting interviews with and about Irish writers he produced a series of portraits (published in 1972 by the BBC as *Irish Literary Portraits*) which, he hoped, would 'build up a composite picture of Ireland as it was more than half a century ago, of the literary renaissance which flowered so magically and died so mysteriously'. He also published a series of articles and booklets which provide insights into his poetry and personality ('Balloons and Maggots', 'The Dance of Words'), and his native province ('An Ulster Protestant', 'Black North'); wrote the text for *Ireland in Colour* (1957), and printed privately a personal miscellany called *Essex Roundabout* (1963). The articles about Ulster character and the political situation, which appeared in journals like *The Bell* and the *New Statesman*, and his British Council booklet, *The Ulstermen and their Country*, must strike anyone who reads them now – after twenty-five years of political confusion and terrorist violence – as broadminded, astute, prescient. In *Collected Poems* Dan Davin's 'Introductory Memoir' gives a detailed, often funny, account of the slow failure of the projected *The Character of Ireland*, a collection of essays which he was to co-edit with Louis MacNeice. This selection ends with Rodgers's unfinished 'Epilogue' to the never-completed book.

In 1966 Rodgers took up a visiting professorship at Pitzer College in Claremont, California, for a period of one year. Thanks to his success and popularity as a teacher, his contract was renewed for another year. One of the more spectacular events he organised was a week-long Irish Festival which featured, among others, Conor Cruise O'Brien, Máire Mhac an tSaoi and Benedict Kiely. Because no funding was available for a permanent position at Pitzer, Rodgers moved on to a part-time job at California State Polytechnic College. In England in the summer of 1968 he was diagnosed as suffering from colonic cancer, and underwent major surgery. He managed to return to California that autumn, but became seriously ill again in January 1969, and died on 1 February in the Los Angeles County General Hospital. His ashes were flown to Belfast and, after a memorial service in the First Ballymacarrett Presbyterian Church which he had attended as a boy, he was buried in Loughgall.

At the memorial service it was Seamus Heaney who read a brief selection from Rodgers's poetry. Northern Irish poets of my vintage revered Rodgers along with Louis MacNeice, John Hewitt, Patrick Kavanagh. In 1963 Derek Mahon read a paper on MacNeice to the Philosophical Society of Trinity College, Dublin. The honoured guest was Rodgers, and MacNeice's widow Hedli sat in the audience. I spoke to the paper. Using the briefest of notes, Rodgers talked entertainingly, affectionately, perceptively about his friend and colleague. It was a sparkling performance. Later we gave him milky Nescafé in my college rooms. Although he had drunk a good deal of whiskey that day, it had not been all that evident during his address. And he got up the following morning at seven o'clock to finish an article for the *New Statesman*. When I joined the Arts Council of Northern Ireland in 1970, I discovered on file a brief commissioned report in which Rodgers surveyed the local literary scene and praised the new generation of Ulster poets who had just started to get their work published. He had clearly read all of us with interest and sympathy. The Board of the Arts Council had earlier decreed that because literature was practised by amateurs, financial support should not be given to writers. The generous enthusiasm of Rodgers's report helped to prepare the way for the literature programme which I was later to initiate.

W. R. Rodgers is a latter-day metaphysical who apprehends the divine through the senses, The Word through words. I have already quoted what the Reverend Fry said at the poet's ordination: 'If he seems to speak with unusual power, be sure that he paid a great price for that freedom. He got it through the furnace.' In 'that freedom' Rodgers enlists 'all the bells and hullabaloos of joy'; carollings, fiddles, flutes, trumpets, flowers; images of dance; the rhythms of day and night; the seasons and their festivals; all weathers; lakes, waterfalls, rivers, fountains, cataracts; the altering perspectives of haze and mist; an archetypal bestiary of bulls, hares, hounds, hawks, larks; classical mythology; and the story of Christ. In his best poetry we find 'The Word made flesh, melted into motion'. Although Rodgers seeks to demonstrate how 'God can be sought in a golden rain/ Of levity and fireworks', he also knows that

> ... the god has always a foot of clay, and the soul
> Grows in soil, the flower has a dark root.

Introduction to W. R. Rodgers, *Selected Poems*, edited by Michael Longley (Loughcrew: Gallery Press, 1993)

'IN THE BEAUTIFUL WHITE RUINS':
JAMES WRIGHT

A few years ago I copied into my commonplace book Dante Gabriel
Rossetti's 'The Woodspurge'. Here are its last two stanzas:

> My eyes, wide open, had the run
> Of some ten weeds to fix upon,
> Among those few, out of the sun,
> The woodspurge flowered, three cups in one.

> From perfect grief there need not be
> Wisdom or even memory:
> One thing then learnt remains for me, –
> The woodspurge has a cup of three.

A poem has really to get under my skin before I feel the urge to write
it out in longhand. By a pleasing botanical coincidence 'The Woodspurge' was soon followed by James Wright's 'Milkweed', which I quote
in its entirety:

> While I stood here, in the open, lost in myself
> I must have looked a long time
> Down the corn rows, beyond grass,
> The small house,
> White walls, animals lumbering toward the barn.
> I look down now. It has all changed.
> Whatever it was I lost, whatever I wept for

Was a wild, gentle thing, the small dark eyes
Loving me in secret.
It is here. At a touch of my hand,
The air fills with delicate creatures
From the other world.

I love both poems for the risks they take and for the way they sound so closely together the notes of sorrow and celebration. But in comparison with Wright's free verse do not Rossetti's octosyllabics creak a bit? Does not Wright's line 'Whatever it was I lost, whatever I wept for' embody feelings of loss with an appropriateness of cadence which it would be much harder to achieve within Rossetti's metrical grid? 'Wisdom and 'memory' seem to me inadequately earthed by the poet's voice, with the result that they escape from his mouth and float out of sight above his head as the abstractions they are. Wright's line brings to puzzled surmise all the physicality of a heavy sigh.

I hear Wright's voice in my head and with my inner ear I imagine its accent and accompanying emotional wobbles. Because he is talking to me so directly, I am inclined to believe every word he says. Likewise, in their matter-of-factness his mystical moments convince. 'A Blessing', his beautiful psalm about two Indian ponies encountered 'Just off the highway to Rochester, Minnesota', concludes famously:

I would like to hold the slenderer one in my arms,
For she has walked over to me
And nuzzled my left hand.
She is black and white,
Her mane falls wild on her forehead,
And the light breeze moves me to caress her long ear
That is delicate as the skin over a girl's wrist.

> Suddenly I realise
> That if I stepped out of my body I would break
> Into blossom.

(What unexpected grace that awkward comparative, 'slenderer', gives the line!) Twenty-five years ago when Wright was parodied in the *Review*, the ending of this poem provided ammunition. I sniggered along with the rest. On this side of the Atlantic we were embarrassed by what appeared to be unselfconscious, even shameless outpourings. We were wrong of course. Wright is a highly self-conscious artist whose formal early verse shows great metrical and stanzaic skill in the traditional modes. Although, like so many American poets, he found liberating the example of William Carlos Williams and his 'reply to Greek and Latin with bare hands', he was well-versed in the cultures of Greece and Rome. He went on to learn from Chinese poetry, from German expressionism and Spanish surrealism. Going abroad – even within the confines of one's library – is as good a way as any of discovering the value of home. Attentive to the procedures and noises of foreign poetry, Wright catches the life of America with a precision that validates his vaults into the mystical and the surreal ('I am lost in the beautiful white ruins/ Of America'). Here is most of 'Twilights':

> The big stones of the cistern behind the barn
> Are soaked in whitewash.
> My grandmother's face is a small maple leaf
> Pressed in a secret box.
> Locusts are climbing down into the dark green crevices
> Of my childhood. Latches click softly in the trees. Your hair is gray.

Lyric loveliness, yes: but at its core Wright's imagination is robust, disenchanted, omnivorous. 'Ohioan Pastoral' ends like this:

> The limp whip of a sumac dangles
> Gently against the body of a lost
> Bathtub, while high in the flint-cracks
> And the wild grimed trees, on the hill,
> A buried gas main
> Long ago tore a black gutter into the mines.
> And now it hisses among the green rings
> On fingers in coffins.

If he is great, it is because his poetry is potentially home for everyone and everything. A good example is 'Autumn Begins in Martins Ferry, Ohio':

> In the Shreve High Football stadium,
> I think of Polacks nursing long beers in Tiltonsville,
> And gray faces of Negroes in the blast furnace at Benwood,
> And the ruptured night watchman of Wheeling Steel,
> Dreaming of heroes.

Half of me admires this American determination to jettison the iambic beat and rhyme schemes and along with them the safety-net of irony, the meshes of which are pulled into shape by such formal tensions. 'Walking naked' Yeats called it. Then everything depends on timing, on an inherent sense of rhythm, on having a good ear. (And at his best Wright has perfect pitch). The aim is to be plain and open-faced and big-hearted. The risk is sentimentality. The reward is revelation. James Wright reminds us, as did his teacher Theodore Roethke, that even at the end of this century religious poetry remains a reasonable aspiration.

This time, I have left my body behind me, crying
In its dark thorns.
Still,
There are good things in this world.
It is dusk.
It is the good darkness
Of women's hands that touch loaves.
The spirit of a tree begins to move.
I touch leaves.
I close my eyes, and think of water.

This poem should sound ridiculous. Somehow or other it doesn't. It is called 'Trying to Pray'.

Poetry Ireland Review 43/44 (Autumn/ Winter 1994)

MEMORY AND ACKNOWLEDGEMENT

Last week I returned to my old school to retrieve a copy of a letter my father had written in 1953 to the headmaster. He was replying to a proposition that my twin and I, who were thirteen years old at the time, might join the school's combined cadet corps – the CCF. My father conceded that the training and discipline would be very good for the boys, but ended his letter as follows: 'I recall that as a result of being a cadet myself, I found myself with the British Expeditionary Force in France in 1914 at the age of seventeen years and although I do not regret it, I do hope history will not repeat itself. Accordingly I do not feel that they should join. Yours sincerely . . .' Shortly before he died (in 1962), my father broke his silence about his war-experience. His stories have helped to shape my imaginative landscape. In each of my six collections there are poems based on my memories of his memories. One memory was of his travelling through Europe, after the war, helping to spread anti-German propaganda. He disliked telling official lies, and thought that Goebbels had learned from British propaganda.

In November 1993 my wife and I spent the last day of a visit to Germany in Weimar where as good tourists we wandered round the homes of Schiller and Goethe. Twenty minutes up the road lies Buchenwald – one of history's filthiest spots in the midst of memories of the Enlightenment. Our British Council host offered to take us there. And there we went. It would be impertinent in a short essay to give details of the nightmare that only partially but still unendurably lingers in that place. The Museum at Buchenwald is crammed with mementoes of humiliation and abandonment, which should be allowed to bear silent witness on their own. But a notice was pointed out to us, an official apology for bias. The party line of the discredited East German regime had been that in Buchenwald Nazis imprisoned and tormented Communists. Little mention was made of what Germans had done to Jews. This sprawling memorial to the most extreme suffering had been used to tell a bare-faced lie which the new government was gradually correcting.

When we went outside, we noticed a wreath of poppies, a British Legion wreath, exactly the same as those laid at more familiar war memorials. British prisoners were among the many nationalities who suffered in Buchenwald. Although there were hundreds of terrible things to remember, that wreath and the official apology were what I later found words for. 'Buchenwald Museum' is a very short poem about historical revisionism, about trying to remember truthfully:

> Among the unforgettable exhibits one
> Was an official apology for bias. Outside
>
> Although a snowfall had covered everything
> A wreath of poppies was just about visible.
>
> No matter how heavily the snow may come down
> We have to allow the snow to wear a poppy.

When I wear a poppy I do so in remembrance of millions of lost lives, and not as a political gesture. I hate it when the wearing (or the not wearing) of a poppy is politically construed. Where poppies are seen as pro-British badges, they have sometimes been ripped from lapels. This act of aggression would be countered by another act of aggression, which I record in a second epigrammatic piece. Within the poem, as a coda to its brevity, I describe in two lines what happed in Belfast, in Royal Avenue, when wounded soldiers returned from France in 1918 – an ambiguous occasion. This poem is called 'Poppies' and it is meant to relate to that snow-covered, disappearing wreath in Buchenwald:

I

Some people tried to stop other people wearing poppies
And ripped them from lapels as though uprooting poppies
From Flanders fields, but the others hid inside their poppies
Razor blades and added to their poppies more red poppies.

II

In Royal Avenue they tossed in the air with so much joy
Returning wounded soldiers, their stitches burst for joy.

As Alistair Thomson and the Popular Memory Group have noted, 'Memories are painful if they do not conform with the public norms or versions of the past.' The historian Jane Leonard is presently engaged in brilliant research, which is rescuing from willed amnesia parts of our common past and giving them back to us. The sub-title of her essay 'Facing the "Finger of Scorn"' is 'Veterans' Memories of Ireland After The Great War'. Leonard writes:

> Those [veterans] who applied for cottages and smallhold-
> ings under the 1919 Irish Land Act were threatened and
> boycotted. In some cases, their homes were vandalised
> and set on fire. Cultural boycotts included the refusal to let
> former hurlers and Gaelic football players rejoin the Gaelic
> Athletic Association if they had served in the war . . . . The
> extremes of intimidation included beating, mutilation,

> punishment shooting, expulsion from Ireland, prolonged
> kidnapping and ultimately murder. During the period
> from 1919 to 1924 upwards of 120 ex-servicemen were
> killed... Some of these veterans were undoubtedly intelli-
> gence agents for the police and military forces. However,
> the vast majority appear to have been killed simply as a
> retrospective punishment for their Great War service and
> because, as ex-servicemen, they formed a marginalised
> and unwelcome group in Irish society. (See *War and Memory
> in the Twentieth Century*, ed. Martin Evans & Kenneth Lunn.)

The embarrassment and defensiveness, the reticence and fear of these
Irish ex-servicemen and their families seem tragic to me when I
measure their self-denial against my own schoolboyishly straightforward pride in my father's war record. Towards the end of her essay
Leonard comments:

> They matured into middle age and retirement, aware that
> they were excluded from the national cultural identity
> forged after independence in 1922. This identity declared,
> in the words of a popular ballad:

> > 'Twas better to die 'neath an Irish sky
> > Than at Suvla or Sedd el Bahr.

> The Irish who survived Gallipoli and the Western Front
> 'backed the wrong horse', in joining the British forces, as
> one of them recalled. The same veteran recognised that his
> British Army service was compromised by the Easter
> Rising and post-war revolution in Ireland, but he regretted

that the history textbooks used by his children and grandchildren were silent on the extent of his generation's
participation in the war.

Many other memories from the 1920s and later have been buried. It
can be painful to bring to light what has been repressed – the expulsion of Catholics from the shipyards and from streets in Belfast, for
instance, the expulsion of Protestants from West Cork. It is more painful to remember a civil war than an uprising. There are dozens of
ballads about Easter 1916 and the War of Independence, hardly any
that come out of the Irish Civil War. But even the Easter Rising was
beginning to cause some official embarrassment when its seventy-
fifth anniversary came around in 1991. The Irish Government was
reluctant to give even oblique support to the IRA by commemorating
too vigorously the militant republicanism that gave birth to the State.
And people were also recalling how in West Belfast some of the
coat-trailing (that is to say, tricolour-trailing) in 1966 at the fiftieth
anniversary of the Rising had provided an opening for Ian Paisley and
had contributed to the untwisting of the blue touch-paper for the
Troubles.

At the time this underplaying of a central historical moment
seemed wrong to me. It was as though Yeats's great, ambiguous refrain
'A terrible beauty is born' was being diluted into 'Yes, something
rather exciting and significant did happen round about then'. A mean
between uncritical glorification of the past, and frightened repression,
is what we should be seeking. So I accepted an invitation to take part
in one of the commemorative events, a marathon poetry read-in in
the GPO. I'm pretty certain that Padraic Fiacc and I were the only writers to travel down from the north that day. In the queue of readers I
was proud to take my place between one of the key figures in the

197

revival of poetry in Irish, Máire Mhac an tSaoi, and Michael D. Higgins (then, Minister for Arts, Culture and the Gaeltacht; now, President of Ireland). Without comment I read elegies for people killed in the Troubles. I saluted the leaders of the Easter Rising, and then, partly because the presence of such as Higgins and Mhac an tSaoi gave me the courage to be myself, I said that, coming from Belfast, I felt Irish sometimes and sometimes I felt British. I sensed that the large crowd took little or no exception to what I was saying. Indeed, they seemed quite sympathetic to what amounted to my declaration of dual allegiance.

This, for me personally, is a small pre-echo of what happened at Islandbridge some weeks ago when John Bruton became the first Irish Taoiseach to acknowledge Ireland's great debt, not only to Britain and the other Allies for doing the fighting in the Second World War, but also the thousands of Irishmen and women (Catholic and Protestant) who donned British uniforms to defeat Fascism. Who was not moved to see on television the old soldier in his beret and clinking medals smiling and saying, 'I never thought I'd see the day'? He had been given back a fuller sense of himself and the freedom to be truly himself among his fellow citizens. The presence of Tom Hartley of Sinn Féin was seen by everyone, including me, as admirable, significant and very welcome. But the soul-searching is only beginning. In a speech last month in University College, Cork, Gerard Delanty said: 'It is a matter of great regret that this country has not participated in the collective remembering of the Holocaust and the defeat of fascism. It would be a fine contribution to a European identity if more public persons had followed the lead of the Irish Prime Minister, Mr Bruton . . . Ireland like the rest of Europe was aware that the Jews were doomed.' Delanty quotes these words of Conor Cruise O'Brien: 'We shut the doors, knowingly and deliberately. All of us, Britain, the US, France, us, everyone. Our only defence, as Ireland, is that we were no worse than the others. That is quite true, but it is hardly enough to entitle us to that high moral plane we so often claim for ourselves.' Delanty concluded: 'Instead of a probing of unexamined consciences on the extent of Irish anti-Semitism and . . . pro-fascist sympathy, we have had the grotesque attempts to promote the 150th anniversary of the Irish famine as an "Irish Holocaust".'

To equate the Famine with the Holocaust is to devalue both. I want to know everything there is to know about the Famine as well as everything there is to know about the Holocaust. But in 1945 would it not have been impossible, offensive even, to commemorate the hundredth anniversary of the Famine in some of the politicised ways in which it is being processed today? Is this also an evasion of responsibility for recent painful Irish history? I remember in the late 1960s joining a civil rights demonstration in Belfast, and then leaving it in despair when the crowd started to use the Nazi salute and shout at the police 'SS-RUC! SS-RUC!' This wasn't remembering. This wasn't even knowing. The SS would have strung us up from the lamp-posts.

Two months ago in Tullamore, a small town in the middle of Ireland, it was my honour to take part in an ecumenical church service in memory of all who had died in the Troubles. It was televised north and south. For many of us the most moving part of the service came when a procession of townsfolk carried down the central aisle large card-board placards on which a woman from Dungannon had single-handedly written out every one of the names of the victims – children, civilians, politicians, paramilitaries, civil servants, soldiers, policemen, even miscarried babies. Parents who had lost children contributed to the televised service. So did a widow whose husband had been blown to pieces; a policeman who had lost both his legs. Sharing a few pints with some of them afterwards, I felt humbled by their lack of bitterness. These people who had suffered so much had subtle, complicated things to say about rehabilitation and forgiveness. Among all the talk of peace process and peace dividend (and even peace prizes) the victims and their relatives can so easily be overlooked.

That long list of names should become a litany – a litany of the dead. The word itself – 'litany' – suggests three things: enumeration, repetition, penitence. Concepts such as 'a clean slate' or 'drawing a line' are offensive. If we are not ever to know who bombed Enniskillen and Birmingham, Dublin and Monaghan, we can at least go on asking 'Where are all the missing bodies of the last twenty-five years? Where have they been buried?' In the ghastly paramilitary argot these are the 'bog jobs'. Amnesty does not mean amnesia. We Irish are good at claiming a monopoly on human suffering. We are good at resurrecting and distorting the past in order to evade the present. In Ireland we must break the mythic cycles and resist unexamined, ritualistic forms of commemoration. If we don't, it will all happen again.

Irish Review 17/18 (Winter 1995)

This article was based on a talk given at a symposium, 'Reconciliation and Community: The Future of Peace in Northern Ireland', organised (in June 1995) by The Foundation for a Civil Society and The University of Ulster.

THE FIRST AND THE TWELFTH OF JULY

As a boy watching the Twelfth of July procession on the Lisburn Road, I used to wait with particular commitment for the banners commemorating the Battle of the Somme. In March this year my wife and I visited some of the First World War battlefields and cemeteries in Northern France. As an Ulsterman haunted by the Somme, but also for personal and literary reasons, I had dreamt for a long time of making this pilgrimage. My father who hailed from Clapham Common had joined up as a youngster in 1914. By the age of twenty he had received the Military Cross and was in command of a company of soldiers even younger than himself. As I grow older, the nightmare that he lived through looms ever larger in my imagination. My wife's first publication was an edition of the poems of Edward Thomas who died at the Battle of Arras in 1917. For many years she in her criticism, and I in my poetry, have tried to honour the creativity with which young writers such as Edward Thomas, Wilfred Owen, Siegfried Sassoon, Isaac Rosenberg, Charles Sorley faced death in the trenches. We drove to the small out-of-the-way graveyards in which Owen and Thomas lie buried, and to the wall on which Sorley's name is inscribed. He and Rosenberg were probably blown to bits: their only remains, literary remains. These were the ghosts we knew. Then there were the millions of other ghosts. We found it all unendurably moving.

It is in the nature of cemeteries to become overgrown, their inscriptions blurred by lichens and mosses. But here the headstones blaze white and clean and in the middle distance turn into a fall of snow. Immaculately mown lawns and dainty flowerbeds add to the feeling that these sorrowful vistas were laid out only yesterday by some omnipresent gardener from a British suburb. They both unsettle and console. The atmosphere aches with pain and anguish. The tact of the overall design as conceived by Sir Edwin Lutyens miraculously makes room for the heartbreak in millions of homes. Every detail is simple and clear-cut, without a hint of jingoism or triumphalism. Here and there an unknown German soldier lies buried beside his English or Scottish or Irish foes, bringing to mind the famous line in Owen's great poem 'Strange Meeting': 'I am the enemy you killed, my friend.'

The rows of war graves amount to a huge silent lamentation. Millions of names have been recorded in a strange unison, as it were, a low-pitched, continuous, internalised moan in which discriminations as to rank, class, religion, nationality are annulled. We did not detect a wrong note until we arrived at the memorial to the 36th Ulster Division close to the place where they made their heroic attempt to reach Thiepval and take the Schwaben Redoubt on 1 July 1916. The wrong note is not struck by the memorial itself: an exact replica of Helen's Tower at Clandeboye where the soldiers trained before going to France, the first and last journey abroad for so many of them. In that offensive five and a half thousand men were killed or wounded or went missing. In its recollection of County Down meadows the memorial gathers to itself every town and village in Ulster that was afflicted. At once foreign and familiar, it stands in its own small park and boasts a tea room at the rear.

Outside the front wall, however, and close to the entrance gate, a black and mean-looking obelisk commemorates the Orangemen who died in the Great War. This recent effort to improve on the 36th Ulster Division memorial contradicts the tenderness and nostalgia with which, in 1921, Helen's Tower was reproduced among the wounded fields of France. Aesthetically a disaster, an ugly lump of prose that detracts from the poetry of its setting, the obelisk is appropriately kept outside the enclosure of remembrance, beyond the pale. Out of touch, out of proportion, this monument to bad taste affronts Lutyens's profound vision and the unobtrusive, attentive, fastidious management of the cemeteries from day to day and over the years. Whereas desolation on an unprecedented and multi-national scale produced the cemeteries, tribal assertion thrust the obelisk onto the scene. Our present Troubles lurk behind its inadequate cover. It seems to be an attempt at tit-for-tat commemoration, a reply to Padraic Pearse's claim: 'The Fools! The Fools! The Fools! They have left us our Fenian dead.' Veneration for the dead of the Somme has degenerated into a necrophilia that mimics the necrophilia of political enemies. Two graveyard cultures vie with one another.

A failure of the imagination, the obelisk symbolises much that has gone wrong with Orange and Unionist culture. Those who trampled on the graves in Drumcree churchyard last year trampled on the graves in France. Those who march on the Twelfth of July this year should ask themselves to what extent they are in danger of destroying the values they ostensibly seek to maintain.

Contribution to *The Twelfth: What it means to me*
(Ulster Society, July 1997).

Note: The obelisk has since been moved to a less obtrusive position behind Helen's Tower.

'THE STILE BY THE HOLLY':
EDWARD THOMAS

Several years ago my wife, Edna, and I and our friend Ronald Ewart visited Edward Thomas's grave at Agny on the outskirts of Arras. Suddenly, shockingly, we found his headstone in the small cemetery. We stood just feet away from the skull that had contained the brain that had produced the lines that had filled our minds for many years. In that moment we loved him and mourned him. Listening to the bird-song and the rustle of the surrounding trees, we wrote our names in the visitors' book. Edna added the four lovely lines of 'Thaw'. By the time we returned to Agny three years later, I had visited the *Anthem for Doomed Youth* exhibition in the Imperial War Museum, and had gazed at Thomas's crinkled notebook and his pocket watch, stopped at the instant of his death in a shell-blast at the beginning of the battle of Arras on 9 April 1917. The more one learns, the more painful the fact of his death becomes. Walking away from the poet's narrow plot was more difficult this second time.

* * *

Like everyone else, I have suffered periods of writer's block – two of them protracted and painful. I have no idea where poetry comes from or where it goes when it disappears. It is a mystery most vividly brought home to us by Edward Thomas's life and achievement. He made his living as a writer of prose – country books, criticism, biographies, anthologies – and a ferocious routine of reviewing. Some of this huge output is good and the best of it nourished the poems that were waiting to be born. But he considered himself a hack, a drudge. As we know, he was released into his true calling by, first of all, Robert Frost's friendship and then by the Great War: the muse that killed him. The poetry existed as a subterranean current. It had to come. So, strangely, Edward Thomas's poetic career began with writer's block. The one hundred and forty poems he wrote in the last two years of his life are a miracle. I can think of no body of work in English that is more mysterious.

* * *

When he first came to Belfast in 1973 to give a reading, I took Douglas Dunn to the Crown for a drink. 'What's Edna working on just now?' he asked. 'She's preparing an edition of Edward Thomas's poems.' 'Och,' Douglas exclaimed: '"Tall Nettles" – that's the sort of poem you dream about writing.' I have read 'Tall Nettles' hundreds of times. It is brand new every time – 'worn new', to quote Thomas's poem 'Words'. Somehow 'the dust on the nettles' seems capable of registering everything. 'Anything, however small,' Thomas wrote, 'may make a poem. Nothing, however great, is certain to.' 'Aspens', for instance, celebrates the tree itself, but also manages to be an *ars poetica* and an elegy that covers the war and 'village' England – 'the inn, the smithy and the shop'. The weaving syntax communicates psychological commotion and foreboding. (And who has used adverbs more compellingly than Thomas does in the penultimate line: 'ceaselessly, unreasonably'?) He is a master of the short lyric. His quatrain poems contain whole worlds: 'Thaw' with its dizzying alternation of perspectives; 'The Cherry Trees' and 'In Memoriam: Easter, 1915', which are compressed lamentations for the dead and missing of the Great War. *Multum in parvo*. Better than any other poet, Edward Thomas shows that miniature is not the same as minor.

* * *

In April 2005 I sat beside Edna at a heavy mahogany table in the New York Public Library's marvellous Berg Collection. A white-gloved attendant brought us the field-notebooks into which Edward Thomas had scribbled nature-notes for his prose works. New York seemed a strange setting in which to follow the poet-to-be as he wandered in pre-war Hampshire, Wiltshire or Gloucestershire, scrutinising the birds and the flowers and obsessively describing the weather of nearly a hundred years ago. I got an electric charge touching the pages he had touched. Almost as exhilarating was my unexpected ability to decipher his tiny, cursive script. I felt at home with his handwriting. I was able to help Edna decode several knotty passages. I was taken back thirty years to when she was working on her annotated edition, *Poems and Last Poems,* and I helped her to transcribe material from files of newspaper cuttings in the Thomas archive in Cardiff. Now, waiting in an airport coffee shop to fly back to Europe, I wrote this quatrain and called it 'Footnote':

> I deciphered his handwriting for Edna
> In the Berg Collection, and helped them both
> To rise above the table-top's green baize
> When Edward 'grasped the stile by the holly'.

* * *

We went on a pilgrimage to Thomas territory in March 2004. In Wiltshire we walked around Stonehenge, and spent the night in Manor Farm in the middle of the Avebury Stone Circle. We must have looked like house-hunters or nosey parkers as we inspected Thomas's Hampshire homes: Berryfield Cottage, Yew Tree Cottage and Wick Green (The Red House). We took a bunch of Mothering Sunday daffodils to the memorial stone above Steep. And on the crest of a muddy Gloucestershire hillock planted with cabbages we looked down on Oldfield House, where Thomas stayed in August 1914, and beyond it, across dips in the landscape, to Little Iddens where Robert Frost then lived. Past those hedges and along those lanes the two poets had strolled together and talked 'of flowers, childhood, Shakespeare, women, England, the war'. When Frost returned to Little Iddens as an old man in 1957, he could not bring himself to cross the threshold. Lovers of Thomas's poetry stand waiting behind him. His 'Iris by Night' complements Thomas's 'The sun used to shine':

> Then a small rainbow like a trellis gate,
> A very small moon-made prismatic bow,
> Stood closely over us through which to go.

* * *

I have written several poems about Edward Thomas. In 'Poetry', an unrhymed sonnet from *The Weather in Japan*, I consider the friendship of poets, the relationships between them over the years, and their posterity:

> When he was billeted in a ruined house in Arras
> And found a hole in the wall beside his bed
> And, rummaging inside, his hand rested on *Keats*
> By Edward Thomas, did Edmund Blunden unearth
> A volume which 'the tall, Shelley-like figure'
> Gathering up for the last time his latherbrush,

207

Razor, towel, comb, cardigan, cap comforter,
Water bottle, socks, gas mask, great coat, rifle
And bayonet, hurrying out of the same building
To join his men and march into battle, left
Behind him like a gift, the author's own copy?
When Thomas Hardy died his widow gave Blunden
As a memento of many visits to Max Gate
His treasured copy of Edward Thomas's *Poems*.

I felt honoured to be one of several poets who read their poems and talked about Thomas at the Conference held in St Edmund's Hall in March 2005. On that day we were this great poet's posterity and in our different ways we showed that Edward Thomas's presence is everywhere: 'The past hovering as it revisits the light'.

'Afterword' to *Branch-Lines: Edward Thomas and Contemporary Poetry*,
edited by Guy Cuthbertson and Lucy Newlyn
(London: Enitharmon Press, 2007)

'SWEET RUB-A-DUB': RUTH STONE

All things come to an end.
No, they go on for ever.
                    – Ruth Stone

Over the years I have accumulated twenty or more anthologies of American poetry. In not one of them is Ruth Stone's work represented. Since the British publication last year of the marvellous *What Love Comes To: New and Selected Poems*, I have read only one review. This is a shocking state of affairs. Ruth Stone's poetry is profound and beautiful. It will alter the way you consider the art. Here is the title poem from her 1959 volume *In an Iridescent Time*:

> My mother, when young, scrubbed laundry in a tub,
> She and her sisters on an old brick walk
> Under the apple trees, sweet rub-a-dub.
> The bees came round their heads, the wrens made talk.
> Four young ladies each with a rainbow board
> Honed their knuckles, wrung their wrists to red,
> Tossed back their braids and wiped their aprons wet.
> The Jersey calf beyond the back fence roared;
> And all the soft day, swarms about their pet
> Buzzed at his big brown eyes and bullish head.
> Four times they rinsed, they said. Some things they starched,
> Then shook them from the baskets two by two,
> And pinned the fluttering intimacies of life
> Between the lilac bushes and the yew:
> Brown gingham, pink, and skirts of Alice blue.

I quote the entire poem because the weave of its argument and imagery is uninterruptible. I gasped when I first read it. Only after several readings (some aloud to friends) did I fully register the rhymes. While some of these feel quite spontaneous, others are clearly more worked for, like embroidery, deliberate and yet organic. Local felicities, touches of genius – 'sweet rub-a-dub', 'a rainbow board', 'fluttering intimacies of life' – keep the poem well away from the sentimental or merely heart-warming. The stunning last five lines cry out to be learned by heart which would not be difficult: they are unforgettable.

What Love Comes To is a generous sampling. It contains poems from ten of Ruth Stone's collections, the work of sixty years. Her most recent slim volume begins the book. The earliest poems come second, and so on. The last section *In the Dark* dates from 2004. Stone seems to have been her own true self from the very beginning and has remained true throughout a long career. Although she can be a sparkling improviser, versatile and various, she has not gone in for the sudden stylistic *volte face* (which is so often a symptom of spiritual shallowness). If you choose from her poems at random, they miraculously knit one with another. The intertwining of themes and approaches makes this large book (360 pages) read like one long poem.

Stone's adventurous, highly original work draws on lyric poetry's customary preoccupations, with an overwhelming emphasis on death (and the dead):

> The sensible living
> aren't interested in the dead,
> unless there is money in it.
> So little you can do with them.
> What they say is in your head.
> They visit in dreams but turn their backs

when you beg them to stay.
They are never hiding in your closet.
Empty jackets, loose sleeves yawn
on the hangers. Their cold feet
that they rubbed and rubbed
with their long sensitive fingers,
before they put on their socks,
never come back with their fine
fitted bones to warm your bed.

('How it is')

A detail like 'fine/ fitted bones' helps to create a tone of voice that is both intimate and distancing. The devastating ordinariness of 'socks' is the clincher. This is unsettling poetry, sometimes humorous, often heart-breaking. The central cataclysmic event in Ruth Stone's life was the suicide of her young poet-husband in 1959. He returns again and again to haunt these pages, the 'brief and inconceivable other': 'O mortal love, your bones/ were beautiful. I traced them/ with my fingers.' And here is the plain, shattering opening of 'Turn Your Eyes Away':

The gendarme came
to tell me you had hung yourself
on the door of a rented room
like an overcoat
like a bathrobe
hung from a hook;
when they forced the door open
your feet pushed against the floor.

Then, within the space of six lines Stone manages two dizzying modulations, and follows these with a further crashing of chords when she recalls her young husband's dead body in the morgue:

> Inside your skull
> there was no room for us,
> your circuits forgot me.
> Even in Paris where we never were
> I wait for you
> knowing you will not come.
> [. . .]
> How could I have guessed
> the plain-spoken stranger in your face,
> your body, tagged in a drawer,
> attached to nothing, incurious.

There are further dips and swirls, unendurable memories of love-making. The candour and passion make commentary feel like a desecration – like 'the rush of the El-train/ jarring the window' at the end of the poem. Stone is a great death poet. I'm not sure if that's the same thing as being an elegist. There is nothing of the formal threnody in her work, no requiem hush. Death just happens to be one of her everyday characters.

Now in her mid-nineties and still writing, Ruth Stone is drawn to Eros as much as to Thanatos. She is a devout and sometimes hilarious celebrant of life and the things of the earth, its plants and animals, creation's beauty ('the wing language of April') as well as its terrors ('snakes with useful toads/ still kicking in their guts'). She solemnises with high jinks:

Laughter from women gathers like reeds in the river.
A silence of light below their rhythm glazes the water.
They are on a rim of silence looking into the river.
Their laughter traces the water as kingfishers dipping
circles within circles set the reeds clicking;
and an upward rush of herons lifts out of the nests of laughter,
Their long stick-legs dangling, herons, rising out of the river.

('Women Laughing')

Home is Ruth Stone's imaginative base: 'The floors and the cupboards slanted to the West,/ the house sinking toward the evening side of the sky'. The sense of a real woman in a real place, of a genius in her house, lends her poetry much of its radiance and mystery: 'Those endless closets and halls/ in the brain where the unknown hides; that open for a/ moment and then close again. That is where the/ poems come from.' (How delicately the last two unexpected enjambments correct whatever drift there might have been towards grandiloquence). She lets us into her world – her Vermont household with its furniture and utensils, its porch and garden and orchard, her relationships with relatives like Aunt Harriett and Aunt Mabel, with neighbours, with her three daughters who live nearby: 'my Indian corn, my maize,/ my seeds for a ruined world;/ Oh my daughters'. We gaze with the poet through her kitchen door to the landscape and the seasons and the stars in the sky, 'the outer planets/ the fizzing sun'. Within the space of a few lines this poet's vision swerves from the domestic to the cosmic. Images and vocabulary drawn from the natural sciences mingle with echoes from fairy tale and nursery rhyme.

Not all her poems are knock-outs. An even more rigorous selection might have increased the potency of *What Love Comes To* (and made room for a much-needed index of titles and first lines). But I may be wrong. We would probably then have lost some of that insouciance and freewheeling story-telling gift which contrasts so well with her more gnomic intensities. On the cover there's a photograph of the poet in her extreme old age, a portrait of heart-wrenching beauty, a magical reflection of the poetry within. Sharon Olds provides an enthusiastic preface in which she suggests that Ruth Stone's poems 'shine in their place within her generation, among the pioneering women (Bishop, Brooks, Rukeyser)'. For myself, I have not, for a very long time, been so captivated by a newfound body of work. To quote Sharon Olds again: 'This volume should help more of us find her; we are hungry for her. Ruth Stone's poems are the food the spirit craves.' I must give this wonderfully gifted poet the last word. Here are the closing lines of 'Before the Blight', one of dozens of soul-sustaining creations:

> My lips whispered over the names of things
> in the meadows, in the orchard, in the woods,
> where I sometimes stood for long moments
> listening to some bird telling me of the strangeness of myself;
> rocked in the sinewy arms of summer.

Poetry Ireland Review, 102 (December 2010)

HELEN LEWIS:

A Time to Speak

'There are many people who have given their lives to dancing. But there are not too many who can truthfully say that dancing saved their lives. Yet that is what happened to me.' Helen Lewis survived the Jewish ghetto of Terezin, and then Auschwitz. In *A Time to Speak* she describes the escalation of horrors, and then the merciful sequence of flukes that brought her against all the odds to live in Belfast in 1947. For many years a respected choreographer and teacher of dance in the city, she founded the Belfast Modern Dance Group in the early sixties. Her artistic response to the Holocaust was first of all expressed through dance, in such works as *Phases* and *There is a Time* – dance theatre that would have seemed rather avant-garde in the Northern Ireland of the time.

Encouraged by her sons Michael and Robin, Helen started to write *A Time to Speak* in 1986, composing it in longhand for her husband Harry to type out on his antique Olivetti. In a letter to me Robin Lewis says: 'it crystallised many years of oral recounting to her family ... The birth of her first grandchild, Daniel, in October 1986 was almost certainly the stimulus which led her to create a permanent written record of her experiences for another generation.' Helen asked me to look over her work. I felt honoured when heavy envelopes started dropping through our letterbox containing drafts of the chapters that would eventually become her astonishing memoir. We would meet in my home or just down the road in her house to look over each new instalment. Harry would pop his smoky head round the door. 'Who'd have thought I had married such a pearl,' he would quip. Helen was a natural stylist and storyteller. I was no more than a French polisher. I recommended Helen's book to Anne Tannahill of the Blackstaff Press who later described the publication of *A Time to Speak* as the highlight of her career. With a passionate foreword by Jennifer Johnston, the book appeared in October 1992. Enthusiastic reviews and articles followed and it became an Irish bestseller, serialised on RTE, published in America, and in translation in Italy and the Czech Republic.

In *A Time to Speak* Helen Lewis maps Hell, and in so doing gives us an irreproachable work of art. Guiding us over the nightmare ground she doesn't put a foot wrong. Her voice remains low-key, her style simple. Such modest utterance conceals the agony of recollection. It is heroic to bear witness as Helen does to the very nadir of human experience. Without raising her voice in bitterness or anger, she tells us about the transports in suffocating cattle wagons; the casual allocation of life and death in what were called 'selections'; starvation and disease; the interminable roll calls in all weathers; the crazy, perverted rules; dysentery and lice; the deadly whims of the all-powerful; beatings and torture and executions; the death marches in which prisoners and guards 'were bound to each other by hate, fear and degradation'.

Again and again Helen chooses just one or two images to convey the horror: the hour in the washhouse spent 'snatching the precious trickle of water from each other'; or, at the midday meal, 'the angle of the ladle' on which life itself depended, because 'if the ladle was lying fairly flat on the surface you got a bowl of warm water with a faint aroma of what might have been. But if the ladle plunged vertically into the barrel, it came up with turnip, a bit of barley, perhaps even the odd potato'. The storyteller in Helen knows that when the world is surreal – 'all reason and logic gone' – the details speak for themselves. In Auschwitz 'nature had died, alongside the people. The birds had flown

from the all-pervading black smoke of the crematoria and their depar-
ture had left a silence that was like a scream.'

The earlier chapters of *A Time to Speak* show how the Nazis first
confused and diminished those whom they were going to destroy. The
Nuremberg race laws, introduced by Hitler in September 1935, were
regularly augmented over the next decade and enforced mercilessly.
Germany's cankered authoritarians passed laws for confiscating from
Jews their bank accounts, their homes, their jewellery, their radios and
even their pets. We witness in these pages civilisation disintegrating as
step by step it abandons the Jews. Helen writes: 'Public parks, swim-
ming pools, theatres, cinemas, restaurants and coffee houses were all
forbidden.' Their ration cards were worth much less than those given
to everyone else. Travel was restricted to special carriages and certain
hours. The introduction of the yellow star, to be worn in public at all
times, meant that 'we were visible targets for anyone who chose to
abuse or attack us'. Prolonged humiliation on such a scale was very
cunningly planned. It led inexorably to ultimate abasement: tattooed
numbers instead of names; identities obliterated in slave labour and
the gas ovens. The Final Solution was, among other terrible things, a
bureaucratic triumph.

A Time to Speak wins through in the end as a celebration of life and
art. At its heart are the wonderful pages where Helen relates how she
was saved, for a while at least, by her gifts. Exhausted and close to
death, she found herself involved in one of those weird cultural events
which the Nazis occasionally set up in order to complicate the nightmare – a ballet performed by inmates of the death-camp:

> After half an hour the *valse* from *Coppélia* had assumed
> some form and shape. This in itself was remarkable in the
> circumstances, but what had taken place inside myself was

miraculous. I had forgotten the time and the place and I had even forgotten myself. I hadn't noticed that it had become quiet in the hall, that the other rehearsals had stopped and that everyone was standing round watching. When, finally, I stopped, I was happy and fulfilled: where there had been chaos, there was now a dance. The girls were delighted, there was a burst of applause and shouting; the shouting became a refrain: 'Dance for us, please dance for us.'

The trance held. I took off my wooden shoes, the excellent accordionist played a South American tango, and I danced. Where was the hunger, the fear, the exhaustion? How could I dance with my frostbitten feet? When I finished they hugged and kissed me, calling me their 'star' and lifting me up on their shoulders. Some gave me bread and a bit of margarine and even jam.

'Where there had been chaos, there was now a dance': that extraordinary statement might be the motto of this book.

From Auschwitz Helen was sent to work on the construction of an aerodrome in the satellite camp of Stutthof near Danzig. The Red Army was now closing in, avengers as well as liberators. Those prisoners who could stand up were evacuated in January 1945, sent on what, in hindsight, we call a death-march. 'If the guards had been rational human beings, they would have run away and saved themselves. But, instead, they stayed with us, faithfully obeying their orders to the last, orders to hate and torment us and in the end to kill us.' Helen recounts the terrifying trek over ice and snow, her spur-of-the-moment escape and the beginnings of her recovery. She returned to Prague that summer, and learned by chance that her husband Paul had died in Auschwitz. She also lost her mother and many aunts and uncles and cousins in the Holocaust. A letter arrived in October, 'a letter from Harry, from that faraway city in foreign lands, Belfast'. Helen had known Harry since childhood in Trutnov. He had fled from Czechoslovakia with his parents in 1939, and settled in Belfast where he and his father had friends and contacts through the linen industry. Harry wrote to Helen after finding her name on a list of survivors issued by the Red Cross. They were married in Prague in June 1947, and came to live in Belfast. 'I spent the first two years learning to understand that strange place, its language, customs and people'. She used to joke with me: 'In Belfast the Catholics are more so, the Protestants are more so, and even the Jews, my dear, are more so!' Despite being safe now, she was tormented by a recurring nightmare. 'It stopped, never to return again, after the birth of our first child, Michael, in 1949.'

A Time to Speak is about 'the greatest nightmare ever dreamed by man', to quote the novelist Ian McEwan who read the book in typescript. Helen Lewis fought for breath in history's filthiest corner. She survived to teach young people dancing in Belfast and to give the world this devastating testament. She died in Belfast when it was snowing on New Year's Eve 2009.

Foreword to second edition of *A Time to Speak*
(Belfast: Blackstaff Press), July 2010

ROBERT GRAVES

When Derek Mahon and I were undergraduates at Trinity College Dublin, we inhaled poetry with our Sweet Afton cigarettes. From the beginning Robert Graves emerged as one of our heroes. We read his poems aloud to each other, counting the beats with our hands and scattering cigarette ash into the gully of the 1959 *Collected Poems* (my favourite Graves volume to this day, with our ash lingering as faint smudges between the pages). As a master of the singing line, complex syntax and stanzaic pattern, Graves was an ideal focus for two apprentices. After fifty years, the poems we loved then have lost none of their radiance: they continue to astonish, and are the heartbeat of this selection.

At the same time we were delighting in the louche narratives of Graves's historical novels *I, Claudius* and its sequel *Claudius the God*. Their erotic episodes and insouciant scholarship ensured that these books enjoyed something of a vogue among the repressed classicists of Trinity College. We shared our copies of the two-volume Penguin *Greek Myths*, and some of us read his other novels, *Wife to Mr Milton, King Jesus, Homer's Daughter*. For its insights into the nature of poetic experience we turned to *The White Goddess* as a kind of religion sub-stitute, and pilfered its image hoard for our own poems. From the library we borrowed Graves's criticism – *The Common Asphodel, The Crowning Privilege*. As a literary critic he was far more lively than anyone we had read before. Mischievous, irreverent, combative, he appealed to our youthful iconoclasm. We cringed guiltily and with masochistic pleasure as he drubbed some of our favourite poets – Yeats, Dylan Thomas – and others we cared for less – Pound and Eliot. Here the debunking outsider is at full throttle:

> It is an extraordinary paradox that Pound's ignorant, inde-
> cent, unmelodious, seldom metrical Cantos, embellished
> with esoteric Chinese ideographs – for all I know, they may
> have been traced from the nearest tea-chest – and with
> illiterate Greek, Latin, Spanish and Provençal snippets . . .
> are now compulsory reading in many ancient centres of
> learning.

Perhaps the prose volume that made the deepest impression was his memoir *Goodbye to All That*, in which Graves revisits the psychic quagmire of the trenches. This awakened my own memories of my father's infrequent reminiscences: he had joined the London Scottish as a boy-soldier in September 1914 and miraculously survived. He was wounded and gassed, and he won the Military Cross. For five decades, in each of my poetry collections, I have been following in his footsteps (and in Graves's). *Goodbye to All That* was not published until 1929. Graves took his time, as did the other major Great War memoirists, Siegfried Sassoon and Edmund Blunden. The terrible subject matter needed time to settle to an adequate imaginative depth. Yes, we hero-worshipped Graves for his astonishing productivity, his enthusiastic learning and independence of mind, his often outrageous and sometimes preposterous opinions, his protean range. But, at an altogether higher altitude, we venerated his poetry. Graves maintained that his prose mountain paid for the inner adventure of poetry: 'Prose books are the show dogs I breed and sell to support my cat.'

* * *

Not many poets can produce such commanding, resonant, unforgettable opening lines: 'We looked, we loved and therewith instantly/ Death became terrible to you and me. . .'; 'All saints revile her, and all sober men/ Ruled by the God Apollo's golden mean . . .' I have such lines by heart to this day. Graves lays down the law majestically, and with a chasteness of utterance which, paradoxically, owes something to 'Apollo's golden mean'. Yet his line is flexible, at times improvisatory, jazzy even: 'Never be disenchanted of/ That place you sometimes dream yourself into . . .' Or, from 'Mid-Winter Waking': 'O gracious, lofty, shone against from under,/ Back-of-the-mind-far clouds like towers'. The metre seems to dissolve in 'blue' notes, the syntax tantalisingly to unravel. In his search for the right word, the vocabulary can become intoxicatingly eccentric, lending the texture of some of his poems a strange brocaded richness. In an early poem, 'Lost Love', we find 'clashing jaws of moth/ *Chumbling* holes in cloth . . .' Has 'discontinuance' ever been used in a lyric poem before? It gives a magical lift to the stunning last line of 'The Second-Fated': 'A moon-warmed world of discontinuance'. If the exact word does not exist, Graves will invent it, or (see 'back-of-the-mind-far' above) he will create uncanny compounds. 'The Troll's Nosegay' contains 'Cold fog-drawn Lily, pale mist-magic Rose . . .' In 'The Last Day of Leave' a virtuoso compound comes at the poem's climax: 'blind-fate-aversive afterword'.

This poet is able to take daredevil risks because he has perfect pitch:

> She tells her love while half asleep,
>   In the dark hours,
>   With half-words whispered low:
> As Earth stirs in her winter sleep
>   And puts out grass and flowers

Despite the snow,
Despite the falling snow.

Between the last two lines there's something akin to a change of key from major to minor (except that the whole poem is in the minor key). The mood floats between keys in a way Chopin would have appreciated. In this and other exquisite lyrics – 'Love Without Hope, 'The Narrow Sea' – Graves is a virtuoso at turning on a sixpence. A connoisseur of riddles and spells and nursery rhymes, he has learned much from the works of Anonymous (and Walter de la Mare):

Allie, call the children.
    Call them from the green!
Allie calls, Allie sings,
    Soon they run in:
First there came
Tom and Madge,
    Kate and I who'll not forget
How we played by the water's edge
    Till the April sun set.

Why is this so heartbreaking? Graves's preternaturally acute ear returns us magically to childhood's half-remembered arcanum. Lewis Carroll or Edward Lear would have been proud to write 'The Untidy Man', an overlooked macabre little gem which I have included here: 'He had rolled his head far underneath the bed:/ He had left his legs and arms lying all over the room.' (Might this be a sublimated battlefield memory?) Childhood inspires some of his best known pieces, such as the edgy 'Warning to Children' in which he invokes 'the fewness, muchness, rareness,/ Greatness of this endless only/ Precious

world . . .' and makes it feel like a Pandora's box. 'The Death Room' hits
the exact note for the wakefulness and fears of everyone's childhood:
'an inconclusive/ Circling, spidery, ceiling craquelure,/ And, by the
window-frame, the well-loathed, lame,/ Damp-patch, cross-patch,
sleepless L-for-lemur . . .' Graves can cheerfully free himself from the
restraints of the perfected lyric to tell stories ('Welsh incident': 'I
was coming to that . . .') or indulge his taste for grotesquerie as in
'Ogres and Pygmies': 'They had long beards and stinking arm-pits,/
They were wide-mouthed, long-yarded and great-bellied . . .' As a rule,
the rhythm is consummately pitched, however free-wheeling the
lines.

* * *

Robert Graves was born in London in 1895 of mixed 'Irish-Scottish-
Danish-German' parentage. His father, Alfred Perceval Graves, himself
a poet, was Irish. His mother was German and related to the historian
Leopold von Ranke. Through two world wars Graves's German
connections were such an embarrassment that he protected himself
by insisting on his Irish paternity. (In the Foreword to his 1959 *Collected
Poems* he writes that his poems 'remain true to the Anglo-Irish poetic
tradition into which I was born'.) He attended a succession of preparatory schools where he learned to 'keep a straight bat at cricket, and to
have a high moral sense'. His public school was Charterhouse, which
he found 'conventional, hypocritical and anti-intellectual'. Graves left
school a week before the outbreak of war in 1914, and joined the Royal
Welch Fusiliers as an officer. He served in France from 1915, and fought
at the Battle of Loos and the Battle of the Somme. Of Graves's school
generation one in three died in the war. On his twenty-first birthday
he was himself reported killed in action and letters of condolence were

dispatched. Though he detested the officer caste, he always respected courage and soldierly values. More than was the case with the other war poets (an exception being Ivor Gurney of the Gloucestershires), he professed an open-faced, almost naive regimental loyalty. His attitude and tone were not necessarily those which we associate with 'protest poetry': 'I like feeling really frightened and if happiness consists in being miserable in a good cause, why then I'm doubly happy.' Being a 'jolly young Fusilier' mattered deeply to Graves; and at his memorial service in London in December 1985 'The Last Post' was played by a Royal Welch Fusilier.

In *Goodbye to All That* the prose sometimes approaches the condition of poetry, as in this description of No Man's Land:

> I looked at the German trenches through a periscope – a distant streak of sandbags . . . The enemy gave no sign, except for a wisp or two of wood-smoke where they, too, were boiling up a hot drink. Between us and them lay a flat meadow with cornflowers, marguerites and poppies growing in the long grass, a few shell holes, the bushes I had seen the night before, the wreck of an aeroplane, our barbed wire and theirs. Three-quarters of a mile away stood a big ruined house; a quarter of a mile behind that, a red-brick village – Auchy – poplars and haystacks, a tall chimney, and another village – Haisnes. Half-right, pithead and smaller slag heaps. La Bassée lay half-left; the sun caught the weather-vane of the church and made it twinkle.

Graves wrote several exceptional war poems which his older self ignored or suppressed ('The Patchwork Quilt', the touching poem which I have placed as an epigraph to this selection, was never published). Perhaps the future devotee of the White Goddess regretted their homoeroticism. Perhaps he feared that they compared unfavourably with the war poems of Siegfried Sassoon and Wilfred Owen. He enjoyed a bumpy friendship with Sassoon, to whom 'Two Fusiliers' is addressed. And Graves pleaded loyally on his behalf when Sassoon made his famous declaration against the prolongation of the war. He probably saved Sassoon from court-martial and prison by arranging to have him admitted as a neurasthenic patient at Craiglockhart Hospital outside Edinburgh. There Sassoon met Wilfred Owen, as did Graves when he visited Sassoon. The poets read and absorbed each other's poems. In the history of English poetry this was a momentous coincidence of talent, with Graves a crucial part of it. Graves is among the poets of the Great War commemorated on the stone in Poets' Corner in Westminster Abbey. His strongest war poems deserve to be read alongside those of his peers. 'A Dead Boche' shocks like a harrowing war photograph: 'he scowled and stunk/ With clothes and face a sodden green'.

Some of Graves's war poems were written in retrospect. Published in 1925, 'A Letter from Wales' is a rich, complex, informally cadenced meditation on war and friendship, on death, identity and poetry; it ends with the *cri de coeur*: 'How am I to put/ The question that I'm asking you to answer?' In 'Recalling War' (included in *Collected Poems*, 1938) Graves reviews the ghastly waste: 'War was return of earth to ugly earth,/ War was foundering of sublimities,/ Extinction of each happy art and faith/ By which the world had still kept head in air.' Again, but this time with no grandiloquence, 'The Last Day of Leave' (subtitled '1916' and collected in 1948) suggests the horror in a beautifully understated drama:

But when it [the sun] rolled down level with us,
Four pairs of eyes sought mine as if appealing
For a blind-fate-aversive afterword –

'Do you remember the lily lake?
We were all there, all five of us in love,
Not one yet killed, widowed or broken-hearted.'

In *The Great War and Modern Memory* Paul Fussell, discussing what he calls 'The British Homoerotic Tradition', touches on 'the unique physical tenderness, the readiness to admire openly the bodily beauty of young men, the unapologetic recognition that men may be in love with each other.' He quotes Graves's 'sensuous little ode', 'Not Dead', written to the memory of David Thomas, a young man loved by both Sassoon and Graves, in what Graves considered his transient public-school homosexual phase ('pseudo-homosexual', as he put it): 'Walking through trees to cool my heat and pain,/ I know that David's with me here again.' The last lines are: 'Over the whole wood in a little while/ Breaks his slow smile.' John Keegan ends his great history *The First World War* with this profound meditation:

> Comradeship flourished in the earthwork cities of the Western and Eastern Fronts, bound strangers into the closest brotherhood, elevated the loyalties created within the ethos of temporary regimentality to the status of life-and-death blood ties. Men whom the trenches cast into intimacy entered into bonds of mutual dependency and sacrifice of self stronger than any of the friendships made in peace and better times. That is the ultimate mystery of the First World War. If we could

understand its loves, as well as its hates, we would be nearer understanding the mystery of human life.

Although he did not like to be called a war poet, the story of Great War poetry is incomplete without the war poems of Robert Graves. His war poems are love poems in their way.

* * *

Home on leave before the armistice, Graves married the artist Nancy Nicholson, daughter of William Nicholson, the painter. They had four children. After the war he briefly attended St John's College, Oxford. In his thesis for a B.Litt, published as *Poetic Unreason*, he argues that there is in poetry a 'supralogical element' and that the 'latent associations' of the words used in a poem often contradict its prose sense. He was, again briefly, Professor of English at Cairo (on the recommendation of T. E. Lawrence). The war left Graves shell-shocked, mentally scarred for many years: 'the fear of gas obsessed me: any unusual smell, even a strong smell of flowers in a garden, was enough to set me trembling . . . the noise of a car back-firing would send me flat on my face, or running for cover.' His marriage failed, and in 1926 he left his wife and four children to live in Majorca with the American poet Laura Riding. They collaborated as critics on such books as *A Survey of Modernist Poetry* and *A Pamphlet Against Anthologies*. They founded the Seizin Press and published a select list of finely produced books and the critical miscellany *Epilogue*. Riding's megalomaniac personality, powerful intellect and uncompromising theories overwhelmed Graves. He was in thrall. In her sympathetic biography *Life on the Edge* Miranda Seymour describes the relationship:

From now on, he dedicated himself to protecting her reputation, honouring her with gifts, and showing an unquestioning deference to her wishes ... Riding's inflexible certainty about what was right and what was wrong provided him with values in which he could trust. He honestly believed that her supervision was making him into a better – because a more honest – writer.

In his study *Swifter Than Reason: The Poetry and Criticism of Robert Graves*, Douglas Day asserts: 'The influence of Laura Riding is quite possibly the most important single element in his poetic career.' This goes too far, but Day is right to add that 'some of his best work was done during the years of his literary partnership with Laura Riding'. In 1939 she ended the bizarre alliance that had lasted for thirteen tumultuous years. Graves continued to admire her – 'a perfect original'. She had helped him to concentrate his lyric power, and she inspired some fine love poems. But Laura Riding had also exhausted him. He now needed to compose himself, to quieten down.

He married Beryl Hodge, formerly the wife of one of his collaborators Alan Hodge, and in 1946 returned with her and their children (they eventually had four) to live in Deià in Majorca where, apart from occasional forays to England and America to give lectures, he remained for the rest of his life. This was a fruitful time for Graves and, in addition to distinguished prose, he wrote some of his finest poems: 'Mid-Winter Waking' ('Stirring suddenly from long hibernation,/ I knew myself once more a poet . . .'); 'Theseus and Ariadne' ('High on his figured couch beyond the waves/ He dreams . . .'). Might the first of these be an oblique reproach to Laura's ferocious domination, and an expression of gratitude for Beryl's 'sudden warm airs'? In 1961 he was elected Professor of Poetry at Oxford in succession to W. H. Auden;

and in 1968 he was awarded the Queen's Gold Medal for Poetry.

* * *

Love poems such as 'With Her Lips Only', 'A Former Attachment', 'Pure Death'. 'Never Such Love', 'The Thieves', 'Through Nightmare' will live as long as the language lives. They are irradiated, of course, by sexual desire but also by Graves's investigations for *The White Goddess*. In 1948 he completed this 'historical grammar of poetic myth', which Richard Ellmann calls 'a matriarchal study of history, personality and poetic inspiration'. This idiosyncratic amalgam of studious survey and imaginative surmise resembles Yeats's *A Vision* which, Yeats said, gave him 'metaphors for poetry'. In the introduction to *Graves and the Goddess* Ian Firla and Grevel Lindop write: 'Neglected by most academic scholars of modern poetry, alternately celebrated and reviled by feminists, banished from the syllabus in departments of classics, Celtic studies, and anthropology, *The White Goddess* has nonetheless exerted a persistent influence in these and many other fields for more than half a century and has continued, above all, to be a central source of inspiration for poets, the more potent for remaining hidden.' They quote Keith Sagar: 'The single most important influence which Ted Hughes offered to the intellectual development of Sylvia Plath as their relationship began in 1956 was a fully worked-out belief in the poetic mythology of Robert Graves's *The White Goddess*.'

So, what is it all about? In the first chapter Graves explains:

> The theme, briefly, is the antique story ... of the birth, life, death and resurrection of the God of the Waxing Year; the central chapters concern the God's losing battle with the God of the Waning Year for love of the capricious and all-powerful Threefold Goddess, their mother, bride and

layer-out. The poet identifies himself with the God of the Waxing Year and his Muse with the Goddess; the rival is his blood-brother, his other self, his weird. All true poetry . . . celebrates some incident or scene in this very ancient story, and the three main characters are so much a part of our racial inheritance that they not only assert themselves in poetry but recur on occasions of emotional stress in the form of dreams, paranoiac visions and delusions.

Many of Graves's finest poems are rooted in this vast, multi-faceted compendium with its Ogham stones, sacred animals and magic trees, its backdrop of Greek and Celtic, Hebraic and Egyptian mythologies. 'To Juan at the Winter Solstice' links, in a rosary of seven stanzas, themes and images from the book. Here is the penultimate stanza, lines heavily freighted and yet exquisitely melodious:

> Much snow is falling, winds roar hollowly,
> The owl hoots from the elder,
> Fear in your heart cries to the loving-cup:
> Sorrow to sorrow as the sparks fly upwards.
> The log groans and confesses:
> There is one story and one story only.

In his *Third Book of Criticism* Randall Jarrell sums up Graves's devotion to the White Goddess. Affectionate and amused though it may be, this essay annoyed Graves:

> All that is finally important to Graves is condensed in the one figure of the Mother-Mistress-Muse, she who creates, nourishes, seduces, destroys; she who saves us –

or, as good as saving, destroys us – as long as we love her, write poems to her, submit to her without question, use all our professional, Regimental, masculine qualities in her service. Death is swallowed up in victory, said St Paul; for Graves Life, Death, everything that exists is swallowed up in the White Goddess.

Graves himself could put it very simply: 'A Muse-poet falls in love, absolutely, and his true love is for him the embodiment of the Muse.' Or, yet again: 'There is one story and one story only/ That will prove worth your telling.'

* * *

'Where are poems? Why do I now write none?' Graves laments in the late poem 'At the Gate'. 'Where have my ancient powers suddenly gone?' In his old age Graves, in Paul O'Prey's words, 'attempted to maintain his poetic gifts by consciously exposing himself to the vicissitudes of romantic love; between 1950 and 1974 he "experienced" the Goddess through four different "muse-possessed" women.' Beryl must have been a very tolerant wife.

In the introduction to his finely judged *Selected Poems* of 1985, O'Prey, who knew Graves well, writes:

> Unfortunately, when the time came to edit the 1975 edition of the *Collected Poems*, Graves, by then in his eighties, felt he could no longer trust his own judgement so decided to publish *all* the later poems: this not only made the book 'top-heavy' but meant that the 'real poems', as he calls them, were obscured among the rather large quantity of 'mistakes and digressions'.

By and large I have followed O'Prey's 'decluttering'. In many of the later poems Graves seems to be flying on automatic pilot; the lines go clickety-click like a Rubik's Cube; the rhythmic resolutions fail to cover up emotional gaps and flimsy argument. He blurs the focus of *The White Goddess* and reduces this (for him) religious text to a highfalutin rigmarole that can sometimes look like an alibi for an old poet's philandering with younger women. The results can be tiresome and embarrassing. 'How It Started' concerns 'a wild midnight dance, in my own garden': 'In the circumstances I stayed away/ Until you fetched me out on the tiled floor/ Where, acting as an honorary teenager,/ I kicked off both my shoes.' But even in the doldrums of his final phase gusts of inspiration blow, as in 'Three Times in Love' ('You have now fallen three times in love/ With the same woman . . .'); and 'Crucibles of Love' in which Graves in his old age continues to ask leading questions: 'From where do poems come?'

* * *

'Since the age of fifteen poetry has been my ruling passion and I have never intentionally undertaken any task or formed any relationship that seemed inconsistent with poetic principles; which has sometimes won me the reputation of an eccentric.' In his singleminded devotion to his poetic vocation and the fortitude it required of him, Graves most resembles W. B. Yeats. They could both be preposterous. But, to borrow Auden's line from his elegy for Yeats: 'You were silly like us: your gift survived it all.' I first read Graves in *The Penguin Book of Contemporary Verse* (1950). Kenneth Allott's clearheaded opinion in the prefatory note to his generous selection still seems spot-on: 'The poetry of Robert Graves is in some ways the purest poetry produced in our time, waving no flags, addressed to no congregation, designed neither to comfort nor to persuade. It is poetry with roots in everyday experience, but it always has the quality of making that experience new, pungent, and exciting.'

Graves's influence is multifarious. If *The White Goddess* (perhaps disturbingly) impressed Hughes and Plath, Graves influenced Philip Larkin and the so-called 'Movement' poets in other ways. In *The Movement*, his study of English poetry and fiction of the 1950s, Blake Morrison writes: 'Though all the Movement looked to Graves as a poet who had shown the possibilities inherent in a non-Modernist tradition, different members of the group responded to different qualities in his work.' Philip Larkin had his own slant. Reviewing *Steps* in the *Manchester Guardian* in 1958, he is somewhat agnostic but ultimately affirming: 'Neither respectful nor vulgar, unlettered nor pedantic, unbalanced nor entirely sane, Mr Graves is as good a poetic mentor as the young are likely to get.' My two favourite titles for 'poet' are the Scots word *makar* and Horace's *musarum sacerdos*, 'priest of the Muses'. Again and again Robert Graves brilliantly succeeds in uniting craft and vision:

> We spell away the overhanging night,
> We spell away the soldiers and the fright.

Introduction to Robert Graves, *Selected Poems*,
edited by Michael Longley (London: Faber, 2013)

234

FRANK ORMSBY

Way back in the early 1970s I was in charge of the literature programme of the Arts Council of Northern Ireland. The newly formed Literature Committee was considering an application from the *Honest Ulsterman* magazine for a grant to publish Frank Ormsby's first poetry pamphlet, *Ripe for Company*. Recently returned to Belfast from his fifteen-year exile in Coventry, John Hewitt was the most considerable personage around the table, the elder statesman of Irish poetry, 'the daddy of us all' as James Simmons christened him. 'Listen to this,' he said, and proceeded to read aloud 'Mrs G. Watters', a poem about absence and isolation:

> The letters still come for Mrs Watters,
> who must, at one time, have warmed this house
> and lived as we do. Mostly small matters –
> the rolled calendar that, had she stayed,
> might hang now where I drew the rusted nail,
> the catalogues, the last gas bill unpaid . . .

'This is exactly the sort of thing we should be supporting,' he said. We all agreed, and a small grant was unanimously recommended.

Ripe for Company grew into *A Store of Candles*, Ormsby's first full collection, which was published by Oxford University Press in 1977. Mrs Watters was joined by other household ghosts. In 'Moving In' a home's previous tenants inhabit every corner. A young couple discover that

> The first act of love in a new house
> is not private. Loving each other

> we are half-aware of door and mirror.
> Our ecstasy includes the bedside chair,
> the air from the landing.

In 'Landscape with Figures' real people behave like apparitions. They are nearby and yet so far away. Our hearts go out to them, but there is 'No sight that might have softened/ on the eye the scene's/ relentlessness.' From early on something desolate and unsettling shades this poet's vision, counteracting his warmer compulsions. Much of Ormsby's finest poetry explores the 'sadness of dim places, obscure lives,/ ends and beginnings,/ such extremities.'

But he is far from being a melancholy artist. Those who have attended his poetry readings will know how funny Ormsby can be. Think of the witty account of boyhood sexuality in 'My Friend Havelock Ellis', or of McQuade the goalie: 'When McQuade went up for a ball/ he came down with snow on his heels.' The serious message of 'Sheepman' would be lost without its humour. Wes Davis, the editor of *An Anthology of Modern Irish Poetry*, is spot-on when he writes: '"Sheepman" maps the Catholic/ Protestant divide onto the range wars of the American west, where a sheep farmer in cattle country, like his fellow outcasts the Mexicans and half-breeds, "must wear that special hangdog look,/ say nothing".' Ormsby's lightness of touch licenses the exciting note of defiance at the poem's close:

> When I skirt
> the rim of cattle drives, salute me,
> and when I come to share your bunkhouse fire,
> make room.

Frank Ormsby, like most of his contemporaries, approaches political themes obliquely. For all his documentary proclivities, when he touches on the Troubles he steadfastly avoids the poetry of the latest atrocity (to adapt a phrase used by Conor Cruise O'Brien). Throughout his career he has been a vigorous enemy of what in Northern Irish literary circles we call 'Troubles trash'. Art is the opposite of propaganda, he implies. As poet, critic and editor, he appeals to what Louis MacNeice calls our 'generous instinct'. In one of his finest poems, art's role in atrocious times is symbolised by the work of war photographers during various wars:

> Working with one eye closed or heads buried
> under their drapes, they focus to preserve
> the drowned shell-hole, the salient's rubble of dead . . .

Halfway through 'The War Photographers' a powerful note of disenchantment rings out: 'The worst has happened, they confirm the worst'. But, despite war's abominations, photographer and poet are still able to capture 'enough of sky/ to suggest the infinity of angles', and to 'confirm' magnificently and against all the odds 'the loved salience of what is always there:/ flower of Auschwitz, bird of the Western Front'.

A remarkable sequence of thirty-five war poems is at the heart of Ormsby's second collection and provides its title, *A Northern Spring*. Here he imagines the lives and afterlives of the American troops stationed in his native Fermanagh in the months leading up to the Normandy landings of 1944. In one deft stanza he gives us some sense of the multitude and its diversity:

> Meatpackers, truckers, longshoremen from Maine
> Slav lumberjacks, tough immigrants at home

>on the wharves of the East River,
>a negro lad who lied about his age
>in Jackson, Missouri.

The ghosts speak with heartbreaking exactitude: 'I died in a country lane near Argentan,/ my back to a splintered poplar'; 'I stepped on a small landmine in the bocage/ and was spread, with three others, over a field/ of burnt lucerne'; 'They buried me in an orchard at St Lô/ on a pillaged farm.' Compassion and humour suffuse the sequence. Each individual soldier is brought back to life, his drollery and lamentations. We eavesdrop on memories of home and families and sweethearts, while the interwoven landscapes of Ulster, America and France make a disconcerting backdrop. Ormsby returns to his themes of war and peace and art in 'Apples, Normandy, 1944', a tender portrait of a war artist. His companions remember him saying: 'I'm sick drawing refugees./ I want to draw apples', and they picture him

>striding past old dugouts
>towards the next windfall –
>sketchbooks accumulating as he becomes
>the Audobon of French apples,
>or works on the single apple
>– perfect, planetary – of his imagination.

I have already quoted the first two lines of 'I Died in a Country Lane', a distressing dramatic monologue delivered by a soldier who has been blown to bits, an excoriation of racism (and, by implication, sectarianism):

>The bits they shipped to Georgia at the request
>of my two sisters were not entirely me.
>If dead men laughed, I would have laughed the day

the committee for white heroes honoured me,
and honoured too the mangled testicles
of Leroy Earl Johnston.

These are horrifying lines. The 'Northern Spring' sequence is a major achievement.

From his earliest work, Ormsby has favoured a natural shapeliness. The critic Eve Patten praises 'his defiant attachment to economy of form'. In the introduction to *The Hip Flask*, his anthology of short poems from Ireland, Ormsby describes the lyric poem as 'an insight distilled or crystallised, the essence of a mood or emotion caught with memorable concision, the verbal equivalent – linguistic, aphoristic, epigrammatic – of the brushstroke which evokes the fuller picture, the splash and its ripples.' That's Ormsby's *ars poetica* in a nutshell. A plain-speaking, down-to-earth utterance may be the norm, but it teeters on the verge of taking flight, and sometimes gives way to an exquisitely refined lyricism. Here in its entirety is 'Helen Keller':

> Brighter than gold trumpets, swords of light,
> tougher than mailed fist or splendid spur
> and softer than pelts in young fur-traders' hands.
> White as the white wings lifting from the ark,
> those fingers moving in a soundless dark.

This profound poem (its five lines filling the page) begins Ormsby's third, and most intimate, collection. *The Ghost Train* charts the joys and griefs and anxieties of family life. He laments his father and celebrates his daughter's conception and birth. In the elegies – 'The Gatecrasher', 'One Saturday' – the complexities of the father-son relationship unfold in lovingly selected anecdote, real and imagined. In 'The Gap on my

Shelf' Ormsby writes: 'What floods my head is dislocated light/ and rain at the window'. 'Dislocated light' could be watchwords for this poet's *oeuvre*. In 'A Paris Honeymoon' Claude Monet's waterlily paintings in L'Orangerie become part of a dizzy erotic whirl that generates a matchless moment:

> Primordial blossoms. Watery nebulae.
> Blurred, breathless features in a spawny hush,
> gathering towards us, miming the kiss of light.

This volume develops with a happy inevitability. In a sequence of cradle-songs Ormsby writes in anticipation of the child's birth – 'Lullaby', 'You: The Movie', 'The Names' – and then welcomes her into the world: 'We wrap you in your name./ Peace is the way you settle in our arms.' These, the quietly triumphant closing lines of 'Helen', echo a complicated poem which comes earlier in the sequence. To quote Eve Patten again: 'The Easter Ceasefire' involves 'a direct and pointed political metaphor, a systematic process of reference to the long and difficult "gestation" of the peace process in Northern Ireland during the 1990s . . . Against this backdrop, preparations for the birth are tinged with tension and anxiety. Expectation takes on a double meaning . . . the parallel between peace negotiations and fear of miscarriage is drawn into an uncomfortable poem-in-waiting . . .'

> In the fraught silence between
> might-be and might-have-been,
> we edged towards Saturday and the hoped-for all-clear.

In his fourth collection, *Fireflies*, Ormsby returns to America, 'places touched in passing, their secret withheld'. Animated by the sheer size of the country, freighted with an abundance of local particulars –

trains, freeways, cemeteries, bridges, bars, diners, dams – these are extended ode-like meditations on history and heritage, past and present:

> The present is a thicket of sound, the dust of industry
> a fine web in the trees, an invisible drift
> across parkways, the new towers of White Plains.

The poet registers the anxiety of post 9/11 America when he prays for 'sunlit-/ for-a-while-stormless, tomorrows' (the prayer invigorated by the chiasmic boldness of those compound adjectives.) The background music in 'At the Lazy Boy Saloon and Ale Bar' is a symphony of exotic trade names for beers: 'Victory Golden Monkey, Eye of the Hawk'. This exuberant poem concludes: 'Glasses will tilt to receive/ our soul-beer, our personal amber, the wheat of our dreams'. *Fireflies* is perhaps Ormsby's most experimental volume. Has he ever been more hilariously freewheeling than in 'The Gate': 'We swing on the thought of a gate in the middle of a field'? The richer acoustic of the American sequence enhances some of the Irish poems, 'The Whooper Swan', for instance, a rare excursion to the western seaboard:

> Though earthbound, landlocked, I never lacked till now
> the gift of a coastal childhood, or missed a life
> edged with Atlantic: sea-self, sky-self, land-self
> among the dunes in late autumn, balance restored
> by the rich plaint, the vibrant ochone of the whooper swan.

In contrast, the skinny stanzas of 'The Rabbit' and 'Small World' (a rosary of haiku-like lyrics) anticipate the shapes and sounds of the new work at the end of this *Selected Poems*.

Between *Fireflies* and *The Ghost Train* there was a gap of fourteen years. Where poetry comes from, and where it goes when it disappears, remain mysteries. During this long silence Frank Ormsby was serving literature in other ways. For forty years he was a brilliant and popular teacher of English at the Royal Belfast Academical Institution where he became eventually Headmaster of the English Department. For twenty years he edited *The Honest Ulsterman*, a scruffy, irreverent, much-loved, indispensable literary magazine which published early poems by many writers who are now well known. Anyone who wants to unravel Ulster's cultural and political tangles could do no better than study Ormsby's landmark anthologies *Poets from the North of Ireland* and *A Rage for Order: Poetry of the Northern Ireland Troubles*. A labour of love, his compendious *Collected Poems of John Hewitt* remains the standard edition of this crucial *oeuvre*. Other important anthologies include *The Hip Flask* and *The Long Embrace*, a collection of Irish love poems. Few people have done more for poetry.

Compared with the orchestral riches of *Fireflies* ('where-are-we-now/ dalliance with night, such soothing restlessness') some of the New Poems in the last section may read like minimalist gestures. But miniature is not the same as minor. Though formally pared down, this later work remains emotionally capacious. Here is the pitch-perfect nearly-free verse of 'Bog Cotton':

> They have the look
> of being born old.
> Thinning elders among the heather,
> trembling in every wind.
> My father turns eighty
> the spring before my thirteenth birthday.
> When I feed him porridge he takes his cap off. His hair,
> as it has been all my life, is white, pure white.

The poet's rural childhood, a whole way of life, is conjured up in a handful of words: 'A blue flame,/ a whiff of paraffin,/ a mild hiss' ('The Tilley Lamp'); 'the family pisspots/ airing in the rhododendron' ('Home is the Hero'); 'our main source is a leafy well in the woods' ('Water'). The mood swings from affection to disenchantment and worse. The family goat is called, improbably, 'Judy':

> That's our goat Judy
> in Chagall's Self Portrait with Goat.
> That's her again, the goat
> with the 'Semitic face'
> in Umberto Saba's poem.
> We petted her in the garden.
> We drank her milk.
> We put her children to death.

Frank Ormsby belongs to that extraordinary generation of Northern Irish poets which includes Ciaran Carson, Medbh McGuckian, Paul Muldoon and Tom Paulin. He is a poet of the truest measure. In his poem 'Some Older American Poets' he might be imagining our embrace of his own wonderful gifts:

> I can't get enough of you, bright-eyed and poetry-mad
> in the fields next to the cemetery, where you drop to your knees
> before the first flower in the world, where you lift your hands
> to that bare cry among brambles, the original bird.

Introduction to Frank Ormsby, *Goat's Milk: New and Selected Poems*
(Hexham: Bloodaxe Books, 2015)

PART 4

OTHER ARTS

THE ARTS IN ULSTER

Confronted with tragedy in his own community, as he has been in Ulster, the artist might be inclined to question the validity or at least the usefulness of his vocation, to assume that when the usual patterns of life are disrupted, he has failed personally in some way. Although I am certain that no true artist can possibly avoid such doubts, I find relevant here an analogy of Cyril Connolly's. He compares art's relationship with the community to the influence, on the body, of certain glands. Small and seemingly unimportant they may be, but when they are removed the body dies. The range and depth of artistic activity in Ulster are in themselves symptoms of its continuing liveliness – even though it is this very vitality which most creative people here would wish to qualify and refine, just as surely as they recognise it as one of the sources of their energy. The political explosion was preceded, as is so often the case, by an artistic efflorescence. The sixties began and continued with a surge of creativity, which might have prevented, and certainly suggested, the upheaval with which they were to end. The Ulster artist has been no less successful than anyone else as diagnostician and physician.

Indeed, his achievements have been underestimated. I have heard many charges similar to those drummed up by the popular dailies during the last war: 'Where are the war poets?' Too many critics seem to expect a harvest of paintings, poems, plays and novels to drop from the twisted branches of civil discord. They fail to realise that the artist needs time in which the raw material of experience may settle to an imaginative depth, where he can transform it, and possibly even suggest solutions to current and very urgent problems by reframing them according to the dictates of his particular discipline. He is not some sort of super-journalist commenting with unfaltering spontaneity on events immediately after they have happened. Rather, as Wilfred Owen stated over fifty years ago, it is the artist's duty to warn, to be tuned in before anyone else to the implications of a situation.

And the warnings came. They came in Sam Thompson's play about sectarian division in the shipyard, *Over The Bridge*; in Gerard McLarnon's apocalyptic vision of violence, *The Bonefire*; in John Hewitt's long poem, *The Colony*, written twenty years ago, which explores the position of the 'Planter'; in many of Louis MacNeice's ambivalent poems about Ireland; in the novels of Brian Moore and Maurice Leitch; in Derek Mahon's fine poem, 'In Belfast'. Mahon, I think, speaks for all Ulster artists when he writes:

> One part of my mind must learn to know its place –
> The things which happen in the kitchen houses
> And echoing back-streets of this desperate city
> Should engage more than my casual interest,
> Exact more interest than my casual pity.

Warnings generally go unheeded. Art seldom changes things. Two wise lines from W. H. Auden's 'New Year Letter' provide at least an alibi:

> Art is not Life, and cannot be
> A midwife to Society.

Besides, the artist has other duties to perform apart from his painful role as a Cassandra. He has a duty to celebrate life in all its aspects, to commemorate normal human activities. Art is itself a normal human activity. The more normal it appears in the eyes of the artist and his audience, the more potent a force it becomes. In Ulster the abnormality of a cultural apartheid sustained to their mutual impoverishment by both communities is still only gradually being corrected. Artists at least appreciate what W. R. Rodgers has called the 'creative wave of self-consciousness' which occurs 'wherever two racial patterns meet'. Unlikely to countenance a meeting in which all the colours run so wetly together that they dissolve into toneless uniformity, the artist is in fact uniquely qualified to demonstrate how both our cultures can define themselves by a profound and patient scrutiny of each other. To quote Auden again:

> . . . all real unity commences
> In consciousness of differences.

From Introduction, *Causeway: The Arts in Ulster*, edited by Michael Longley (Belfast: Arts Council of Northern Ireland, 1971)

COLIN MIDDLETON

Colin Middleton is probably the most accomplished painter Ireland has yet produced. A Belfast artist once declared to me, almost angrily and certainly with envy, 'Middleton can do just about anything with paint.' But his protean abilities and endless inventiveness serve a very patient exploration of preoccupations which have remained constant over the years. Broadly speaking, these are the female archetype and the qualities of place, though I suspect that Middleton would hate to be thought of as either a landscape or a figure painter. His female figures suggest the contours and textures of fields and hills, as do the sculptures of Henry Moore whom Middleton greatly admires. The texture of various woods may also be evoked, as in the recent *Ash* and *Sycamore*, which are ostensibly studies of the female form. The female form may take root completely and become a tree which harbours owls, the breasts growing like fruit, or merely recline in serene celebration of the drumlins and shallow valleys of County Down.

In an interview I had with Middleton for the *Irish Times*, he said, 'What gives my work continuity is the constancy of the female archetype, no matter how many the disguises – the mother figure, the mother and child, the reclining figure, the single tree against a hill'. He thinks of the archetype as a symbol, a link between what is articulate and inarticulate, between what is known and unknown. The symbol is a communicating vessel.

And what Middleton communicates to us is an unselfish and unclouded devotion to the beauty he sees in landscape and in woman. Some of his recent pictures must be almost unique in modern painting for their apparent freedom from intrusive neurosis – a quality rare at any time but especially rare this century. One finds it in Chaucer, in Villon, perhaps, and in Bach's *Goldberg Variations* or Beethoven's *Waldstein Sonata*. Relish and enjoyment soar in an act of untroubled worship. Middleton's finest landscape-cum-figure paintings are masterpieces, energetic purveyors of an equable joy.

Though place is for Middleton of utmost importance, he is not a sketch-book artist – he doesn't go out for a day's sketching. There is probably no need to, for his knowledge of the Ulster countryside is deep and extensive. He knows all the country roads and can describe from memory certain areas with minute exactness. The landscapes of Antrim and Down have settled to an imaginative depth where mnemonic sketches would be unnecessary. Middleton does, however, clutter the mantelpieces of his home with shells, pebbles, feathers, driftwood. As he rolls them over in his hands, these objects become direct links rather than reminders. He treasures them for their textures, their hints of a drystone wall in one place, the line of a plantation of trees in another. One of his most remarkable pictures, *Cybele*, has the feel of driftwood about it, and recently he has been experimenting with pencil-rubbings of fern and bracken and leaves. One of the pleasures of studying Middleton's work is the identification of the influence of his two favourite counties: a quite abstract composition proclaims its origins in the limestone and basalt of Antrim, another its allegiances to the gentler attributes of Down. Middleton's pictures are more like chips off, than representations of, Ballycastle and north Antrim, or Newcastle and the Mournes.

Technically, Middleton is a master. He himself claims that his years as a damask designer taught him much about pattern and how to work quickly. But I'm sure this explanation is partly a salute to craftsmen he admires. Perhaps the close precision of his surrealist paintings helped to develop his technical capacities. Whatever the reasons, his dexterity is magical. Most of his pictures exhibit complete control and knowledge of his medium. And this has come after years of patient study (he is not interested in artistic happenings). He has a profound respect for the materials he works with, and his painting is a slow exploration of their qualities. It is significant that, when for economic reasons he has not had a large supply of paints, he has made a virtue of necessity and released to its full potential pigment applied thinly and very sparingly to boards which he has carefully prepared before-hand, scraping lines and polishing surfaces. Some of his richest and most resonant pictures have hardly any paint on them at all. A dozen separate and laborious processes involving traditional and improvised tools (and even fingers and thumbs) disguise the fact that Middleton has used only one or two colours. He can take a colour through an infinite number of gradations, paint an all-brown picture that dazzles.

Though primarily known as a painter, Middleton is also a very fine draughtsman – whether he is working with pencil, charcoal, linocuts or etching. I am surprised that there has not been a really comprehensive exhibition of his drawings, or that some have not been included in recent shows of his paintings. A few Northern Ireland institutions have commissioned him to decorate their buildings with impressive murals. Typically, before starting work on these, Middleton trudged the locale in search of pebbles or shells or whatever to arrange in his patterns, thus letting the place assist in its own commemoration. Middleton also writes poetry, and was represented by two poems in the *Faber Book of Irish Verse*. He claims, however, that his poetry has now become a philosophical aid to the painter, a catalyst. In poetry he may cross-examine and converse with himself privately – he no longer publishes.

Middleton's father was one of the first men to introduce Impressionist painting to Ireland, and his earliest enthusiasm was for Monet and Pissarro. Later on, Van Gogh was a powerful influence. Middleton has, over the years, painted Impressionist, Expressionist and Surrealist pictures. He finds it easy to understand the criticism often levelled at his work – that he changes his style too often, and is derivative. He disagrees, of course, and, for my own part, I find great consistency in his work. His personality is obvious in paintings from all his phases, the only work which does not appeal to me being the Surrealist paintings of the early forties. It is certainly odd that one of the qualities most suspect in an artist today is versatility. With so many painters methodically and unswervingly ploughing their separate half-acres, it is refreshing to have an artist like Middleton who feels free to learn from anyone he has admired. To admire is to learn. The painters who mean most to him are Piero della Francesca, Vermeer, Cézanne and Mondrian ('my four evangelists'), and he would add to these Ben Nicholson and Henry Moore. Middleton believes that a period as complex psychologically as ours demands of an artist diversity and versatility.

It was undoubtedly his need to be varied, his appetite for change, which led Middleton to opt out of the art-world circuits. For a number of years he was contracted to a London gallery, but he now works as an art-master at Friends School, Lisburn. This was a characteristically brave decision, which meant complete artistic freedom, although he obviously finds it frustrating having to spend so much time away from the easel. And since Middleton is an artist who likes to work out an idea or theme in a sequence of paintings, exhausting all the possibilities, discovering what he has just completed as well as what he is about to attempt, interruptions of any kind must be particularly menacing. Be that as it may, he is amazingly prolific, always getting on with the job. When he can do nothing else he is busy preparing canvases and boards. Even when he is reading a magazine, he turns it upside down, folds pages, searches for shapes and patterns. He can produce a delightful, whimsical collage out of a mousetrap, a walnut, wire and a few dots of paint. Everything is done with extraordinary deftness.

Nowadays, the artist is hemmed-in by temptations and dangers. Middleton, as I have implied above, seems to have come clear of these. Symptomatic of this are the low prices at which he insists his pictures are sold. Nothing matters more to him than the wide currency of his work – especially within his native Ulster. He was particularly pleased when one of his paintings was bought for an old people's home built near to the scene represented in the painting. He is, therefore, continually extending the imaginative estate of the community in which he lives. This is surely the ancient and proper role of the artist – true art must always be to some extent local: the so-called International Style in painting reflects little but the dominion of the dollar and pound sterling.

Middleton will finish my article for me. I quote from an introductory note he wrote for the catalogue of his most recent exhibition in Belfast:

> These paintings are the product of the interaction of two basic concerns of the painter; with the moods and qualities evoked in him by certain places; by the intimate nature of the rocks, pebbles, trees and plants as much as by the configuration of the mountain, mud flat or cockle strand – and with the essential nature of the materials which he uses, namely chalk, glue, wax and stains.
>
> The keynote is simplicity of statement . . . Contrary to the more readily accepted notion that images are abstracted or reduced from objects or groups of objects, here the dominant archetypes are coaxed from the amorphous materials and move toward realisation in much

the same way as the elements work upon wood and stone; a process of erosion; the polish of wind and rain, the action of sand or the trace of a thorn . . .

Dublin Magazine 6, 3–4 (Autumn/ Winter 1967)

GERARD DILLON

Gerard Dillon's new show at the Tom Caldwell Gallery, Belfast, is both immediately charming and deeply satisfying. Something of a mixed bag, perhaps, with work from the early fifties nudging more recent paintings, it nevertheless somehow benefits from this. We are aware throughout of a vital and engaging personality and a consistent but developing vision. We can trace the infinite shifts and adjustments as the artist, in picture after picture, has tackled the problem of controlling and re-interpreting the handful of images which seem to dominate his mind.

The most notable of these is, of course, the Dillon Pierrot. This figure casts both his light and his shadow across whatever companions are sharing the picture, and against backcloths which range from the dream-like and ill-defined to the realistic – trees, haystacks, fields and so on. Pierrot is clearly Dillon's mask, in the Yeatsian sense; but he is more than this: severely reduced to basics and yet amazingly flexible and various, Pierrot has become a sort of ideogram of humanity, through which the artist can interpret an impressive range of emotions. He stands isolated and forlorn in a familiar landscape or dances wildly at the ends of the earth or floats disturbingly through space or sits quiescent beside a sweetheart. He can be menacing, his reveller's mask like an executioner's, or wryly Chaplinesque. He is 'L'Allegro' and 'Il Penseroso' rolled into one, a real and important discovery, the chief keeper of the map and compass with which this remarkable artist faces and explores the unknown.

The earlier oils are of considerable interest. These take for their subject matter everyday life – an Italian woman washing or hanging up clothes, a boy drawing, a young soldier in an untidy bedroom. With tact and delicacy Dillon nudges prosaic and seemingly intractable material towards the condition of poetry. He has, indeed, the uncanny knack of releasing the poetry which lies locked up in such objects as socks and slippers and coat-hangers – grandchildren, these, of van Gogh's old boots! Of this group I particularly liked *Funeral in Connemara* and *Back Streets of Belfast*.

Some of the more recent oils struck me as being less satisfactory, especially the nudes. These look like academic, life-class drawings transposed with too much facility into vaguely surrealist and stylised settings – incongruous, out of place. But I guess that they are work in progress, that Dillon has still to come to imaginative terms with the female form, the most powerful of images – has still to let it settle to a depth in his mind and in his mind's eye. *Yellow Nude with Pierrot Tree*, the best of this series, hints at possible future riches, and suggests that Pierrot may have found a daughter and heir. The recent *Self-Portrait with Pierrot* is the latest in a long line of distinguished Dillon self-portraits. With its Pierrot figure and a yellow nude in the background it summarises nicely the whole show. If the title, 'The Poet of Irish Painting', means anything, then Gerard Dillon lays serious claim to it.

Irish Times, 13 April 1971

'PLAYTHINGS FOR THE SOUL':
THE PAINTINGS OF FELIM EGAN

This world is not conclusion – Emily Dickinson

Felim Egan's paintings and sculptures come into being according to their own laws of growth. He prefers to make his own stretchers, to feel for himself whether the cotton or linen is too light or too loose, a sailor adjusting sails. In order to build up a robust texture, he mixes his paint with ground stone and resin, then brushes it violently until the acrylic dries. As he puts it himself, he 'stretches a colour in all directions'. He does this flat on the floor, avoiding runs, keeping things under control. The process is for him as precarious as watercolour. Layers of different colours are applied in a way that allows each colour to insinuate itself and contribute to a complicated glow. He paints around and away from areas where he senses images may occur, although at this stage he thinks of these as 'negatives' only. If they are to play a positive role by providing the occasion for colour, wax may be applied to bring them forward, just as sanding will make them recede – like stained-glass windows taking in the sky or doors that lead into a shadowy room. Painting for Egan is all about surface, about keeping images 'in front' or 'behind', about controlling the space.

It pleases him that for his sculptures he will make images out of the wax he applies to his canvases; and that the bronzes which emerge from the 'lost wax' process in the foundry will be echoed in the bronze shapes he inserts into the works painted on wooden panels. These cross-references seem crucial to an artist who, rather than concentrate on one piece at a time, prefers to let works interact in a group so that they can generate their own energies; who chooses at regular intervals to visit the proposed gallery space and let the imagined emptiness provoke new ideas. Of course, this particular exhibition consists of more than one space or 'emptiness'. In each room and in the connecting corridor, different aspects are revealed, five bronzes accompany the ten large canvases; the watercolours are shown on their own, as are the wooden panels. This gives us a wonderful sense of the artist finding his way through his preoccupations, his passage within and between works evidence of the practical and mysterious ways in which an *oeuvre* accumulates.

The other presence which permeates this show is Sandymount Strand, its high tides lapping the sea-wall just a few yards from Egan's house. Standing there you feel as tall as the horizon and the oil-tanker at anchor in the middle-distance. You can see for miles. As the tide goes out it shapes the sand which is then marked by wormy scribbles and the prints of birds. That's how it will look until the next high tide. Most days Egan goes with his dog on the same walk over a landscape which never stays the same. He may stroll out a mile towards the horizon, and he can find his way in the dark. This intertidal zone influences his rarefied, humorous vocabulary of circles, lines and triangles, his fleeting references, the gestures we register somewhere between glimpse and after-image. He lets things happen, then reduces detail, stripping his images down. Perhaps this is his way of facing up to the immensity of nature on his own doorstep. He sets the minutiae of life in an endless vista. He shows us 'how full emptiness really is' as John Ashbery observed. Or, as the great American poet Emily Dickinson put it:

> The Brain – is wider than the Sky –
> For – put them side by side –
> The one the other will contain
> With ease – and You – beside –

The Brain is deeper than the Sea –
For – hold them – Blue to Blue –
The one the other will absorb –
As Sponges – Buckets – do –

The Brain is just the weight of God –
For – Heft them – Pound for Pound –
And they will differ – if they do –
As Syllable from Sound –

Released from the prison of geometry, Egan's quirky shapes behave, as he himself reports, like 'wee characters'. Though each picture or sculpture becomes its own microcosm, other realities find room within. Choreography and orchestration do not seem inappropriate metaphors for describing Egan's procedures. Contrapuntal, harmonious, sonorous, these works have been born out of the struggle between inventiveness on the one hand and a deliberately restricted range of theme on the other. The rich tonalities depend on a frugality of means. In addition, it seems that the potent mysteries of megalithic drawing, Ogham stone, hieroglyphic, pictogram have been invoked.

Amid so much sophistication we sense the primitive responses that drive riddle and spell. The urgencies of the graffiti-scribbler joust with the elegance of the calligrapher's gestures. At an even more literal level the boogying lines suggest germination, spring shoots, vegetal stirrings, as well as musical notation; the triangles, gull-prints perhaps, or tree-tops; the circles, sun and moon. In the sculptures, which play with scale by keeping mere handfuls of material well out of reach on tall pedestals, the circles change into pebbles, stones, permanent snowballs, what you will. Bronze could hardly be more light-hearted. Suspended between the earth and their counterparts in the sky, these most characteristic creations are indeed 'playthings for the soul'. This is a phrase from a poem of mine called 'Stilts': it concludes with a mythologised portrait of my father's father, a carpenter who

> Comes from another town
> With tools and material
> To manufacture stilts
> And playthings for the soul.

Felim Egan has never been more true to the Japanese concept of *karumi*, not a brush-stroke too many. His habitual understatement grows more assured, his spare lyricism more eloquent. Purged of rhetoric, Beckettian almost, earthy and yet ethereal, his is a pianissimo world where whimsy swells into vision. These new pieces are clearly the fruits of prolonged contemplation. But however deliberate they may be, they excite us because Egan remains open to the unexpected, precariously balanced between experience and intuition, detachment and involvement, plan and passion. As he moves through his middle years, he appears more generous with himself, more open. By now he is the figure we can nearly make out in the landscape, and the atmosphere is charged. He is unlikely to confront us face to face. Instead, it is his heroic task to show us – in Emily Dickinson's extraordinary phase – 'the Faces of the Atoms'.

Introduction to Catalogue, Felim Egan: Exhibition at Irish Museum
of Modern Art, Dublin, January 1996

PATTERNS & PARABLES:
THE PAINTINGS OF BRIAN FERRAN

As a young man, Brian Ferran's interest in Irish mythology was awakened when he encountered those stone carvings which ghost our countryside in surly dialogue with the high crosses that superseded them. In the carved heads of the Fermanagh Basin and the stone figures of Boa Island he discovered one of his most enduring themes. His images took shape in response to those mysterious, eroded carvings. It seems important that in the first place the confrontation should have been intuitive, and the old presences allowed their stony silence. The artist looked long and hard at the figures before he made a study of them.

Initially more interested in the narrative line, he read Lady Gregory's translations and the straightforward mythological reconstructions of J. J. Campbell before graduating to the ferocities of Thomas Kinsella's prodigious version of the *Táin Bó Cuailnge* (The Cattle Raid of Cooley), the central saga of the Ulster cycle and one of the oldest stories in European vernacular literature. Helen Hickey's scholarly survey, *Images of Stone,* provided the artist with more than a gazetteer of the landscape of carved effigies. He went on pilgrimages to every one of the hundred or so statues and idols which she had located. Hickey's researches helped the artist to people his imagination and to put faces on the characters of the *Táin*: on the warriors, the boasters and the slaughterers; on Conchobor, Fergus, Cú Chulainn; on those who ages ago got bogged down in dynastic conflict and were the first, though not the last, to turn the fields of Ulster into killing fields.

At about the same time Ferran was attracted to the *Book of Kells* and the other great illuminated manuscripts, as well as experiencing a youthful, pre-Raphaelite desire to breathe new life into the medieval concept of chivalry. Although the antiquarian inklings of the pre-Raphaelites and the rainbow microcosms of the ancient parchments do indeed colour Ferran's mythological pictures, he does not as a rule allow them to soften those intimations of death and violence which give this strand of his work its muscle.

'Essentially I'm a pattern-maker who knows a little about colour', is his own modest analysis. And again: 'I still believe in the old-fashioned notion that every picture tells a story'. These two simple statements add up to something rather complex: the tension between, on the one hand, the abstract nature of a pattern and, on the other, a story's need for representation, for the figurative. This generates in Ferran's work a ceremonial character, which only occasionally hardens into the heraldic. His technique illuminates rather than illustrates the stories, and it lives up to the grandeur of legend. Despite the chromatic bravura – the prevalence of red, orange, crimson, indigo, gold – the final effect often appears crepuscular. Sometimes there's even a glimmering hint of heroic camp-fires.

Although he seldom moves into total abstraction, Ferran admires such masters of abstract expressionism as Mark Rothko and de Kooning for the way they 'make colour speak'. And he remembers with affection his own earliest beginnings as a maker of patterns – abstract patterns – 'saving up all the little bits of sweet papers and wrapping paper and anything that had a silver or a gold flash in the sunlight or had a nice smooth surface. I kept them, stuck them down, made pictures out of them and impressed my primary school teacher.' When as a teenager he discovered cubism, the process by which Braque and Picasso ingeniously manoeuvred into pictures the words

263

and textures of pieces of newspaper awoke memories in the young artist. For several years Ferran made collages, until he grew dissatisfied with the fragility of the work – with what seemed to him its built-in obsolescence. But the method has left its mark in the letters and words that from time to time interrupt his later compositions. And he continues to collect in portfolios newspaper photographs, cuttings, bits and pieces that might feed the mind.

The mature Ferran believes that a painting should be made to last. For many years he has used traditional materials – oil paint, gold leaf – and he also relishes what he calls 'the swift response' of acrylic. He used to think of drawing and painting as distinct exercises – the paint-ing a translation of the drawing onto a larger scale. Now he prefers to work directly onto whatever surface is to hand, mainly canvas – an altogether riskier business, but for this artist the ultimate excitement. He admits that sometimes the 'glare' of a large open canvas space can be so intimidating that it will require a wash of sepia or red or blue to tame it. The picture suggests its own scale and finds its own flow as one mark follows another.

In a 1993 essay on the artist, Brian Fallon writes: 'In the last twenty years the political upheaval in the North has been inescapable, in fact a dominant reality; and while Ferran does not preach or posture he is plainly a man with a social conscience.' Like the Northern Irish poets, he would seem to prefer an oblique approach when responding to tragic events in his own community. Even his images of Orangemen have been mellowing (maturing, one is tempted to suggest) in his bulging portfolio of ephemera from twenty-five years of Twelfth of July parades. A year ago he had nearly completed two pictures of Orange processions, but the turbulence at Drumcree in July 1995 kept him from adding even one brush stroke, the finishing touch. It is as though the Orangemen march in Ferran's pictures only with the consent of the warriors from his Táin series and the heroes from his later explorations of themes drawn from the 1798 Rebellion.

Two strange works ignited Ferran's fascination with 1798, the first a naïve but spectacular canvas (in the National Gallery, Dublin) of the Battle of Ballynahinch by Thomas Robinson, a jobbing English portrait painter who plied his trade in Belfast and Dublin. True artists are seekers as well as finders. Ferran tracked down his second source in the Linen Hall Library, a pamphlet with the wondrous title: *McComb's Guide to Belfast, the Giant's Causeway, and the Adjoining Districts of the Counties of Antrim and Down, with an Account of the Battle of Ballynahinch and the Celebrated Mineral Waters of that Neighbourhood*. It gives an account of Elizabeth Gray of Killinchy, a young girl of extraordinary beauty who had gone into battle with her brother and lover, and perished fleeing from the field. A man called Jack Gill cut off her gloved hand with his sword, and then she was shot through the head by Thomas Nelson of Annahilt. So the story goes, and its shadow stretches right up to the present day. Boldly, but with tact, Ferran depicts Betsy Gray as a nude figure, terribly vulnerable among the guns and uniforms. The horror of war is poetically intimated rather than displayed voyeuristically.

Brian Ferran's continuing preoccupations with the *Táin* and Irish mythology, with the 1798 Rebellion, and with contemporary tribal manifestations bestow on his *oeuvre* an impressive coherence. Though his work is universal in its appeal, these paintings could only have been produced by an artist living in Ulster through the last twenty-five grim years. In addition, his studies of the female nude and the fine landscapes he has painted in Ireland and abroad, give this retrospective exhibition an even more generous aspect. He has returned again and again to his several themes and explored them with an increasing intensity. He has looked disorder in the face, and come through purposefully to create against the odds works of commemoration and celebration.

Introduction to Brian Ferran, *Patterns and Parables: Paintings 1966–1996*:
Catalogue of exhibition at RHA Gallagher Gallery, Dublin, 1996

'THE FIRE IN THE WINDOW': THE PAINTINGS OF DAVID CRONE

'In painting, gesture must attach itself and become its opposite'
– Peter Lanyon

When I stand in front of a David Crone canvas I think of windows and mirrors, an interplay of reflections that brings the outdoors inside and, beyond the glass, the indoors outside. The boundaries between interior and exterior dissolve. One might say that among the contents of the artist's home near Spa in County Down are mirror images of the garden, hedges in the middle distance, drumlins and Slieve Croob and, farthest afield, sun and clouds. For me, Louis MacNeice's unsettling late poem 'Reflections' suggests what seems to be happening in Crone's early work and right through his career to more recent paintings such as 'Pool' and 'Field':

> ... The standard
> Lamp comes thrice in my mirror, twice in my window,
> The fire in the mirror lies two rooms away through the window,
> The fire in the window lies one room away down the terrace,
> My actual room stands sandwiched between confections
> Of night and lights and glass and in both directions
> I can see beyond and through the reflections the street lamps
> At home outdoors where my indoors rooms lie stranded ...

Crone combines two (or more) familiar scenes so that they metamorphose each other and invoke the strange and unknown. His vantage points open out into nature, its mysteries as well as its manifestations. And, in return, the world in view spurs him to look into his own soul. Crone's art is more complicated than the merely descriptive or representational: it is profoundly psychological. He internalises what he sees, as his titles sometimes suggest – *Fantasy, Interior*. In pictures such as *The Great Big City* and *Shop Window* the Belfast of security gates and peace walls, the busy streets and passers-by, are absorbed into a vision that feels moral as well as aesthetic. When the Troubles disrupt the scene, Crone has preferred an oblique approach, as the commanding compositions *Victim, Tourist and Model* and *Demolished Building* demonstrate. He prefers us to view his concerned expression out of the corner of the eye.

David Crone was brought up, as I was, on Belfast's Lisburn Road. The Bog Meadows just across the railway line, froggy ponds next to the perimeter-fencing around Windsor Park football ground and, only a short bicycle ride away, the Lagan towpath, Barnett's Park with its big white house, the Minnowburn, the canning factory at Newforge – all of this introduced us to a terrain where the urban and the rural impinged on each other with an incongruity so intense it obliterated comfortable concepts of the suburban. Isolated linen villages, locomotive yards (his father worked as an engine driver on the Great Northern Railway), barges heaped with coal, lock-keepers' houses created their own peculiar 'soul-landscape', to borrow Samuel Beckett's lovely coinage. Meanwhile, to the south Strangford Lough and the Ards Peninsula beckoned, to the north the Glens of Antrim.

The Ulster countryside, geologically multi-layered and historically dense, suits this artist's cast of mind. He makes soul-landscapes out of County Down's enfolding drumlins and the basalt sheets of the Antrim plateau. Those intense greens, heathery glows, the yellow blaze of gorse and broom charge his palette – though he eschews facile lyricism and wryly insists that, when you look closely at its constituents, a green field isn't green at all. His brush inscribes field-patterns, traces of settlement and enclosure, quarries, forgotten mills and kilns, rusty fences, man's fleeting presence. Runny surfaces offset the solidity of his compositions and remind us of water eroding rock, the spread of lichen and moss, rain. The element of chance comes into play in the art as in nature. Ultimately the paint becomes its own subject matter.

A year before I agreed to write about David Crone's art, I composed a love poem, which happens to visit his territory. Very recently I discovered in the Ulster Museum his painting *Rocks and Vegetation*. It was indeed a validation and a delight to read in the note on the wall that this picture had been conceived at Glenariff:

> If the hut still existed, I would take you there
> To contemplate the waterfall at Glenariff
> Through three panes of glass the colour of dawn
> And noon and sunset, a cobwebby perspective,
>
> A windy, wide-open snug, a shrine to daylight,
> Our time together measured by water falling
> And the silence beneath the roar, a pebble
> That rotates and dwindles in its rumbling hole.

Nowadays much of the landscape (and townscape) painting produced in this country celebrates an Ireland that never really existed. It consoles too easily and stops us thinking. In his energetic engagement with the world Crone defies such complacency. A thundery disquietude hangs over even his brightest creations. His watchful, edgy, ambiguous work suggests that everything – from wild flower to boulder, from graffito to stone cross – is provisional. David Crone's wonderful paintings commemorate the interim.

Introduction to Catalogue, David Crone: Retrospective Exhibition, Ulster Museum, Belfast, January 2000

DOMESTIC CORNER – NORTHERN LIGHTS: THE PAINTINGS OF JEFFREY MORGAN

I

Jeffrey Morgan learns how to look at an object by drawing it. For him drawing is a probing discipline that frees the artist from the bondage of mannerism. Although in his paintings he makes his own rules, creates his own worlds, one senses that the enchantment usually starts in pencil or charcoal studies; that, from beginning to end, working from life is the chief inspiration. In Morgan's case practice does not make perfect. The more he returns to a sitter, an object, a view, the more questions he finds to ask. It is as though, just out of sight, there will always be another piece of information waiting to reward his pursuit. He has worked on some of these canvases for five or ten years, and yet they retain their original spontaneities. Sitting for a long time in front of the same picture can be just as risky as any splashy brief encounter.

II

In *The Striped Dress* the window-shutters are half-closed and cut out everything except the sky. A solitary figure looks out at the view which we cannot share with her; nor can we see her face. We make do with what light comes through and the shadows it casts. The wispy jet-trail which comments on the moment, on the woman who seems neither trapped nor free, is an artist's flourish as well as death's signature. She epitomises what lies hidden at the back of the mind, and she conjures up feelings of intense longing. Although this is a study in stillness, things visible and invisible come together in a disturbing psychic dance.

271

One suspects that in *Night Painting – Full Moon* the woman (the artist's wife) is sitting in the lovingly portrayed house across the street, in the room where a light burns – in two places at the one time. Thus the artist turns the idea of home inside out, and measures the closenesses and distances of domesticity. Here is the muse, her dress with its pattern of blue sky and white birds a reminder of daytime. Her uncompromising expression softens in *The Duck, The Spiral* to suggest, as do all true muses, the sister and the daughter as well as the wife. Will the old toys disappear when she adds to her repertoire the role of the mother? Is the red tape a humorous allusion to the logarithmic spiral which catches us all in the end?

The muse expresses herself through her clothes, and these influence the moods of the pictures, random catalysts. When seen as a sequence these works, though the opposite of casual, comment on the chanciness of the whole enterprise and of anyone's life. In so doing they capture miraculously the sacred penumbra that surrounds everyday objects – sponge-ware bowls, books, hats, old toys, garments, a smoothing-iron. The domestic interiors, the outdoor vistas, the townscapes, each with its single beautiful female figure, reflect the artist himself, his state of mind, his reverie. An anxious or complacent gesture would break the spell. The artist and his muse must keep coming and going, changing places – presences, absences.

III

Jeffrey Morgan's art is an affair of tensions, of contradictions. He returns to the same subjects in order to remake them and renew himself. The randomness of the things which clutter his life contributes to the evolving design. The mystery derives from the precision. He takes pains to explain his passion. He seems detached from his obsessions. He documents his vision. He improvises deliberately. His pictures make no empty promises and take nothing for granted. This is work of a very high order.

Introduction to Catalogue, Jeffrey Morgan: Exhibition at Arts Council Gallery, Belfast, July-August 1991

IN DEFENCE OF BILLIE HOLIDAY

In a recent issue of *The Honest Ulsterman* the artistry of Billie Holiday was questioned. I spring to her defence with more faith in my gallantry than in my jazz scholarship or musical criticism. When she is given less than her due, Billie seems to demand from her admirers enthusiastic and devoted defence. Her status as a cult figure and the tragedy of her life explain this partly, and I for one am affected by both. But the main cause is of course her singing – its uneasy blend of vulnerability and power, its capacity for resolving shocking tensions without a hint of assertiveness, its grim but saving ambiguities, its very stylish courage.

I bought my first Billie Holiday LP partly because of the dazzling line-up of accompanying musicians, partly out of curiosity. The first few times I played it I was unimpressed. I found her singing featureless, uncharming, rather harsh – in short, not particularly musical. It took a long time for the penny to drop, but when it did I bought all the available recordings and played them continually. Billie Holiday's is not the easiest music to come to terms with.

There are several reasons why this should be so. She indulges in no specious displays of virtuosity as do Ella Fitzgerald or Lena Horne; she often flattens and manipulates the melodic line and takes liberties with the lyrics, so that someone used to, say, Bing Crosby's interpretation of a popular song will hardly recognise it, or, if he does, may feel affronted; in many of her best recordings she is part of a well-blended ensemble rather than a featured star-singer; much of her raw material consists of Tin Pan Alley ephemera, songs of unbelievable banality which in 1969 have no life whatsoever outside her embodiment of them; she sings harshly about harsh realities: her voice, in terms of the number of octaves it can span, does not have great range; she is honest, uncompromising and disquieting.

Billie made her first recording with Benny Goodman in November 1933. The numbers were 'Your Mother's Son-in-law' and 'Riffin' the Scotch', neither of which reveals much of the true Holiday. The songs and their arrangements indicate that Goodman may not have recognised what a profound artist he had employed, or that he was being insensitively commercial. They're pretty lightweight and can't have sold well because Billie had to wait two years before she made another record.

By 1936 Billie was recording regularly with Teddy Wilson and his orchestra, in an attempt by jazzmen to cash in on the growing juke-box industry by presenting jazz interpretations of popular songs, by resuscitating the tiny heartbeat of mediocre tunes and lyrics. Billie's re-creations made her unpopular with song writers and publishers and she was often short of material. But the leading jazz men of the day were quick to recognise her talents, and a bonus of any recording from Billie's best years (mid-thirties to early forties) is the rich assembly of accompanying musicians, some of them artists of genius – Johnny Hodges, Ben Webster, Buck Clayton, Henry 'Red' Allen, Buster Bailey, Hot Lips Page, Count Basie and, of course, Teddy Wilson and Lester Young.

Wilson and Young were her favourite musicians: they accompanied her on dozens of fine recordings. No account of her singing would be complete without reference to their uncanny ability to anticipate or extend her interpretation of a song, the deep and unfailing rapport between instrumentalist and singer. Wilson's piano style is always understated, a delicate, ironic filigree. After a bold opening blast on trumpet or saxophone, which states the tune simply, Wilson weaves a cunning web of arpeggios which suggest fleetingly all sorts of possibilities and open up the song for Billie who then proceeds to reshape it. And, while she sings, Wilson tinkles and caresses in the background. There is something sexual about it all; sexual metaphor is, at any rate, convenient and revealing. If Wilson's piano-playing resembles pre-coital love play, Lester Young's saxophone accompaniment becomes complete love and climax. He is one of the four or five greatest saxophonists jazz has produced, a pioneer whose languorous but forceful playing denies the regular beat and yet pushes the overall rhythm inexorably forward in a style strangely paralleled by Billie's own singing. Between them they create an emotional quicksand of shifting emphases, an alarmingly complete musical-cum-sexual reciprocity. They obviously influenced each other's music profoundly, and many of Lester Young's finest performances are on Billie Holiday recordings.

These partnerships are perfected versions of a response Billie inspired in dozens of musicians. The thirties' recordings possess a fullness and polish which suggest careful rehearsal. But by all accounts they were ad hoc affairs – the sheet music was read in the studio, 'breaks' were allotted, there were a couple of run-throughs, and then the recording. Somehow everything fell into place: the perfection with which singer and instrumentalists again and again inscribe the arc of a song, the abundance of the sound, the comparative rarity of wrong effects, let alone wrong notes, is miraculous – indeed, many songs received in these carefree sessions their definitive renditions. And I doubt very much whether any of the performers realised, at the time, that they were creating great music in which ambition and achievement, plan and practice coincide. It must have been good to play jazz in those days.

Billie sang a lot of good songs very well – songs like 'They can't take that away from me', 'These Foolish Things'. 'The Way You Look Tonight', 'The Man I Love', but generally she is at her best with completely indifferent material that allows her complete freedom to project her own personality and produce a new song. The brilliance of song writers like Gershwin or Kern was inclined to get in the way, to prick her artistic conscience so that often half-way through a number of theirs she seems to lose interest and hand it back to them. And in a witty, clever song like 'A Fine Romance', which has its own clearly defined lines, she can sound uncomfortable.

She was in fact a blues singer, a successor of Bessie Smith and Ma Rainey, rehearsing all over again but in a different setting and in a different mode their themes of loneliness and sexual betrayal. But she had no cultural hinterland as they had, no cotton fields where she could absorb the majestic poetry of rural blues. Instead she grabbed what was at hand – the shallow popular music of the cities and sang the blues through this unlikely medium. She was only doing what jazz had always done (right from the time ex-slaves picked up the instruments jettisoned by the bands of both sides at the end of the Civil War, and tried to play them, just like that) – taking over anything which might be of use, be it brass instruments, military music, violins, harmoniums, jugs, stovepipes, operatic arias, Spanish music, pop songs. In Billie Holiday's regal example is displayed the voracity of jazz, its vitality, its ability to absorb impurities and remain itself, to convert trash into solid musical protein. To deny, as many purists do, that Billie Holiday sings the blues is to mistake origins for essence.

In the last recordings she made before she died in 1959 (she was under arrest on her death bed for drug addiction) Billie can hardly sing at all: with all the know-how and all the feeling and no ability she croaks out a kind of broken recitative over a background of insipid strings and a hellishly heavenly choir. The result is as moving as

277

anything I know in vocal music. No doubt in such a judgement the personality and the legend have become for me inextricably bound up with the singing: but that is what jazz is all about.

Honest Ulsterman, 1969

LISTENING TO GHOSTS

Philip Larkin, *All That Jazz*

This is a useful reference book. The articles are short and many deal with several records at a time, so that as continuous reading it is rather bitty. Indeed, the most satisfying section is the long introduction, which modulates from a sustained attack on modernism in the arts, and on modern jazz in particular, to a moving lament for a Golden Age when jazz (and the other arts, I presume) was expansive and generous. I am sympathetic to his diagnosis of the break-down: 'My own theory is that it is related to an imbalance between the two tensions from which art springs: these are the tension between the artist and his material, and between the artist and his audience, and that in the last seventy-five years or so the second of these has slackened or even perished. In consequence the artist has become over-concerned with his material (hence an age of technical experiment), and, in isolation, has busied himself with the two principal themes of modernism, mystification and outrage.' A focal point of his scorn and despair is the alliterative trio Parker, Picasso and Pound, and anyone who is curious as to the likely complexion of the next *Oxford Book of English Verse*, of which Larkin is editor, should read these pages.

When the negro musician changed from entertaining the white man with jazz to hating him with it, did he merely turn Uncle Tommery on its head? I too am bewildered by what seems to be the 'chaos, hatred and absurdity' of 'the beret-and-dark-glasses boys'. Much contemporary jazz is an expression of the aspirations of the Black Power movement: like Larkin I don't understand these noises – it would be misguided liberalism to pretend that one did. One's ears are insulted, and that, I imagine, is the whole point. Perhaps the musicians are more confused than we are. Perhaps we are passing through a difficult transitional period. Perhaps jazz is dead. I don't know. But as an Ulsterman I find Larkin's blanket term, 'Civil Rights jazz', far too glib a dismissal, and his justifiable nostalgia seems to thin in places to a revealing sentimentality.

When the negro athletes raised their gloved fists on the Olympic podium, I was very moved (if also frightened). Much modern jazz lacks the simple dignity of their gesture, and I share Larkin's sense of loss. But if the abundant humanity of the best moments of the twenties and thirties jazz, which he celebrates so well, are not in some strange way reflected in that moment in Mexico, then I think we are both wasting our time – just listening to ghosts.

Irish Times, 21 February 1970

A PERPETUAL ONE-NIGHT STAND

Some Thoughts on Jazz and Poetry

I can remember the exact moment when the wonders of jazz first grabbed me as a young boy. The English Number One tennis player of the day, Tony Mottram, chose as one of his Desert Island Discs Fats Waller's 'Alligator Crawl'. I was standing in our kitchen at the time (early fifties?), and thrilled to the rolling boogie base of the great stride pianist. As an adolescent I first fell in love with the romantic classics: Tchaikovsky, Rachmaninov, Chopin, Grieg. In the Sixth Form at Inst (the Royal Belfast Academical Institution) I was one of a small group of highbrows who met in each other's homes to listen to the still new-fangled long-playing records, some of them jazz. George Filor favoured Duke Ellington; Terry Gillespie, the Modern Jazz Quartet. The traditional jazz revival of the fifties meant jiving on Saturday nights to Jimmy Compton's Band. (At the school hops there were 'Jitterbugging Forbidden' notices on the walls.) Chris Barber's Dixie-land version of 'Bobby Shafto' was all the rage: and his guitarist Lonnie Donegan went on to become the King of Skiffle, an early example of the pop star/ teenage idol phenomenon. But I was spending my pocket money on records of classical music and regularly attending concerts given by the City of Belfast Symphony Orchestra in the Ulster Hall.

At Trinity College Dublin, jazz was occasionally on the menu but not yet a major preoccupation. I enjoyed some fairly modern stuff in Harry Gilmore's rooms. (Harry, who liked to play along with his records on a muted trumpet, was a Miles Davis devotee.) Johnnie

Wadham, a fellow student and already a thrilling drummer, could be heard beating it out in some of the Dublin dives. My total conversion to jazz came in my twenty-fifth year when marriage and our return to Belfast coincided with my discovery of Solly Lipsitz's celebrated emporium in High Street. Atlantic Records sported no shop front. With the entrance to this dusty cubbyhole at the end of a dark passage-way, and Solly not always in residence, one felt honoured and rather enterprising to be seated on a stool in one of the happiest atmospheres I have ever known – combative conversation, cigar smoke, gossip, jokes, new boxes of records, jazz.

My first purchase was two LPs, *Fats on the Air*, compilations of Fats Waller's radio work recorded on magnetic tapes. These made more room for the expansiveness of this larger-than-life, charismatic show-man than the three or so minutes of the old-fashioned 78s. I loved the drive, the warmth, the apparent spontaneity, the insouciance, the dizzy humour, the hilarious demolition of sentimental material, but I also sensed a dark and unsettling aspect, as though behind the twinkle Waller is issuing a challenge: 'Yes, I'll make you laugh and tap your feet, folks, but not until you've kissed my fat ass!' Waller seamlessly combines sunniness and subversion. Undermining not only the inane Tin Pan Alley lyrics, but our racial and artistic preconceptions as well, he can be very complicated indeed. Sometimes I wish he had performed more often with musicians of his own calibre; that he had left us more of those tracks on which he keeps his mouth shut and just plays as a driving session-man or, as the composer of intricate parlour pieces like 'Handful of Keys', 'Clothesline Ballet', 'Jitterbug Waltz'. But most of the time I'm happy like everyone else to chuckle when Fats Waller sings and jokes. Ebullient perennials like 'Ain't Misbehavin' and 'Honeysuckle Rose' never fail to thrill me. To quote Louis Armstrong: 'Every time someone mentions Fats Waller's name, why you can see the grins on all the faces, as if to say, "Yea, yea, yea, yea, Fats is a solid sender, ain't he?"'

In my first collection, *No Continuing City*, I included a sequence of jazz poems called 'Words for Jazz Perhaps' and dedicated it to Solly Lipsitz. (I cheekily pinched the title from Yeats.) In the first of these, 'Elegy for Fats Waller', I refer to the rumbustious life-style which surely contributed to his death at the grimly early age of thirty-nine. I try to convey the weightless artistry of this hugely overweight man. I take him seriously, but in a way I hope he would have appreciated. His closest friends called him Thomas rather than Fats:

> Lighting up, lest all our hearts should break,
> His fiftieth cigarette of the day,
> Happy with so many notes at his beck
> And call, he sits there taking it away,
> The maker of immaculate slapstick.

> With music and with such precise rampage
> Across the deserts of the blues a trail
> He blazes, towards the one true mirage,
> Enormous on a nimble-footed camel
> And almost refusing to be his age.

> He plays for hours on end and though there be
> Oases one part water, two parts gin,
> He tumbles past to reign, wise and thirsty,
> At the still centre of his loud dominion –
> THE SHOOK THE SHAKE THE SHEIKH OF ARABY.

Or, as James P. Johnson put it in an impromptu obituary: 'Some little people has music in them, but Fats, he was *all* music, and you know how big he was.' The last line of my elegy quotes his own rendition of 'The Sheikh'. The twelfth line is historically, though not poetically, inaccurate. Waller diluted his gin with port. Love of Waller's stride-playing led me to other jazz pianists: his instructor James P. Johnson, who brought together ragtime and classical techniques and got the world dancing the Charleston; Art Tatum who, as jazz's most prodigious virtuoso pianist, was admired by Rachmaninov and Horo-vitz; Earl Hines, whom I first heard competing with Louis Armstrong for elbow room on the Hot Seven recordings from the late twenties, and then – miraculously – in 1966 he dazzled a few dozen of us in the Ulster Hall: an embarrassingly small audience for an artistic giant who over the decades had jousted with most of the greats. The bounce and zing of Earl Hines's improvisations brought tears to my eyes.

Round about this time the Queen's University Festival invited Bud Freeman to Belfast. He performed with an English outfit, the Alex Welsh Jazz Band, and more or less filled the Whitla Hall. With his bris-tly pert moustache this tubby little white man in a grey suit looked more like a vacuum cleaner salesman than a hot saxophonist. He played music that veered from the hardboiled to the brittle and bitter-sweet, in the 'Chicago style', the fruit of the creative collision of black musicians who had migrated there from the south, with white disciples such as Muggsy Spanier, Eddie Condon, Mezz Mezzrow who copied and modified the classic New Orleans sound. Later, tracking down Freeman on various recordings, I uncovered further riches: the tense holler of Max Kaminsky's trumpet, the introverted, sceptical, querulous searchings of Pee Wee Russell's clarinet. In the meantime I wrote 'Bud Freeman in Belfast', the second poem in my jazz suite:

284

Fog horn and factory siren intercept
Each fragile hoarded-up refrain. What else
Is there to do but let those notes erupt

Until your fading last glissando settles
Among all other sounds – carefully wrapped
In the cotton wool from aspirin bottles?

Harry Chambers, who edited the still-undervalued literary maga-zine, *Phoenix* (there was a special Northern Irish issue featuring poems by Heaney, Mahon, Simmons and myself, with drawings by Carolyn Mulholland), and who later founded Peterloo Poets, was living in Belfast in the sixties. He loved jazz nearly as much as I did. The copy of Louis MacNeice's autobiography, *The Strings are False*, which Harry gave to me, is inscribed in green biro with four lines composed in my honour. Harry's quatrain catches the spirit of those days:

I see you smiling, fat, dressed all in brown:
Here you are mimicking that piano jazz,
Here you are swaying on my midnight hearth
Or quoting Irish poetry as the Scotch goes down.

At a party in Harry's flat in Camden Street the music issued from a tinny-sounding portable Dansette record player. I could just pick out through the crush and chatter a heart-stopping voice, a rich contralto, one of the most majestic sounds in all music:

It's raining and it's storming on the sea,
It's raining, it's storming on the sea;
I feel like somebody has shipwrecked poor me.

285

The following day I rushed to Atlantic Records and asked for Bessie Smith albums. Solly told me that Philips had – disgracefully – deleted her from their catalogue. I asked him to order the Columbia set of five LPs from America. (Philip Larkin, through his influential jazz column in the *Daily Telegraph*, helped to persuade Philips to re-issue Bessie Smith some time later.)

It is a miracle how backwoods keening, mainly by men, about sex and betrayal, money and hard times, was transformed by female singers with powerful voices into a universal lamentation, a sound that would encircle the globe. Bessie Smith and other blues singers – Ma Rainey, Chippie Hill, Alberta Hunter – travelled the Southern states providing entertainment in tent shows and on vaudeville stages. Did she realise she was producing great art? The saxophonist Buster Bailey suggests: 'For Bessie singing was just a living. She didn't consider it anything special.' The three-minute span of those early pre-electric recordings clearly helped to concentrate an already potent brew. Bessie Smith came at just the right time, a delta into which tributaries flowed – the blues, ragtime, vaudeville, Tin Pan Alley, spirituals, New Orleans jazz, jazz from Chicago and New York, a developing record industry. But nothing can really explain the glory of her achievement, the golden period of six years or so when she performed to the highest level on dozens of tracks. Even in her bawdy, obstreperous, more knock-about modes her majesty seldom deserts her. She has earned her title, 'Empress of the Blues'. When the youthful Louis Armstrong accompanies her in W. C. Handy's 'St Louis Blues' (which is for anyone who hears it the definitive version), 'Reckless Blues', 'Sobbin' Hearted Blues', 'Cold in Hand Blues', 'Careless Love', the two geniuses generate a high-voltage charge. In my third poem, 'To Bessie Smith', I try to keep in mind the intensity and pathos of her music, her courage and defiance ('I ain't goodlookin' but I'm somebody's angel child'), the sexual surge of her voice, the elemental force of her personality:

> You bring from Chattanooga Tennessee
> Your huge voice to the back of my mind
> Where, like sea shells salvaged from the sea
> As bright reminders of a few weeks' stay,
> Some random notes are all I ever find.
> I couldn't play your records every day.

> I think of Tra-na-rossan, Inisheer,
> Of Harris drenched by horizontal rain –
> Those landscapes I must visit year by year.
> I do not live with sounds so seasonal
> Nor set up house for good. Your blues contain
> Each longed-for holiday, each terminal.

The legendary cornettist Bix Beiderbecke came from a white middle-class family who lived in Davenport on the Mississippi. As a teenager he listened to Bessie Smith, King Oliver, Louis Armstrong and at the deepest level took them all in. But he educated himself by playing over and over again records of the white ensemble The Original Dixieland Jazz Band, and in particular their cornettist Nick La Rocca. (It's ironical that the very first jazz records were cut by these white musicians in 1917.) From the beginning, his cornet sings out from the dimly recorded tum-te-tum throb of a youthful group called the Wolverines. Mezz Mezzrow captures the Beiderbecke magic: 'He played mostly open horn, every note full, big, rich and round, standing out like a pearl, loud but never irritating or jangling, with a powerful drive that few white musicians had in those days.' At the end of his brief career (he died of alcoholism at twenty-eight) Bix was playing with the Paul

Whiteman Orchestra, and scattered his pearls in pretty boring sludge. The Whiteman recordings survive only because Bix made his immortal contribution, hot breaks that are tantalisingly brief, sometimes only several seconds long, miniature versions of the story of his life. Tracks like 'Singin' the Blues' and 'I'm Comin', Virginia' delight me as much as any music. Bix Beiderbecke was the first white man to play great jazz. My parents came from London to live in Belfast. When I wrote 'To Bix Beiderbecke' in my mid-twenties I wondered if I might be the first Englishman to write Irish poetry. This is the fourth poem in my jazz quartet:

> In hotel rooms, in digs you went to school.
> These dead were voices from the floor below
> Who filled like an empty room your skull,
>
> Who shared your perpetual one-night stand
> – The havoc there, and the manoeuvrings! –
> Each coloured hero with his instrument.
>
> You were bound with one original theme
> To compose in your head your terminus,
> Or to improvise with the best of them
>
> That parabola from blues to barrelhouse.

Atlantic Records closed years ago. (Solly Lipsitz who prescribed all those new records with an almost medical precision, remains one of my closest friends.) I now buy early jazz on CDs. Computer-enhanced and digitally re-mastered, seventy-year-old recordings sound as fresh as yesterday. Though my chief enthusiasm continues to be the jazz of the twenties and thirties, I recently fell in love with the quirky melodic lines of Thelonious Monk, one of the original boppers ('The music Pythagorian,/ one note at a time/ Connecting the heavenly spheres', to quote the American poet Charles Simic). And I have been reaching back to the beginning of the century and transcriptions from piano rolls of compositions by Scott Joplin and other ragtime composers. Jazz is huge. That the suffering and degradation of slavery should bring forth so much redemptive beauty is miraculous. The spontaneity of this music must be one of the best antidotes against authoritarian systems that would tell us what to think and how to feel. Its emergence in the century of the jackboot is of the greatest cultural importance. Stalin hated it. The Nazis hated it. They were frightened of swing. Syncopation is the opposite of the goosestep. Perhaps jazz is our century's most significant contribution to the culture of the world.

Writing Ulster 5 (1998)

PART 5

IRELAND CHAIR OF POETRY LECTURES

2007–2010

A JOVIAL HULLABALOO

The great American poet Wallace Stevens begins his poem 'A High-Toned Old Christian Woman' with this line: 'Poetry is the supreme fiction, madame.' In the course of a complex poem he weighs in the scales religious belief and the life of the imagination. Although he clearly prefers the latter, he seems to compromise by suggesting that both end up creating the same thing: 'A jovial hullabaloo among the spheres':

> Poetry is the supreme fiction, madame.
> Take the moral law and make a nave of it
> And from the nave build haunted heaven. Thus,
> The conscience is converted into palms,
> Like windy citherns hankering for hymns.
> We agree in principle. That's clear. But take
> The opposing law and make a peristyle,
> And from the peristyle project a masque
> Beyond the planets. Thus, our bawdiness,
> Unpurged by epitaph, indulged at last,
> Is equally converted into palms,
> Squiggling like saxophones. And palm for palm,
> Madame, we are where we began. Allow,
> Therefore, that in the planetary scene
> Your disaffected flagellants, well-stuffed,
> Smacking their muzzy bellies in parade,
> Proud of such novelties of the sublime,
> Such tink and tank and tunk-a-tunk-tunk,

> May, merely may, madame, whip from themselves
> A jovial hullabaloo among the spheres.
> This will make widows wince. But fictive things
> Wink as they will. Wink most when widows wince.

This evening I shall be talking about how I discovered poetry as a reader and writer of it. I shall be celebrating some of the poems and poets who have mattered to me. 'A Jovial Hullabaloo' will be an autobiography in poetry.

At Malone Public Elementary School in Balmoral Avenue in south Belfast we ten-year-olds recited aloud, as a sort of ragged chorus, David's great lamentation over Saul and Jonathan. I relished the rolling rhythms generated by the strange words, and didn't worry too much about the meaning:

> Saul and Jonathan were lovely and pleasant in their lives,
> And in their death they were not divided:
> They were swifter than eagles,
> They were stronger than lions.
> Ye daughters of Israel, weep over Saul,
> Who clothed you in scarlet, with other delights,
> Who put on ornaments of gold upon your apparel.
> How are the mighty fallen in the midst of the battle!

The New English Bible of 1970 flattens the rhythms in an attempt to be clearer. In the King James Bible (as we've heard) 'Saul and Jonathan were lovely and pleasant in their lives,/And in their death they were not divided'. In the New English Bible this becomes: 'Delightful and dearly loved were Saul and Jonathan;/ in life, in death, they were not parted.' Though not completely dire, this is neither poetry nor prose.

294

It is verbal polystyrene. It is forgettable. The translators of the New English Bible tried to be contemporary, but their version just ended up being temporary. The King James Bible was written to last. It has inspired many poets. It was composed to be memorable. In poetry the meaning cannot be detached from the melody. In Malone Public Elementary School at least one ten-year old's mind was saturated with beautiful words.

In Form III at Inst (the Royal Belfast Academical Institution), when I was fourteen, I was mesmerised by Keats's 'La Belle Dame sans Merci' and by Walter de la Mare's 'The Listeners'. De la Mare bridges the worlds of nursery rhyme and modern poetry:

> 'Is there anybody there?' said the Traveller,
>   Knocking on the moonlit door;
> And his horse in the silence champed the grasses
>   Of the forest's ferny floor;
> And a bird flew up out of the turret,
>   Above the Traveller's head;
> And he smote upon the door a second time;
>   'Is there anybody there?' he said.

That year I chose for my Third Form English Prize the *Collected Poems* of W. B. Yeats, published by Macmillan with a creamy dust-jacket and maroon boards. The choice alarmed my family.

Joe Cowan, a dapper little Englishman with a pert moustache, taught me English in Sixth Form. It was Joe who awakened in me (and, a year or two later, in Derek Mahon) a passion for poetry. There was little or no Irish literature on the syllabus in those days, so Joe xeroxed for us poems by living Irish writers – Patrick Kavanagh, Louis MacNeice, W. R. Rodgers. He would hand around the sheets. 'Read that one aloud for us, Longley,' he'd say. I'd read, and then he'd ask: 'Is the man a poet?' Embarrassed mumbles. 'Is the man a poet? I should say so! I should say so!' And he'd chortle and slap his thigh.

When I was sixteen I first seriously tried to write poetry – a combination of hormonal commotion and aesthetic awakening. But it wasn't until I went to Trinity College Dublin that poetry grew into an obsession. My career as a Classics student was already in serious decline. Perhaps I was looking for something else at which to shine.

At school I had immersed myself in classical music, and explored in a daze of pleasure the beautiful big art books in the library. Now it was poetry, or the idea of poetry, that took me over completely. I filled notebooks with formless outpourings, writing several bad poems a day. The first piece I ever submitted for publication was a crazy prose poem, like a mad dog's howl, which I dropped into the post-box of the undergraduate literary magazine *Icarus*. I wasn't expecting it to disappear forever – but it did, mercifully.

Eventually, in the March 1960 issue of *Icarus* two of my juvenilia were published. After forty-eight years the thrill reverberates still. One of the poems was called 'Marigolds':

> She gave him marigolds
> the colour of autumn
> to keep in his cold room,
> and the late light of autumn
> gilded all their moments.

That Easter I went home to Belfast. My father discovered 'Marigolds'. 'Michael, it's not worth the paper it's printed on,' he said. Over the years I have written obsessively about my father as a boy-soldier in the Great War. Forty years after 'Marigolds' and perhaps in response to his dismissal, I wrote these four lines ('Anniversary'):

> He would have been a hundred today, my father,
> So I write to him in the trenches and describe
> How he lifts with tongs from the brazier an ember
> And in its glow reads my words and sets them aside.

At Trinity Brendan Kennelly, a fellow student already publishing poems, was generous in his praise and encouraged me very early on. He encompassed everything I had been missing. Coming from Belfast, with my English parents and Protestant schooling, I had never encountered anyone quite like him. He was culturally astonishing. Decades later, in a poem called 'The Factory', I evoked the enduring impression he made on me:

> Already the tubby, rollicking, broken Christ
> Talking too much, drowning me in his hurlygush
> Which makes the sound water makes over stones.

Just as I was jostling to lay claim to the title 'college poet', Derek Mahon breezed in from Belfast, a year or two my junior but fully fledged, it seemed, brilliant and self-confident. I was flummoxed. This was one of the best things ever to happen to me. We became good friends. As I have said elsewhere, we inhaled poetry with our Sweet Afton cigarettes – Hardy and Auden and MacNeice. For years the closing lines of MacNeice's 'Mayfly' have been watchwords of mine:

> The show will soon shut down, its gay-rags gone,
> But when this summer is over let us die together,
> I want always to be near your breasts.

It pleased us that Presbyterian Ulster could produce an exotic like the clergyman-poet W. R. Rodgers:

> Dance, Mary Magdalene, dance, dance and sing,
> For unto you is born
> This day a King. 'Lady,' said He,
> 'To you who relent
> I bring back the petticoat and the bottle of scent.'

We had those lines by heart, and still do. We loved Dylan Thomas's fruity recordings. (All the poets of my generation were intoxicated by Dylan Thomas. I could prove this by showing you some very embarrassing juvenilia, my own especially!)

We revered the D. H. Lawrence of the animal poems and the love poems and the great death psalms, and Robert Graves, the Muse-poet supreme. For my twenty-first birthday a friend gave me Kavanagh's *Come Dance with Kitty Stobling*. I have never thought in Irish dynastic terms and I don't see myself or my poetic colleagues in some kind of Irish succession. I dislike literary ancestor worship. But if I *had* to choose two Irish poetic uncles, they would be Louis MacNeice and Patrick Kavanagh. And, as I was beginning to write poetry in the late 1950s, three new English poets published astonishing first collections. I was excited by their largeness of vision and by the way they renovated the language. In 'Wedding-Wind' from Philip Larkin's *The Less Deceived* a young bride soliloquises:

> Can it be borne, this bodying-forth by wind
> Of joy my actions turn on, like a thread
> Carrying beads? Shall I be let to sleep
> Now this perpetual morning shares my bed?

Can even death dry up
These new delighted lakes, conclude
Our kneeling as cattle by all-generous waters?

Lupercal was in fact Ted Hughes's second collection. Of its several spell-binding animal poems, perhaps my favourite is 'The Bull Moses', at once earthy and cosmic:

> Each dusk the farmer led him
> Down to the pond to drink and smell the air,
> And he took no pace but the farmer
> Led him to take it, as if he knew nothing
> Of the ages and continents of his fathers,
> Shut, while he wombed, to a dark shed
> And steps between his door and the duckpond;
> The weight of the sun and the moon and the world hammered
> To a ring of brass through his nostrils.

The third of these collections, *For the Unfallen* by Geoffrey Hill, begins with 'Genesis', which he composed when he was still in his teens. He seems, in part, to be writing about the genesis of poetry itself:

> Against the burly air I strode
> Crying the miracles of God.
>
> And first I brought the sea to bear
> Upon the dead weight of the land;
> And the waves flourished at my prayer,
> The rivers spawned their sand.

And where the streams were salt and full
The tough pig-headed salmon strove,
Ramming the ebb, in the tide's pull,
To reach the steady hills above.

The coincidence of these three poets of genius marks a pinnacle in the history of English poetry. It was a good time to be an apprentice.

At Trinity we bought the early collections of Thomas Kinsella, John Montague and Richard Murphy as they came out from the Dolmen Press. We took in Baudelaire and Brecht. Thanks to the Penguin Modern European Poets series you could for a few shillings give yourself a rudimentary education in European modernism: the great Russians – Ahkmatova, Pasternak, Mandelstam, Tsvetayeva – four poets sustaining one another in the sub-zero chill of Stalin's Russia, a sodality of imaginations; and Apollinaire and Ungaretti – especially, so far as I was concerned, the poems they wrote as soldiers in the Great War. We looked to the precocious Rimbaud, and were only half joking when we said that we would consider ourselves failures if we hadn't published our first slim volumes by our early twenties!

Here are the first two stanzas of Derek Mahon's 'In Belfast' (which he has re-christened 'Spring in Belfast'):

Walking among my own this windy morning
In a tide of sunlight between shower and shower,
I resume my old conspiracy with the wet
Stone and the unwieldy images of the squinting heart.
Once more, as before, I remember not to forget.

There is a perverse pride in being on the side
Of the fallen angels and refusing to get up.

We could *all* be saved by keeping an eye on the hill
At the top of every street, for there it is,
Eternally, if irrelevantly, visible –

When Mahon's poem was published, the Professor of English, Philip Edwards, wrote it out on the blackboard for his students. I felt envious when I heard that. In this poem and in other early pieces like 'Subsidy Bungalows' and 'Glengormley' Mahon shows that the shipyards and the working-class estates of Belfast are just as much a part of the Irish landscape as the Donegal hills or the wilds of Mayo.

In my Trinity rooms we listened again and again to the Harvard Poetry Library recordings of American poets – Robert Frost reading 'After Apple-Picking', the lilt of e. e. cummings, and Wallace Stevens (still my favourite reader of poetry) reciting 'The Idea of Order at Key West':

Oh! blessed rage for order, pale Ramon,
The maker's rage to order words of the sea,
Words of the fragrant portals, dimly-starred,
And of ourselves and of our origins,
In ghostlier demarcations, keener sounds.

We gutted the work of Robert Lowell, Theodore Roethke, Hart Crane. 'In Memoriam', the first of my elegies for my father, was sparked off by Lowell's autobiographical sequence *Life Studies*. And I am still excited by his early masterpiece 'The Quaker Graveyard in Nantucket':

You could cut the brackish winds with a knife
Here in Nantucket, and cast up the time
When the Lord God formed man from the sea's slime
And breathed into his face the breath of life,

> And blue-lung'd combers lumbered to the kill.
> The Lord survives the rainbow of His will.

My most ambitious early poem 'The Hebrides' (which I wrote towards the end of 1964) takes its bearings from 'The Quaker Graveyard' and mixes equal measures of George Herbert and Hart Crane.

In some of his most brilliant poems Herbert creates a repeated pattern of lines of different lengths. In his poem 'Peace', for instance, the metrical pattern consists of lines of ten, four, eight, six, ten and four syllables. Painfully difficult they may be, but these complicated stanzaic shapes with fixed rhyme schemes generate jazzy syncopations and blue notes. Here is a stanza from George Herbert's 'The Flower', one of the loveliest poems in the language:

> And now in age I bud again,
> After so many deaths I live and write;
> I once more smell the dew and rain,
> And relish versing: O, my onely Light,
> It cannot be
> That I am he
> On whom Thy tempests fell all night.

This is lyrical writing of an aching, almost unbearable refinement. Can poetry get any closer to the grain of the language? In my inner ear such quietude attracted the tidal surge of some lines by Hart Crane – from the second poem in his great sequence 'Voyages'. Like 'The Flower', 'Voyages II' is a poem that has just about everything:

> Bind us in time, O Seasons clear, and awe.
> O minstrel galleons of Carib fire,

Bequeath us to no earthly shore until
Is answered in the vortex of our grave
The seal's wide spindrift gaze toward paradise.

George Herbert and Hart Crane might seem odd bedfellows, the Anglican vicar communing with his God and the suicidal lover of sailors cruising the waterfront, but they seem to get along fine in my poem 'The Hebrides':

Here, at the edge of my experience,
Another tide
Along the broken shore extends
A lifetime's wrack and ruin –
No flotsam I may beachcomb now can hide
That water line.

[. . .]

Beyond the lobster pots where plankton spreads
Porpoises turn.
Seals slip over the cockle beds.
Undertow dishevels
Seaweed in the shallows – and I discern
My sea levels.

'The Hebrides' is dedicated to Eavan Boland. Derek Mahon introduced me to her in 1964. She held forth about poetry with extraordinary flair and authority. She challenged me. Indeed, she intimidated me. I have never been much good in intellectual debate. I think Boland noticed how few opinions I have. In answer to her questioning I wrote 'The

Hebrides', and dedicated it to her. I remember reciting it to her in a Dublin pub – by heart. I meant it to be both gift and confrontation. The subtext was: 'This is as brilliant as I shall ever be.' I hope that our minds meet on the Hebrides.

In the anthology *Watching the River Flow* (1999) I write about the cultural apartheid that operated between the two Dublin universities:

> Extraordinarily, there was next to no literary interchange between TCD and UCD (let alone Cork where Eiléan Ní Chuilleanáin was a student). If we Trinity poets were learning from each other, how much more skilled and versed we might have become had we jousted with the likes of Michael Hartnett, Eamonn Grennan and, later, Paul Durcan who were inhabiting a parallel universe in Earlsfort Terrace.

Poetry did bring us all together in the end, but long after our college days.

Towards the end of my Dublin sojourn I shared with Mahon a malodorous basement flat in Merrion Square. I describe the Beckettian scene in my memoir *Tuppenny Stung* [1994] and I record that: 'These were fulfilling rather than happy times. Our friendship and our abilities were often stretched as far as they could go.' By this time Mahon had published some extraordinarily accomplished poems. I owed much to his brilliant practice, his verve and edginess. But I myself had been travelling quickly, without taking a breath, from my rather wan juvenilia to the aspiring shapes of my first reasonable poems.

I was punch-drunk when I arrived back in Belfast in 1963. So at first I didn't accurately register Seamus Heaney's early poems. They sound so natural it is easy to miss their originality – poems such as

'Digging' and 'Death of a Naturalist', which were dissected at sessions of the now over-mythologised Belfast Group. Initially I had no desire to attend the Group. Prompted, I now know, by Heaney, Philip Hobsbaum the prime mover invited my fiancée and me along.

I began to enjoy what was for me as a lapsed classicist a new experience – practical criticism. In *Tuppenny Stung* I refer to 'the kitchen heat of the discussions', and suggest that friendship 'remains for me the most important legacy of The Group. The poetry would have happened anyway. But Hobsbaum brought some of us together and generated an atmosphere of controversy and excitement.' After one fierce disagreement (not, I might add, at a Group meeting) I walked backwards out of a crowded room, shouting at Hobsbaum and, from a parcel under my arm, dropping sticks of rhubarb on to the floor!

Perhaps Hobsbaum's hot advocacy of Heaney's work got in the way of my own appreciation of it – but only initially. Images such as the frogs at the flax dam 'Poised like mud grenades, their blunt heads farting' or the butcher's-shop turkey invoked as 'A skin bag plumped with inky putty' or the clothes of the milk-churners 'spattered/ with flabby milk' – such images have been lodged in my synapses ever since those early days. It is as though the particulars of life on an Ulster farm were inventing a language for themselves – a dialect that our senses seem always to have known. Take, for instance, 'Cow in Calf':

> Slapping her out of the byre is like slapping
> a great bag of seed. My hand
> tingled as if strapped, but I had to
> hit her again and again and
> heard the blows plump like a depth-charge
> far in her gut.

Depth-charges, indeed. Awakenings. In a barn on a hot summer's day something almost religious can happen, something both visionary and matter-of-fact:

> A scythe's edge, a clean spade, a pitch-fork's prongs:
> Slowly bright objects formed when you went in.

Was I bit high-handed with my new friend? Heaney held his ground in any case, and stood up to Mahon and me when we were being bossy one evening. I can still hear him saying: 'I'd love to write like you boys but I've got to go on my own and write my kind of poems.' Wonderful. Nevertheless, I sense that his move from the early paragraph-like poems to the sculpted quatrains of 'Follower' and 'Personal Helicon' owes something to what Mahon and I were attempting. In 'Personal Helicon', his beautiful lyric about wells and boyhood and imagination, the poet sinks an artesian well into the reader's subconscious and 'set[s] the darkness echoing':

> One, in a brickyard, with a rotted board top.
> I savoured the rich crash when a bucket
> Plummeted down at the end of a rope.
> So deep you saw no reflection in it.
>
> A shallow one under a dry stone ditch
> Fructified like any aquarium.
> When you dragged out long roots from the soft mulch
> A white face hovered over the bottom.

The poetry we wrote then, indeed much of the poetry that has since emerged from the North of Ireland, has been dismissed by unsympathetic critics under the heading 'the well-made poem'. This is meant as a pejorative term, but it is in fact tautological. Any poem that works – be it expansive in Walt Whitman's style or tightly packed à la Emily Dickinson – is bound to be well made. You might as well talk about a 'well-made flower', or a 'well-made snowflake'.

Yeats said that he wrote in form because if he didn't he wouldn't know when to stop. Like Samuel Beckett I prefer the word 'shape' to 'form'. At Trinity during a course on Aristotle's *Poetics* our Greek professor W. B. Stanford told us to come back the following week with our own definitions of poetry. Mine was: 'If prose is a river, then poetry's a fountain.' I still feel that's pretty good because it suggests that 'form' (or 'shape') is releasing rather than constraining. The fountain is shapely and at the same time free-flowing. The American poet Stanley Kunitz puts the case for form perfectly: 'A badly made thing falls apart. It takes only a few years for most of the energy to leak out of a defective work of art. To put it simply, conservation of energy is the function of form.'

I introduced Mahon to Heaney, and Heaney introduced me to James Simmons. Simmons melded the energies of popular culture with his own lyric gifts. The best of his work – poems like 'Stephano Remembers' and 'From the Irish', songs like 'The Silent Marriage' and 'Claudy' – will live on. He founded *The Honest Ulsterman* in 1968 and, after a while, handed the editorship over to Michael Foley and Frank Ormsby. Foley (who favoured the more demotic Simmons) christened Mahon and Heaney and me The Tight-Assed Trio. (It might be worth recalling that *The Honest Ulsterman* School of Literary Criticism went in for fine shades of discrimination: there were three types of bad poetry: Shite, Dogs' Shite and Mad Dogs' Shite.)

In the early 1970s, at the beginning of my stint as Literature Officer with the Arts Council of Northern Ireland, Ormsby and Foley called to discuss their grant with me. I had just published in the *New Statesman* two verse letters – one addressed to Mahon, the other to Heaney.

307

I had submitted to *The Honest Ulsterman* a third verse letter (addressed to James Simmons). I foolishly presumed they'd be delighted to print it. The supplicant editors told me: 'Those two poems in the *New Statesman* were bad enough; but with this third one to Jimmy Simmons you've disappeared up your own arse completely!'

The Tight-Assed Trio was kept on its toes. In the late 1960s Heaney showed me some poems by a schoolboy called Paul Muldoon. A little later in 1968 I met Muldoon after a poetry reading in Armagh. Eventually he joined the BBC as a producer, and I embarked on another exacting friendship. No sooner had the Tight-Assed Trio begun to work out how things might be done, than a brilliant new generation came along hell-bent on deconstructing our best efforts – Paul Muldoon, Medbh McGuckian, Ciaran Carson, Frank Ormsby, Tom Paulin.

I am now grateful for that challenge – and for the stimulation of the next group of Northern poets – Peter McDonald, Sinead Morrissey, Leontia Flynn, Nick Laird, Alan Gillis. (The work of an even younger cluster of live wires was recently showcased in the locally published anthology *Incertus*.) So, there has been little or no opportunity for self-congratulation or self-importance. This has been a lucky chance for me, a gift of life. Who was it who suggested that self-importance inscribes its own gravestone?

Over the years my poetry has become simpler. When I revise I seek to simplify and clarify. An ideal poem, for me, would be 'Tall Nettles' by Edward Thomas. A poet I first read at Trinity, he has by now moved to the centre of my imaginative life:

> Tall nettles cover up, as they have done
> These many springs, the rusty harrow, the plough
> Long worn out, and the roller made of stone:
> Only the elm butt tops the nettles now.

This corner of the farmyard I like most:
As well as any bloom upon a flower
I like the dust on the nettles, never lost
Except to prove the sweetness of a shower.

Like George Herbert, Edward Thomas possesses the poetic equivalent of perfect pitch. I have revisited 'Tall Nettles' hundreds of times. Like all true poems it is always brand new – 'Worn new/ Again and again', as Thomas himself says in his poem 'Words'. Regarding subject-matter he made a statement which I consider crucial: 'Anything, however small, may make a poem; nothing, however great, is certain to.'

Edward Thomas was killed at the Battle of Arras in April 1917. Other geniuses died in the Great War: Wilfred Owen, Isaac Rosenberg, Charles Sorley. I revere these lost soldier-poets as well as those who survived the slaughter – Siegfried Sassoon, Robert Graves, Edmund Blunden, Ivor Gurney. It is wrong to confine such writers to the dubiously simplified category of 'war poet'. When I read a poem like Owen's 'Insensibility' or Rosenberg's 'Dead Man's Dump' –

None saw their spirits' shadow shake the grass,
Or stood aside for the half used life to pass
Out of those doomed nostrils and the doomed mouth

– I picture the young Sophocles and the young Aeschylus trudging under the weight of their kitbags through the terrible mud.

In terms of scale there is no way we can compare the Troubles with the industrialised devastation of the Great War. But I am reminded of the War Poets when I consider my contemporaries and our apprenticeships in a damaged society. Owen's desperate desire to befriend and impress Sassoon feels familiar to me; as does the poetic transformation that Sassoon's (and Graves's) encouragement brought about in Owen's writing. After the war Graves and Sassoon befriended and helped Edmund Blunden; and then, in his turn, Blunden edited collections of Wilfred Owen's and Ivor Gurney's poems. As they tried to make sense of the nightmare of the trenches the War Poets were listening to each other.

In the early 1970s poets here were as dumbfounded as most people by the ferocity of the violence. Seamus Heaney has written of the 'search for images and symbols adequate to our predicament'. And in 1971, in a survey of the arts in Ulster called *Causeway,* I suggested that the poet 'would be inhuman if he did not respond to tragic events in his own community and a poor artist if he did not seek to endorse that response imaginatively . . .' I added that the poet 'needs time in which to allow the raw material of experience to settle to an imaginative depth . . . He is not some sort of super-journalist commenting with unfaltering spontaneity on events immediately after they have happened. Rather, as Wilfred Owen stated, it is the poet's duty to warn . . .'

In such monumental poems as 'Easter, 1916', 'Meditations in Time of Civil War', 'Nineteen Hundred and Nineteen', W. B. Yeats loomed large, an inescapable exemplar. More than any other poet he helped us to find our way through the minefield. Like Wilfred Owen in the trenches, Yeats demonstrated that the complex, intense lyric is capable of encompassing extreme experience:

> Now days are dragon-ridden, the nightmare
> Rides upon sleep: a drunken soldiery
> Can leave the mother, murdered at her door,
> To crawl in her own blood, and go scot-free . . .

We did not write in Yeats's shadow, as some would have it, but in the lighthouse beam of his huge accomplishment.

To be a poet is to be alive to both precursors and contemporaries. As regards my contemporaries from Northern Ireland, this may have been so in a further sense as poets here, with their different backgrounds and perspectives, reacted to the Troubles. Poems are aware of each other. No poem is a solo flight. In his wonderful lyric 'The Friendship of Young Poets', the Scottish poet Douglas Dunn conjures up an ideal scene:

> There is a boat on the river now, and
> Two young men, one rowing, one reading aloud.
> Their shirt sleeves fill with wind, and from the oars
> Drop scales of perfect river like melting glass.

The American poet and critic Randall Jarrell famously tells us: 'A good poet is someone who manages, in a lifetime of standing out in thunderstorms, to be struck by lightning five or six times; a dozen or two dozen times and he is great.' And Rilke says somewhere: 'You ought to wait and gather sense and sweetness for a whole lifetime . . . and then, at the very end, you might perhaps be able to write ten good lines.' The enterprise often feels like a long wait for something that does not necessarily happen. In 'How Poetry Comes to Me' the American Gary Snyder writes a poem about writing a poem:

> It comes blundering over the
> Boulders at night, it stays
> Frightened outside the
> Range of my campfire
> I go to meet it at the
> Edge of the light . . .

It is mysterious why some people write good poems and then stop; and mysterious why others persist. I think being a poet is different from being a writer. Some poets are writers as well but they are usually protecting a core. Poetry can't be created to order. You can't write your way out of a poetic block. I have no idea where poetry comes from, or where it goes when it disappears. Silence is part of the enterprise.

For me Keith Douglas is a pivotal and still underestimated figure in modern poetry. As an undergraduate he was encouraged by Edmund Blunden. In 1944 he died on the Normandy beaches. He was only twenty-four. When he was barely twenty, Keith Douglas had this to say:

> Poetry is like a man, whom thinking you know all his movements and appearance you will presently come upon in such a posture that for a moment you can hardly believe it a position of the limbs you know. So thinking you have set bounds to the nature of poetry, you will soon discover something outside your bounds which they should evidently contain.

Moving one's 'bounds' as a writer of poetry involves, invariably, the renewal of rhythms. To quote Yeats again: 'As I altered my syntax, I altered my intellect.'

I myself am drawn more and more to poets who do things that I can't do. I have been enjoying the New York School of poets who came into prominence mid-century, at the same time as the Abstract Expressionists: in particular Frank O'Hara, James Schuyler and Kenneth Koch (whose reading here in Belfast I introduced a few years ago. There's an elegy for Koch in *Snow Water*). Frank O'Hara finds hilarious ways to be serious. He invites us, as Yeats puts it, to get down off our stilts. In his cod manifesto, 'Personism', he discusses poetic form:

312

As for measure and other technical apparatus, that's just common sense: if you're going to buy a pair of pants you want them to be tight enough so everyone will want to go to bed with you.

(So, perhaps, after all, the improvisatory Frank O'Hara belongs with the Tight-Assed Trio!)

How does a poem like James Schuyler's 'Sleep' work? It was written in a mental hospital. It mentions St Valentine's Day. The poet's eye wanders around the institution and records seemingly random particulars in a mode that manages to be both casual and ceremonious:

> The friends who come to see you
> And the friends who don't.
> The weather in the window.
> A pierced ear.
> The mounting tension and the spasm.
> A paper-lace doily on a small plate.
> Tangerines.
> A day in February: heart-
> Shaped cookies on St Valentine's.
> Like Christopher, a discarded saint.
> A tough woman with black hair.
> 'I got to set my wig straight.'
> A gold and silver day begins to wane.
> A crescent moon.
> Ice on the window.
> Give my love to, oh, anybody.

I don't know many lines as heartbreaking as that last line: 'Give my love to, oh, anybody.'

One thing I have learnt from the New York poets is that good art is often nobly dishevelled. Throughout my fifty years of writing, when the creative buzz comes on, I have felt sizeable, capacious like Walt Whitman; but when I've written the poem and typed it out I realise that I am still Emily Dickinson – the pernickety Emily who, when asked for her opinion of *Leaves of Grass*, said of Whitman, 'I never read his book – but was told that he was disgraceful.'

I have worshipped Emily Dickinson since my Trinity days (there's a poem about her in my first collection). I read Whitman of course, but the penny has only recently dropped. How could I have managed without him for so long? How can there be 'a jovial hullabaloo' without Walt Whitman? He will be the last poet I'll quote from this evening – from his sequence 'Sands at Seventy'. 'To Get the Final Lilt of Songs' is a short poem about old age and about reading and writing poetry:

To get the final lilt of songs,
To penetrate the inmost lore of poets – to know the mighty ones,
Job, Homer, Eschylus, Dante, Shakespeare, Tennyson, Emerson;
To diagnose the shifting-delicate tints of love and pride and doubt
– to truly understand,
To encompass these, the last keen faculty and entrance-price,
Old age, and what it brings from all its past experiences.

For six months in 1993 I was Writer-in-Residence (Writer Fellow) at my old university, Trinity College. From a large number of submitted portfolios I selected for my creative writing workshop a small group of undergraduates. I'm still proud of my choices. Some of those students have gone on to make names for themselves: Caitríona O'Reilly, David Wheatley, Justin Quinn, Sinead Morrissey. (The novelist Claire Kilroy was also a key member of my group.) I have kept in touch with all of them. Sinead Morrissey's achievements and reputation grow apace. She now teaches creative writing here at Queen's. As I begin my professorial sojourn I look to her (and to another brilliant young poet Leontia Flynn) for guidance and inspiration.

Now, as Ireland Professor of Poetry, I feel that I have come full circle. As I start to meet students in the three universities, I am reminded of something the American poet Donald Hall says about his life in poetry. Hall describes the effort to write poetry as having 'conversations with the dead great ones and with the living young.'

Transcript of a lecture given in the Great Hall, Queen's University, Belfast, St Valentine's Night 2008

IN MEMORIAM

Joe Cowan
Alec Reid

'ONE WIDE EXPANSE':
A RETURN TO THE CLASSICS

I

Much have I travell'd in the realms of gold,
  And many goodly states and kingdoms seen;
  Round many western islands have I been
Which bards in fealty to Apollo hold.
Oft of one wide expanse had I been told
  That deep-brow'd Homer ruled as his demesne;
  Yet did I never breathe its pure serene
Till I heard Chapman speak out loud and bold:
Then felt I like some watcher of the skies
  When a new planet swims into his ken;
Or like stout Cortez when with eagle eyes
  He star'd at the Pacific – and all his men
Looked at each other with a wild surmise –
  Silent upon a peak in Darien.

That, of course, is John Keats's great sonnet 'On First Looking into Chapman's Homer'. The 'wide expanse' is open to everyone. Keats, after all, didn't know Greek: he had just discovered 'the realms of gold' in the majestic translations of George Chapman, the Renaissance English poet. Today several translations of the *Iliad* and the *Odyssey* are available in paperback (including Chapman's). Over the last five decades the literatures of Greece and Rome have again become an abundant source for poets writing in English.

For instance, since the 1960s Irish writers have found in Greek tragedy ways of dealing with the Troubles. One thinks of Tom Paulin's *Riot Act* which portrayed the individual – Antigone – confronting authority. Seamus Heaney also turned to Sophocles's *Antigone* (which he called *The Burial at Thebes*) and to *Philoctetes* (which became *The Cure at Troy* with its celebrated chorus:

> History says, *Don't hope*
> *On this side of the grave.*
> But then, once in a lifetime
> The longed-for tidal wave
> Of justice can rise up,
> And hope and history rhyme.

Derek Mahon produced a witty *Bacchae* and in *Oedipus* a sombre conflation of Sophocles's Oedipus plays. In terms of theatrical excitement Brendan Kennelly's *The Trojan Women* has been for me the most thrilling adaptation. Tom Murphy, Aidan Mathews, Frank McGuinness, Brian Friel, Marina Carr and Colin Teevan make it a long list of contemporary Irish writers indebted to the classics – lining up behind Synge and Yeats who called the Greek and Latin authors 'the builders of my soul' – and, of course, not forgetting Louis MacNeice, the brilliance of whose version of the *Agamemnon* must have something to do with his being, out of them all, the only fully fledged classical scholar! (The other plays I've mentioned are, broadly speaking, translations of translations.)

The last few years have seen a steady flow of books about the Classical world. Clearly publishers believe that Classical scholarship sells. In the *Observer* last September Tom Holland wrote: 'People are not stupid – they know when they are missing out on something interesting and important. If the education system fails to give it to them, then it can hardly be surprising that they will look for it elsewhere, in works of popular history, perhaps, and in other media as well.' Feature films and TV dramas come to mind, Hollywood blockbusters and computer games. In his forthcoming edited collection of essays *Living Classics* Stephen Harrison discusses the 'paradox that classical texts have achieved a high profile in contemporary literature at a time when fewer people than ever can read these works in the original languages'. Despite this trend, and after something of a lull, an increasing number of students now want to study Latin and Greek. In 2000, there were a mere 150 non-selective state schools in England offering Latin; now there are more than 500. The British government is in fact putting both languages *back* onto the curriculum. But there is now a shortage of qualified teachers! Seven years ago I (and others) tried to persuade Queen's University to keep Latin and Greek on the curriculum when it had decided to close down the Classics Department. I shall let my letter to the newspapers speak for itself:

As an honorary graduate of Queen's University, I am angered and bewildered by the Academic Council's decision to close down the Classics Department.

With respect to politics, philosophy, language, poetry, drama, architecture, mathematics, the sciences, sport we are all of us three quarters Greek and Roman, whether or not we realise it.

The so-called academic planners who would close down Latin and Greek are wiping out a crucial part of the map by which we know ourselves and find our way.

Have the barbarians arrived? Yes. But, worse, they are in charge.

I pray that the university will think again.

So far, it hasn't shown any sign of thinking again.

Our Professor of Greek at Trinity College, the great W. B. Stanford, used to quote Plato: 'chalepa ta kala' – 'the beautiful things are diffi-cult'. Reading the classics could be tough going – even tougher was trying to compose prose and, sometimes, *verse* in Greek and Latin. I hope that my own poetry has been strengthened by these rigours. Much contemporary writing sounds to my ears syntactically flabby, linguistically impoverished. In losing touch with Latin (and Greek) it has lost its backbone.

II

I have been haunted by Homer for fifty years. Now I would like to say something about what 'that wide expanse' has meant to me. I treasure my battered copy of Stanford's edition of the *Odyssey*. Charlie Fay, our Classics master at Inst, encouraged us to write the date at the end of each book of the *Odyssey* when we had finished reading it. I completed my first, Book X, just before Christmas 1956. There in the pernickety hand of the classical annotator is the date: 17. xii. 56. I was just seven-teen, but like some elderly scholar I filled the margins with notes about the unseen digamma, the gnomic aorist, epexegesis, sociative datives and other technicalities that now mean little or nothing to me. During each class we would slowly translate ten or twenty lines, and then read the Greek aloud. Somehow the Homeric sunshine broke through all that cloudy donkeywork. I loved the sound of the Greek, the bumpy hexameters, the clash of the broad vowels, the way lips and tongue are vigorously exercised, hammer and tongs. And of course I adored the stories.

Fay was an intimidating and sometimes cruel figure. He had me studying the *Agamemnon* when I was only sixteen. He used to knit in class – serious knitting – socks and gloves. Once, when I was half-way through a chorus in the *Agamemnon* – gasping to find the main verb

– he shouted at me: 'Quiet, scum, I'm just turning the heel!' Many years later, when I was well into my fifties, I spotted him in the interval crowd at the Lyric Theatre in Belfast. I thought 'Why the hell not?' and approached him. 'May I buy you a drink, Dr Fay?' He eyed me up and down and sighed theatrically: 'Beneath those whiskers do I discern the idle Longley?'

During the summer holidays Fay attended advanced study courses in Oxford and Cambridge. He came back from one given by the legendary Greek scholar Eduard Fraenkel to tell this teenager about the influence of primitive wedding ceremonies on the choruses of Aeschylus. He pushed me to the limits of my abilities. The Classics for him were character forming like long-distance running. Like playing chess, they were also about being clever. Thanks to the drilling I received at Inst, I was able to survive my first two undergraduate years at Trinity College Dublin without doing much work. My career as a lapsed classicist had begun.

Stanford believed that the *Odyssey* and the *Iliad* had been sung or chanted, and bravely gave us a demonstration.

ἄνδρα μοι ἔννεπε, Μοῦσα, πολύτροπον, ὃς μάλα πολλὰ
πλάγχθη, ἐπεὶ Τροίης ἱερὸν πτολίεθρον ἔπερσε
πολλῶν δ᾽ ἀνθρώπων ἴδεν ἄστεα καὶ νόον ἔγνω,
πολλὰ δ᾽ ὅ γ᾽ ἐν πόντῳ πάθεν ἄλγεα ὃν κατὰ θυμόν,
ἀρνύμενος ἥν τε ψυχὴν καὶ νόστον ἑταίρων.

Stanford deepened my love of Homer as much through the speculations in his study *The Ulysses Theme* as through the scholarly notes at the back of his edition. I became obsessed with James Joyce's *Ulysses*. It was intoxicating to wander from a Stanford lecture on, say, the 'Circe' episode, to the dilapidated Turkish bathhouse on the street behind Trinity College and other nearby sites that Joyce had used as settings for his great novel. My earliest Homer-influenced poems were filtered through the shabby Dublin fanlights of *Ulysses*. In 'Odyssey', Odysseus takes on the characteristics of a seedy Leopold Bloom:

> When I sight you playing ball on the sand,
> A suggestion of hair under your arms,
> Or, in shallows, wearing only the waves,
> I unpack strictly avuncular charms –
> To lose these sea legs I walk on land . . .

And 'Nausicaa' is overshadowed by Gerty McDowell:

> You scarcely raise a finger to the tide.
> Pavilions, those days-off at the seaside
>
> Collapse about your infinite arrest –
> He sees your cove more clearly than the rest.

After these Joyce-inflected poems from the mid-sixties, I didn't really get back onto the Homeric wavelength until 1989/1990 – a gap of more than twenty years – when I wrote a cluster of poems based on Odysseus's complicated reunions with his mother, father, nurse and dog. The first of these, 'Eurycleia', came disguised in prose as my *own* nurse, Lena Hardy. A country girl from County Fermanagh, Lena came to Belfast in 1939 to help my mother look after her twin babies while my father was off at the war. Lena became a surrogate mother. When she left at the end of the war, I was disconsolate. I celebrated her in my memoir 'Tuppenny Stung'. Here is the first sentence: 'I began by loving the wrong woman.' It took me some time to realise that Lena was *my* Eurycleia. When I came to write the poem, the opening line of my memoir did not require much adjustment: 'I began like Odysseus by loving the wrong woman.' The old nurse bathes Odysseus and recognises him when she touches a telltale scar. Loving-kindness irradiates the story:

> Such pain and happiness, her eyes filling with tears,
> Her old voice cracking as she stroked his beard and whispered
> 'You are my baby boy for sure and I didn't know you
> Until I had fondled my master's body all over.'

This poem matters to me because it sparked off the Homeric adventure of my fifties and sixties, my return to the Classics after a quarter of a century. From the outset, in my Homeric poems I pushed against the narrative momentum. The *Iliad* and the *Odyssey* are page-turners. We go on reading to find out what happens next. But in my poems I 'freeze-frame' passages to release their lyric potential.

A week after I had written 'Eurycleia' I was holidaying in a hilltop village in Tuscany. Leaning out of the bathroom window to admire the surrounding mountains I spotted an elderly neighbour tending his vines beyond the last houses. Old Cesare reminded me of my father, then of Odysseus's father. I had brought with me to Cardoso the two Loeb volumes of the *Odyssey* and E. V. Rieu's underrated translation. With these to assist my creakingly unpractised Greek, I wrote 'Laertes' quickly and with a sense of release. Laertes is in mourning for his son Odysseus. He doesn't realise that Odysseus is standing in front of him, alive and well. The poem begins:

When he found Laertes alone on the tidy terrace, hoeing
Around a vine, disreputable in his gardening duds,
Patched and grubby, leather gaiters protecting his shins
Against brambles, gloves as well, and, to cap it all,
Sure sign of his deep depression, a goatskin duncher . . .

The longer lines, sparked off by the Homeric hexameter, let loose new rhythms in my head. And 'duncher', the quaint Belfast dialect word for a flat cap (which caused some alarm among the fact-checkers of the *New Yorker* when the poem was published there) – 'duncher' fixed for me the tone of this fairly free version. The poem ends:

. . . Laertes recognised his son and, weak at the knees,
Dizzy, flung his arms around the neck of great Odysseus
Who drew the old man fainting to his breast and held him there
And cradled like driftwood the bones of his dwindling father.

The eighteen lines make up one long swaying sentence. For reasons I don't fully understand the syntax of many of my poems unwinds through a single sentence. (Perhaps it has something to do with all that time spent on periodic structure in Latin and Greek prose composition.) I also seem obsessively reliant on symmetry. Three weeks after 'Laertes' I wrote a companion piece about Odysseus meeting his mother in the underworld. Another eighteen-line poem in one continuous sentence, 'Anticleia' begins with two long conditional subordinate clauses and ends as a question:

And if, having given her blood to drink and talked about home,
You lunge forward three times to hug her and three times
Like a shadow or idea she vanishes through your arms

And you ask her why she keeps avoiding your touch and weep
Because here is your mother and even here in Hades
You could comfort each other in a shuddering embrace,
Will she explain that the sinews no longer bind her flesh
And bones, that the irresistible fire has demolished these,
That the soul takes flight like a dream and flutters in the sky,
That this is what happens to human beings when they die?

I left out a fair amount of background material. I was not concerned with the narrative. I was looking for an intense lyric to set beside 'Laertes'. The two poems turned out to be the same length and that felt like some kind of endorsement, like a silversmith's hallmark. I compressed the stories to release the personal meaning. Homer enabled me to write belated lamentations for my mother and father.

Homer also empowered me to comment obliquely on the Northern Irish Troubles. I wrote 'Anticleia' when I was in a remote townland in County Mayo called Carrigskeewaun. The landscape there often looks like a sodden Ithaca. Odysseus would have recognised the whitewashed farms and outbuildings. He would have understood the sticky intimate violence of our tawdry little civil war that was to drag on for thirty years. In Carrigskeewaun, with a cardboard box full of translations and commentaries, I started work on the episode where Odysseus slaughters the suitors. I had recently read *The Shankill Butchers*, a study by Martin Dillon of a psychopathic loyalist gang who tortured and murdered many Catholics. These horrors haunted the composition of 'The Butchers'. I admit to this with some reluctance because I do not want to be seen as the literal-minded besmircher of a great literary masterpiece. Lyric treatment of Book XXII's bloodthirsty ferocity demanded tumultuous syntax, twenty-eight fleet-footed alexandrine-like lines straining to the limit in one long sentence. I focused on the similes – 'like fish', 'like a lion', 'like long-winged thrushes', 'like bats' – and I Hibernicised my version with such details as the 'bog-meadow full of bog-asphodels' and 'sheughs' (the Bog Meadows are in west Belfast and 'sheugh' is a Scots word for ditch). My biggest liberty was to skip Book XXIII and reconnect the frenzy of the bloodbath with the eerie opening of Book XXIV. Here Hermes accompanies the suitors' ghosts down into the underworld (in my version I include the souls of the housemaids whom Homer seems to have forgotten about – my little feminist gesture!). I felt very close to Homer. Writing 'The Butchers' was an electrifying experience. I worked on it through the night. I was shaking when I read it aloud to my wife at dawn:

And when they had dragged Melanthios's corpse into the haggard
And cut off his nose and ears and cock and balls, a dog's dinner,
Odysseus, seeing the need for whitewash and disinfectant,
Fumigated the house and the outhouses, so that Hermes
Like a clergyman might wave the supernatural baton
With which he resurrects or hypnotises those he chooses,
And waken and round up the suitors' souls, and the housemaids',
Like bats gibbering in the nooks of their mysterious cave
When out of the clusters that dangle from the rocky ceiling
One of them drops and squeaks, so their souls were bat-squeaks
As they flittered after Hermes, their deliverer, who led them
Along the clammy sheughs, then past the oceanic streams
And the white rock, the sun's gatepost in that dreamy region,
Until they came to a bog-meadow full of bog-asphodels
Where the residents are ghosts or images of the dead.

Sometimes word-play on its own can inspire a translation – the hidden depths of a pun. In 'The Butchers' there was no room for Phemios,

Ithaca's poet-in-residence, and Medon the toastmaster, a rather ridiculous pair who have escaped the rage of Odysseus by hiding. I wanted to give them a comic poem of their own in Ulster-Scots. The word for 'to clean', 'to set in order', is 'redd' in Ulster-Scots (it is still widely used in Ulster). I visualised white walls splashed with blood. The act of cleansing is a bloody one. 'Redd' sparked off the poem 'Phemios & Medon'. Pleading for mercy the cringing poet

> Makes a ram-stam for Odysseus, grammels his knees,
> Then bannies and bams wi this highfalutin blether . . .

I truffled through various Scots-English dictionaries (including the then recently published *Concise Ulster Dictionary* – a rumbustious treasure-trove full of words I was discouraged from using in Primary School!) and I unearthed some marvellous words – 'scoot-hole', 'gabble-blooter', 'belly-bachelor'. I turned 'winged words' into 'highfalutin blether'. For the *wily* Odysseus 'long-headed' sounded just right. Homer's language is, after all, an amalgam of dialects. At the end of the poem Odysseus addresses the toastmaster Medon:

> Long-headed Odysseus smiles at him and says: 'Wheesht!
> You may thank Telemachos for this chance to wise up
> And pass on the message of oul decency. Go out
> And sit in the haggard away from this massacre,
> You and the well-spoken poet, while I redd the house.'
> They hook it and hunker fornent the altar of Zeus,
> Afeard and skelly-eyed, keeking everywhere for death.

The violence towards the end of the *Odyssey* brings us back full circle to the warfare of the *Iliad*. The *Iliad* is probably our greatest poem about war and death. Poetry had to change after the Iliad. It did change, but it didn't get any better! A bit like music after J. S. Bach. Great works of art are packed with smaller works of art for opportunistic painters and poets and composers to purloin. I produced five reflections of the *Iliad* in 1994, mirror fragments. Some of these have a Northern Irish intonation – 'The Helmet' for instance, a short lyric about Hector's farewell to his wife and child. (The loyalist paramilitary leader Johnnie 'Mad Dog' Adair of the UDA referred to his son as 'Mad Pup'. He did, alas, come to mind while I was writing this poem.) When Hector's helmet frightens his baby son:

> His daddy laughed, his mammy laughed, and his daddy
> Took off the helmet and laid it on the ground to gleam,
> Then kissed the babbie and dandled him in his arms and
> Prayed that his son might grow up bloodier than him.

The magical simile with which Homer compares the campfires on the plain of Troy to the night sky has often reminded me of County Mayo where, in the electric-light-free darkness, I can gaze up into the depths of the Milky Way. When I translated this passage, it seemed natural to include in 'The Campfires' some place names and features from my corner of the Mayo landscape:

> There are balmy nights – not a breath, constellations
> Resplendent in the sky around a dazzling moon –
> When a clearance high in the atmosphere unveils
> The boundlessness of space, and all the stars are out
> Lighting up hill-tops, glens, headlands, vantage
> Points like Tonakeera and Allaran where the tide
> Turns into Killary, where salmon run from the sea,
> Where the shepherd smiles on his luminous townland.

Occasionally a poem breaks free into the world at large. In August 1994 there were strong rumours that the IRA were about to declare a ceasefire. I had been reading in Book XXIV the account of King Priam's visit to Achilles' tent to beg for the body of his son Hector. Power shifts from the mighty general to the old king who reminds Achilles of his own father and awakens in him suppressed emotions of tenderness. Psychologically it feels pretty modern. I wanted to compress this scene's two hundred lines into a short lyric, publish it and make my minuscule contribution to the peace process. I got started on 'Ceasefire' by tinkering with the sequence of events. Priam kisses Achilles' hand at the *beginning* of their encounter. I put this at the *end* of my poem and inadvertently created a rhyming couplet. Three quatrains followed. I sent my sonnet to the then literary editor of the *Irish Times*, John Banville, who called 'Stop Press' and published it on the Saturday immediately following the IRA's declaration of a ceasefire from midnight on 31 August 1994.

I

Put in mind of his own father and moved to tears
Achilles took him by the hand and pushed the old king
Gently away, but Priam curled up at his feet and
Wept with him until their sadness filled the building.

II

Taking Hector's corpse into his own hands Achilles
Made sure it was washed and, for the old king's sake,
Laid out in uniform, ready for Priam to carry
Wrapped like a present home to Troy at daybreak.

III

When they had eaten together, it pleased them both
To stare at each other's beauty as lovers might,
Achilles built like a god, Priam good-looking still
And full of conversation, who earlier had sighed:

IV

'I get down on my knees and do what must be done
And kiss Achilles' hand, the killer of my son.'

The sort of lyric I write almost always makes its occasion in private. 'Ceasefire' was an exception. But it seems important to keep at a distance whatever political parallels the story may suggest. It was Homer who spoke to us across the millennia. I was only his mouthpiece.

III

Latin poetry is another 'wide expanse'. We find all the genres there – epic, love lyric, elegy, satire. So far I have not followed my Homeric experiments with translations from Virgil's *Aeneid*; rather, I have opted for chamber music intimacies. As an undergraduate I was drawn to the neurotic and strangely à la mode poetry of Sextus Propertius. I tried to capture in English the ebb and flow of the Latin love elegy. In 'A Nightmare' I used a decasyllabic line (with risky enjambments) and a straightforward rhyme scheme, ABAB. Propertius dreams that his lover is drowning:

> Had they seen you then, the mermaids for envy
>   Would have scolded you, so beautiful and
> One of them, a white girl from the blue sea,
>   Loved by mermen and by men on the land.

In 'Cupid' the line lengths vary and the rhyme scheme is more demanding. If he is destroyed by Cupid, the poet says, and with him

> The little genius which is all I have to show,
>> Who will celebrate the face and curls,
>> The fingers and dark eyes of my girl,
> And who will sing of how softly her footsteps go?

In 1976 I met Betty Williams and Mairead Corrigan in a Belfast pub shortly after they had won the Nobel Peace Prize. I congratulated them on their great honour and on their movement's newspaper *Peace News*, but suggested they were publishing feeble poems in it. 'If you don't like the friggin poems, why don't you write one for us!' Betty Williams demanded. That evening I opened my Loeb edition of Tibullus at – unbelievably – 'Quis fuit, horrendos primus qui protulit enses?' The coincidence galvanised me and over a few intense days I wrote 'Peace'. I translated Tibullus's opening lines as: 'Who was responsible for the very first arms deal –/ The man of iron who thought of marketing the sword?' I chose a ten-line stanza and risked being left with too few lines at the end, or too many. My gamble paid off. There are seven ten-line stanzas:

> I want to live until the white hairs shine above
> A pensioner's memories of better days. Meanwhile
> I would like peace to be my partner on the farm,
> Peace personified: oxen under the curved yoke;
> Compost for the vines, grape-juice turning into wine,
> Vintage years handed down from father to son;
> Hoe and ploughshares gleaming, while in some dark corner
> Rust keeps the soldier's grisly weapons in their place;

The labourer steering his wife and children home
In a hay cart from the fields, a trifle sozzled.

In 'Peace' each stanza is a self-contained argument. I end the poem
with a flourish that stretches but does not, I trust, distort the Latin:

> As for me, I want a woman
> To come and fondle my ears of wheat and let apples
> Overflow between her breasts. I shall call her Peace.

In 1992 I was invited by Michael Hofmann and James Lasdun to
contribute to a collection of versions from Ovid's *Metamorphoses*. For
After Ovid I translated one of the loveliest stories in the world, the tale
of faithful Baucis and Philemon's encounter with the gods and how
Jupiter rewards their hospitality and generosity of spirit. I began at the
end of the poem and worked backwards. Again, as with 'Peace', I was
in luck. The story in my version of 'Baucis and Philemon' progresses
through eighteen self-contained five-line stanzas, many of them little
chronicles of workaday metamorphosis: the embers that turn 'leaves
and dry bark' into flames; the cabbage and smoked bacon 'simmered
in bubbling water to make a stew'; the sofa and mattress that a simple
coverlet transforms into a throne for the gods. The old couple's humility and loving-kindness light up the story and throw a halo around
mundane objects. These 'everyday miracles' set the scene for the
poem's supernatural wonders: the wine jug that 'filled itself up again';
the cottage that 'became a church'; and, finally, the old couple's transfiguration as their wish to die together is granted: 'As tree-tops over-
grew their smiles they called in unison/ "Goodbye, my dear"'. I did not
leave out one of Ovid's affectionate details. And at the close I added
a couple of my own:

> Two trees are grafted together where their two bodies stood.
> I add my flowers to bouquets in the branches by saying
> 'Treat those whom God loves as your local gods – a blackthorn
> Or a standing stone. Take care of caretakers and watch
> Over the nightwatchman and the nightwatchman's wife.'

It is surprising to find in *Metamorphoses* this unironical celebration of a long happy marriage. In their introduction Hofmann and Lasdun give us an astonishing list of what we can normally expect from Ovid's great work: 'holocaust, plague, sexual harassment, rape, incest, seduction, pollution, sex-change, suicide, hetero- and homosexual love, torture, war, child-battering, depression and intoxication'. I agree with them when they say that the stories 'offer a mythical key to most of the more extreme forms of human behaviour and suffering'. I now wanted to explore the weirder zones.

In 'According to Pythagoras' I further compressed the selection Ovid made from the philosopher's teachings. What by modern experimental standards would be judged bad science works wonderfully well as surreal poetry:

> There's a theory that in the grave the backbone rots
> Away and the spinal cord turns into a snake . . .

Occasionally, as in the reference to the hyena's genitalia, an uncanny scientific accuracy takes us by surprise: 'the female mounted by a male/ Just minutes before, becomes a male herself'. (In real life the female hyena does indeed flaunt false male genitals: a power game.) Both the scientific and the surreal appealed to Ovid, and to me. When I had finished 'According to Pythagoras' I counted, to my dismay, twenty-nine lines. With an extra line the poem would have divided perfectly into three ten-line stanzas: my hunger for symmetry again. My wife reminded me of a leitmotif from Douglas Adams's glorious post-Ovidian fantasy *Dirk Gently's Holistic Detective Agency*, and for reasons numerical and poetical I appropriated it:

> The fundamental interconnectedness of all things
> Is incredible enough, but did you know that
> Hyenas change sex . . .

IV

Latin and Greek have been fundamental to my imaginative development. Versions that reflect my preoccupations at a deep level feel to me like my own poems, especially when I combine free rendition of source texts with original lines. An example of this is 'The Evening Star', written in memory of Catherine Mercer (1994–96):

> The day we buried your two years and two months
> So many crocuses and snowdrops came out for you
> I tried to isolate from those galaxies one flower:
> A snowdrop appeared in the sky at dayligone,
>
> The evening star, the star in Sappho's epigram
> Which brings back everything that shiny daybreak
> Scatters, which brings the sheep and brings the goat
> And brings the wean back home to her mammy.

Without Sappho's exquisite fragment, lightly Hibernicised, and the loveliest word I know for evening, 'dayligone', an Ulster dialect word, I could not have broached this heartrending subject.

A group of Greek poets and a group of Latin poets provide me with a coda. My most recent collection *Snow Water* included a poem called 'The Group', a suite of seven short pieces derived from the Loeb *Greek Lyric* series. Each stars a minor poet – Lamprocles, Myrtis, Telesilla, Charixenna. The more obscure the poet, the more I was attracted. Next to nothing is known about most of them. Teetering on the verge of almost total oblivion, they hang on in a few fragments, or as one-liner gags in Aristophanes, or as footnotes in some ancient critic's essay. I chose the title, 'The Group', mischievously, as a red herring which is meant to put researchers of the Belfast Group off the trail for as long as possible. Some readers will look for Seamus Heaney behind 'Ion of Chios, the prize-winning poet' or Medbh McGuckian, perhaps, behind 'hypochondriacal Telesilla'. But they will be missing the point. In its light-hearted way, 'The Group' is concerned with the poetic trade in general and what it involves: careerism, fashion, fame, obscurity, integrity, contamination, factionalism, camaraderie, intrigue, idealism, transitoriness, failure. Groups of poets do not change all that much over the centuries. Charixenna, the last poet in 'The Group', represents us all:

> Oblivious to being out of date,
> Which of us will not appear as dopey
> As Charixenna, oldfashioned pipe-player
> And composer of oldfashioned tunes
> And, according to some, a poet too?

In contrast, most of the poets in my Latin group are very well-known. In his *Tristia* the miserably exiled Ovid gives us a tantalising glimpse of his poetic friends far away in Rome. He misses them, and writes warmly about Propertius and Horace and regrets that Tibullus's early death thwarted their friendship. Virgil he only saw, he says ('Vergilium vidi tantum') but, yes, they all knew each other! In addition to these immortals Ovid names three other members of the coterie who have completely faded away: Macer, Ponticus and Bassus. Three busy literary careers, and hardly a syllable survives. I used Ovid's lines as the basis for a poem I have called 'Remembering the Poets' – it is a playful sonnet about the friendship of poets. Unavoidably, the personalities of my *own* brilliant contemporaries kept crowding in from the back of my mind. The poem expresses brotherly love for *them* and for the poets I converse with across the millennia:

> As a teenage poet I idolised the poets, doddery
> Macer trying out his *Ornithogonia* on me,
> And the other one about herbal cures for snake bites,
> Propertius, my soul mate, love's polysyllabic
> Pyrotechnical laureate reciting reams by heart,
> Ponticus straining to write The Long Poem, Bassus
> (Sorry for dropping names) iambic to a fault,
> Horace hypnotising me with songs on the guitar,
> Virgil, our homespun internationalist, sighted
> At some government reception, and then Albius
> Tibullus strolling in the woods a little while
> With me before he died, his two slim volumes
> An echo from the past, a melodious complaint
> That reaches me here, the last of the singing line.

Transcript of a lecture given in Trinity College Dublin, 28 January 2009

IN MEMORIAM

W. B. Stanford
Donald Wormell

THE WEST

When we were thirteen or fourteen my parents took my twin brother and me on a caravan holiday to Donegal. Donegal, which is *in* the North but *of* the West, might be considered an ideal location for the beginnings of my spiritual education. We were headed in our caravan for Downings on the Rosguill Peninsula. My father misread the map and we parked in the dark by the roadside just beyond Carrigart and only a few miles from our destination. I woke in the morning to a revelation, my first glimpse of wilderness in the Atlantic light. At that moment I discovered my soul-landscape. Close to the seashore at Downings we camped on some grassy machair, our caravan an eyesore for miles around. I would sit on the headland and write ecstatic letters to friends in Belfast about the view across Sheephaven Bay to Marble Strand and Muckish (the first of my holy mountains). Looking back at my passionate desire to share the landscape, I think I can recognise the incipient poet – someone for whom no experience is complete until he or she has written about it, someone who would hope to share the experience with others.

The first great yellow strand to fill my imagination was Tra-na-rossan. The Atlantic Drive winds uphill beyond the village of Downings. It turns rocky corners until, stretching out below and beyond, there is Tra-na-rossan. The strand inspired a nineteen-year-old's first love poem to the Western (or the North-western) landscape:

> We walked on Tra-na-rossan strand;
> the Atlantic winds were wiping the heat
> from the August sun and the stretching sand
> was cold beneath our naked feet ...

In 1965, my wife and I hitchhiked with Derek Mahon around Connemara. Life in Belfast had been demanding and painful because a
friend was having a breakdown. Were we drawn perhaps to the *idea* of
the place? 'Connemara' – and here I quote Tim Robinson – 'Connemara – the name drifts across the mind like cloud shadows on a
mountainside, or expands and fades like circles on a lake after a trout
has risen.' For Louis MacNeice as a child the West glimmered in family
conversation and at the back of his mind: 'The very name Connemara
seemed too rich for any ordinary place. It appeared to be a country
of windswept open spaces and mountains blazing with whin and
seas that were never quiet. But I was not to visit Achill or Connemara
until I had left school. So for many years I lived on a nostalgia for
somewhere I had never been.'

I still feel a bit like that, even though our 1965 trip turned out to be
a prelude to hundreds of journeys along the roads to Westport and
Louisburgh and Leenane. In Galway we boarded the steamer for Inishmore – a very rough crossing – there were no stabilisers on the boat –
belowdecks Mahon and I fought off seasickness with medicinal
brandies. In Kilronan we hired a jaunting car that took us to our guest
house. When we told him we didn't speak Irish, our driver sighed: 'Oh
you're lost. You're Lost.' Was he joking? Perhaps we *were* lost. It rained
most of the time and we huddled in an attic bedroom in our inflam-
mable sleeping bags, chain-smoking. Between showers we walked
around the rocky fields in flashing, soul-irradiating light. Our brief
sojourn would become part of my inner mythology, and part of Mahon's.
We felt sad leaving the island. My eventual response was 'Leaving
Inishmore', the first West-inspired poem of mine to survive: here are
the middle two stanzas:

Miles from the brimming enclave of the bay
I hear again the Atlantic's voices,
The gulls above as we pulled away –
So munificent their final noises
These are the broadcasts from our holiday.

Oh, the crooked walkers on that tilting floor!
And the girls singing on the upper deck
Whose hair took the light like a downpour –
Interim nor change of scene shall shipwreck
Those folk on the move between shore and shore.

Derek Mahon and I returned to the Aran Islands the following Easter
– Easter 1966. On a whim we left the steamer when it anchored in
the bay and were rowed in a currach to the smallest of the islands,
Inisheer. We spotted on the shore someone of bohemian appearance,
pacing up and down, clearly anxious about his mail. We introduced
ourselves. He had read our early poems in the *Dublin Magazine* where
we had read his short story 'Epithalamion'. The friendly stranger, Tom
MacIntyre, was living on the island with his young family. He persuaded
us to stay and arranged our lodgings with a witty woman who served
us with boiled bacon three times a day. On Good Friday, Derek and I
were very moved when we witnessed the islanders, in their best
tweeds, walking on their knees over the stone flags into the church.
Five years later in 'Letter to Derek Mahon' my perspective on all this
may reflect the beginning of the Troubles. I describe us as

. . . tongue-tied
Companions of the island's dead
In the graveyard among the dunes,

Eavesdroppers on conversations
With a Jesus who spoke Irish –
We were strangers in that parish . . .

It is striking that my first collection and the first collections of Derek
Mahon and Seamus Heaney all contain poems about the Aran Islands.
As visitors, as strangers, as outsiders, the three of us in our different
ways were following in the footsteps of J. M. Synge. Perhaps at this
point I should own up to borrowing a sentence from *The Aran Islands*
for a poem of my own about Inisheer. Here is Synge's sentence: 'There
is only one bit and saddle in the island, which are used by the priest,
who rides from the chapel to the pier when he has held the service on
Sunday.' And here is the rather satirical opening stanza of my poem
'The Island':

> The one saddle and bit on the island
> We set aside for every second Sunday
> When the priest rides slowly up from the pier.
> Afterwards his boat creaks into the mist.
> Or he arrives here nine times out of ten
> With the doctor. They will soon be friends.

In 'Synge on Aran' Seamus Heaney invokes Synge as a poetic role-
model:

> There
> he comes now, a hard pen
> scraping in his head;
> the nib filed on a salt wind
> and dipped in the keening sea.

And in 'Lovers on Aran' Heaney beautifully symbolises sexual reciprocity in terms of the landscape:

> Did sea define the land or land the sea?
> Each drew new meaning from the waves' collision.
> Sea broke on land to full identity.

In 'Epitaph for Robert Flaherty', Derek Mahon makes the great American film-maker say of Aran:

> The relief to be out of the sun,
> To have come north once more
> To my islands of dark ore
> Where winter is so long
> Only a little light
> Gets through, and that perfect.

And in 'Recalling Aran' Mahon seems to view the place itself as an artefact, as some kind of aesthetic absolute (both his Aran poems use the word 'perfect'):

> A dream of limestone in sea-light
> Where gulls have placed their perfect prints.
> Reflection in that final sky
> Shames vision into simple sight –
> Into pure sense, experience.
> Four thousand miles away tonight,
> Conceived beyond such innocence,
> I clutch the memory still, and I
> Have measured everything with it since.

The Aran poems of our youth do not seem to me to be escapist. We were drawn to what in my salute to 'Dr Johnson on the Hebrides' I call 'the far-flung outposts of experience'. We yearned for revelation that could well prove unbalancing in its intensity, or, to quote another early poem, 'The Hebrides' – for me the Irish and Scottish west sometimes converge – we coveted 'the privilege/ Of vertigo'.

It is extraordinary how the West continues to draw poets in a spiritual, non-material way. What Yeats began with 'The Wanderings of Oisin' is far from exhausted. Gerald Dawe's most recent collection, for instance, is called *Points West*. For Louis MacNeice in his rhapsodic 'Western Landscape':

> . . . this land
> Is always more than matter – as a ballet
> Dancer is more than body. The West of Ireland
> Is brute and ghost at once.

Richard Murphy first attracted the attention of us 'Western wannabes' with his majestic narratives 'Sailing to an Island' and 'The Cleggan Disaster'. Over the years I have been inspired by his consummate nature poems – 'Storm Petrel', 'Corncrake', 'Sea Holly', 'Seals at High Island'. Paul Durcan often looks West when he contemplates visionary alternatives to a dystopian Ireland. In 'The Seal of Burrishoole', for example, he counters dark forces by imagining an ideal Western burial as a form of spiritual purgation:

> Bury me in the estuary
> When the tide has gone out
> Uncovering the track;
> Under wine-red boughs of mid-winter

And faithful yellow furze;
Where seaweed is all over
And six cows stand apart from one another
Along the spine of the drumlin,
And a sea breeze blows from the west
And in the gap of the estuary
The seal of my death
Poised on rock as it always has been.

My own youthful passion grew into a lifetime's obsession. When I counted them up recently, I was surprised to find that one third of my poems are set in south-west Mayo. This is thanks to David Cabot, the great Irish ornithologist, who allows me to stay in his remote cottage and open my mind to the endless intricacies of the landscape and the Atlantic weather. I fell in love with Carrigskeewan the first time I saw it – nearly forty years ago – from the turn in the road above Thallabaun – a great sandy arena with a meandering channel, the dunes and the lakes and the cottage. I have been going there with my family since 1970. My wife and I have carried each of our three children through the Owennadornaun River and the tidal channel, then across the stretch of sandy grazing behind the dunes to the rickety gate, over the low bridge where brown trout and elvers wait, and up the last rising curves of the path to the white cottage in its little bumpy square of fuchsia hedges and stone walls – and all of this against the backdrop of Mweelrea (my second holy mountain). The first fruits of this love affair were six short topographical lyrics – 'The Mountain', 'The Strand', 'The Lake' and so on – a sequence dedicated to David and Penny Cabot and called, of course, 'Carrigskeewaun'. The sequence closes with 'The Lake', which hopes to make room for all of us outsiders:

Though it will duplicate at any time
The sheep and cattle that wander there,
For a few minutes every evening
The surface seems tilted to receive
The sun perfectly, the mare and her foal,
The heron, all such special visitors.

In his essay on 'Contemporary Irish Poetry' in the *Field Day Anthology of Irish Writing* Declan Kiberd castigates 'the number of poems set on the Aran Islands, or in West Kerry, or on the coast of Donegal – all written by artists who act like self-conscious tourists in their own country'. This kind of thinking makes me feel excluded. So I find reassuring what Derek Mahon says in his essay 'MacNeice in England and Ireland': 'There is a belief, prevalent since the time of Thomas Davis, that Irish poetry, to be Irish, must somehow express the National Aspirations; and MacNeice's failure to do so . . . is one of the reasons for his final exclusion from the charmed circle, known and feared the world over, of Irish Poets. "A tourist in his own country", it has been said, with the implication that this is somehow discreditable. But of what sensitive person is the same not true?' I also find it reassuring that Máirtín Ó Direáin wrote a 'Homage to John Millington Synge'. At the end of the poem he stresses that 'the words' of his people 'will live on in an alien tongue'.

Even Seamus Heaney, for me, hits a wrong note when he criticises the great naturalist, Robert Lloyd Praeger: 'Praeger's point of view is visual, geological, not like Kavanagh's, emotional and definitive. His eye is regulated by laws of aesthetics, by the disciplines of physical geography, and not, to borrow a phrase from Wordsworth, by the primary laws of our nature, the laws of feeling.' Kiberd and Heaney seem to circumscribe who can speak of the west and how it can be

343

spoken of. Praeger's biographer, Sean Lysaght, is surely right when he puts Praeger alongside Yeats, Synge, Lady Gregory and Douglas Hyde as one of the culture-givers of the revival – the nationalist revival. Just as others had turned to archaeology and folklore to rediscover the roots of culture, Praeger, says Lysaght, helped in 'the establishment of Ireland as a biological and geographical territory with an identity of its own'.

Sometimes I find it impossible *not* to view the Western landscape through the eyes of two aesthetic outsiders from Belfast, two painters – Paul Henry and Gerard Dillon. Almost single-handedly Henry created a vision of the West, especially Achill Island, which, with its turfstacks and thatched roofs and currachs, persists in a sort of semi-official way as the state's self-image (or one version of it). At a profounder level, sea and sky do actually combine on certain days in the West as though in a Paul Henry composition. Gerard Dillon who died in 1971, hailed from the Lower Falls district of Belfast, which he depicted magically; but it was in Connemara that he found his soul – on Inishlacken and in the area around Roundstone. My elegy for him, 'In Memory of Gerard Dillon', begins:

> You walked, all of a sudden, through
> The rickety gate which opens
> To a scatter of curlews,
> An acre of watery light . . .

In an *Irish Times* review of his last Belfast exhibition I called him 'the poet of Irish painting' – an overwrought phrase perhaps, but he embodies for me the very idea of the poet as close observer of the natural world. In the poem I describe him as

>   ... an eye
> Taking in the beautiful predators –
> Cats on the windowsill, birds of prey
> And, between the diminutive fields,
> A dragonfly, wings full of light
> Where the road narrows to the last farm.

Gerard Dillon showed me how to find my way from Belfast to the beautiful places. There have been other guides – Synge of course, pioneering ecologists like Praeger and the Field Naturalists, the Edwardian giants (many of them from the North) who carried out the Clare Island Survey of 1909 to 1911. This was the world's first major inventory of a single geographical location. These naturalists were also among the first to recognise the scientific importance of the Burren – that extraordinary place where Arctic and Mediterranean plants co-mingle. Amusingly – and here I quote from Cilian Roden's essay in *The Book of the Burren* – two unionist naturalists joked that the blue Gentian, white Mountain Avens and red Bloody Cranesbill on a Burren hillside were a marvellous reflection of the Union flag 'on the western extremity of the United Kingdom'.

I revere the great geographers of more recent times – Frank Mitchell from Trinity College, Estyn Evans from Queen's University, whom I was lucky enough to meet. I would add to my list brilliant contemporaries such as Charles Nelson with whom I have botanised in County Clare, and Tim Robinson, the Western seaboard's greatest cartographer and philosopher, with whom I have walked around Inishlacken in search of Gerard Dillon's ghost and freshwater wells among the seaweed. Certain books are my bibles: *The Way that I Went, The Aran Islands, Irish Folk Ways, Reading the Irish Landscape, The Burren: A Companion to the Wildflowers of an Irish Limestone Wilderness,*

Setting Foot on the Shores of Connemara, Sailing to an Island.

David Cabot, the custodian of Carrigskeewaun, published in 1999, in the wonderful Collins New Naturalist Library series, his compendious study of Ireland's diverse habitats – from the mountains and peat lands to the sea and the islands. It is called *Ireland*. Four years later his neighbour and our close friend Michael Viney brought out with the Smithsonian Institute his own major study called – yes – *Ireland*: in it he examines the intricate balance of plants and animals, geology and climate. It seems to me astonishing that in the neighbouring townlands of Carrigskeewaun and Thallabaun, on either side of the little Owennadornaun River, a minute apart as the raven flies, two great naturalists should create their masterworks. And that's not the end of it. In 2008 Michael Viney (who of course is also celebrated for his influential column *Another Life* in the *Irish Times*) co-authored with Ethna Viney *Ireland's Ocean: A Natural History* which wonderfully extends the horizons of the Western seaboard into the sea. And he has just published *Wild Mayo*, a vivid guide for layman and visitor. David Cabot's second New Naturalist volume has also recently appeared – *Wildfowl* – a scholarly tome devoted to one of his lifelong obsessions. Cabot and Viney share their landscape with me. It has been my privilege and education to plod along behind them. To the cairn of books I would of course love to add my own *Collected Poems*.

The plants and the animals were what first involved me in Mayo. It was some time before I wrote about the people who live there. 'Mayo Monologues' are four psychologically dark portraits of fictional neighbours – composite characterisations that convey my view (at the time) of human beings in the landscape. In 'Self-heal', the third portrait, a virginal young schoolteacher is molested by a backward boy, to whom she has been teaching the names of flowers:

I wasn't frightened and still I don't know why,
But I ran from him in tears to tell them.
I heard how every day for one whole week
He was flogged with a blackthorn, then tethered
In the hayfield. I might have been the cow
Whose tail he would later dock with shears,
And he the ram tangled in barbed wire
That he stoned to death when they set him free.

I used to consider 'Mayo Monologues' excessively bleak, but not any more, not after so many recent revelations of depravity. Nevertheless, to this day, if I meet on the roads any of the people who might have contributed even a fragment to these composite portraits, I avoid their eyes. At readings I rarely recite 'Mayo Monologues'. I wasn't able to return to this communal zone until I'd got to know Joe O'Toole, one of the few local smallholders who ever admitted to me a love of the wild flowers and the birds – a love which brought us together:

His way of seeing me safely across the duach
Was to leave his porch light burning, its sparkle
Shifting from widgeon to teal on Corragaun Lake.

I was downcast when he died:

This morning on the burial mound at Templedoomore
Encircled by a spring tide and taking in
Cloonaghmanagh and Claggan and Carrigskeewaun,
The townlands he'd wandered tending cows and sheep,
I watched a dying otter gaze right through me
At the islands in Clew Bay, as though it were only
Between hovers and not too far from the holt.

347

'Hover' is the exquisite English word for an otter's temporary resting place. The poem is called 'Between Hovers'. I suppose I see myself as hovering in the west too, and my poems as hovers. Like many an elegy 'Between Hovers' is also a kind of love poem. In my version of the West, love poem and elegy tend to get confused: the erotic and the sorrowful meld together. In 'Above Dooaghtry' (from *Snow Water*) Thanatos makes room for Eros as I give instructions for my funeral and describe the promontory fort where I want my ashes to be scattered:

> Let boulders at the top encircle me,
> Neither a drystone wall nor a cairn, space
> For the otter to die and the mountain hare
> To lick snow stains from her underside,
> A table for the peregrine and ravens,
>
> A prickly double-bed as well, nettles
> And carline-thistles, a sheeps' wool pillow,
> So that, should she decide to join me there,
> Our sandy dander to Allaran Point
> Or Tonakeera will take forever.

I am still only scratching the surface of this small townland. Every time I leave, I wonder will there be any more Mayo poems; but the poems keep arriving. My forthcoming collection, *A Hundred Doors*, will contain another *eighteen* – more than ever – and I haven't finished the book yet! Not just for me but for other poets – Murphy, Durcan, Moya Cannon, Mary O'Malley – the West prompts more than just one kind of poem. As a genre the 'Western poem' can be infinitely capacious. I love Moya Cannon's cosmic Western poem 'Night' which ends with her staring up into the starry sky at

... our windy, untidy loft
where old people had flung up old junk
they'd thought might come in handy,
ploughs, ladles, bears, lions, a clatter of heroes,
a few heroines, a path for the white cow, a swan
and, low down, almost within reach,
Venus, completely unfazed by the frost.

Carrigskeewaun provides me with the template for experiencing all
other places and keeps me sensitive, I hope, to the nuances of locality.
The human habitat in that part of Mayo is precarious, isolated and
vulnerable, its history complex. The landscape is haunted by grown-
over potato-drills, the ghosts of lazy-beds abandoned during the
Famine. The bones of the landscape make me feel in my own bones
how provisional dwelling and home are. In 'Remembering Carrigskeewaun' I say: 'Home is a hollow between the waves,/ A clump of
nettles, feathery winds ...'

In the Mayo poems I am not writing about a cosy community. Nor
do I dwell among the calls of waterbirds and the psychedelic blaze of
summer flowers to escape from Ulster's political violence. I want light
from Carrigskeewaun to irradiate the northern confusion. In Irish
poetry 'the West' is not a pastoral domain outside history and violence.
Think of Yeats's 'Meditations in Time of Civil War', or 'The Closing
Album' by Louis MacNeice, poised on the brink of the Second World
War. Paul Durcan often returns to the West in his critiques of contemporary Irish society. The Civil War, the Anglo-Irish War, two World
Wars, the Troubles have all been refracted through the West. Although
I called my very first Mayo poem 'The West', it is as much about the
North. Here I am sitting in the cottage trying to listen through bad
radio reception for news from Belfast:

> Beneath a gas-mantle that the moths bombard,
> Light that powders at a touch, dusty wings,
> I listen for news through the atmospherics,
> A crackle of sea-wrack, spinning driftwood,
> Waves like distant traffic, news from home . . .

A later poem, 'The Ice-cream Man', also brings together the two parts of Ireland I love the most – Belfast and the Western seaboard. On the Lisburn Road (where I live) the IRA murdered the man in the ice-cream shop. I had been away botanising in the Burren where I had written down in a notebook the names of all the wild flowers I could identify in one day. On my return home I learned of the murder; and my younger daughter Sarah told me that she had bought with her pocket money a bunch of carnations to lay outside the shop. I arranged the lovely flower-names from my notebook into a kind of aural wreath to place beside her bouquet. The poem is addressed to Sarah:

> Rum and raisin, vanilla, butterscotch, walnut, peach:
> You would rhyme off the flavours. That was before
> They murdered the ice-cream man on the Lisburn Road
> And you bought carnations to lay outside his shop.
> I named for you all the wild flowers of the Burren
> I had seen in one day: thyme, valerian, loosestrife,
> Meadowsweet, tway blade, crowfoot, ling, angelica,
> Herb robert, marjoram, cow parsley, sundew, vetch,
> Mountain avens, wood sage, ragged robin, stitchwort,
> Yarrow, lady's bedstraw, bindweed, bog pimpernel.

I mean that catalogue to go on forever, like a prayer. The murder of the ice-cream man violates all nature. The poem is also, partly, an elegy for the flowers themselves, which are under increasing threat.

The whole island is under threat: contaminated lakes, fish-kills, ruthless overgrazing, 'bungalow blight', chemical overkill, building on flood plains, oil spills, inappropriately sited motorways. We are methodically turning beauty spots into eyesores. Even Carrigskee-waun is changing. The stony boreen that leads to the Owennadornaun River has been tarmacadamed. Where we used to wade with our bundles there is now a concrete bridge. We might have seen dippers and sandmartins and sandpipers there; and, in the meadow beyond, butterfly orchids. But the meadow has been turned into a carpark. When a neighbour asked me: 'And how do you like your lovely new carpark, Michael?' I couldn't believe she wasn't joking. Is Nature joking when gale-force winds blow over the two thoughtfully provided Portaloos?

I have a radiant memory of kneeling with my friend the botanical artist Raymond Piper to examine the rare dense-flowered orchid, *neotinea maculata,* in the Burren. We looked up from the peculiar little plant across a magically disappearing turlough to the contours of Mullaghmore (the third of my holy mountains). I don't come closer than this to religious experience. Against the advice of local and national and international environmental organisations, the Office of Public Works was planning in 1999 to build an interpretative centre close to Mullaghmore. This was unnecessary because a centre already existed not too far away. It was also potentially catastrophic. Massive road-widening would have been required to facilitate the tankering-in of fresh water and the tankering-out of sewage. Into the most fragile and intricate of underground water systems the OPW was planning to sink a gigantic septic tank.

Raymond Piper and I got involved in what the *Irish Times* called 'The Battle of Mullaghmore'. We wrote letters to the papers. Raymond deplored 'unnecessary despoliation' and 'irreversible destruction'. I risked sounding boastful or pompous when I said: 'I am a poet whose work is currently represented on the Leaving Certificate syllabus. Many of my poems celebrate the landscape of the West of Ireland. Their very subject-matter is threatened by the absence of intelligent environmental policies.' I pleaded with the minister responsible at the time (Síle de Valera) to listen to the experts, and I asked: 'Does she really want her monument to be a public lavatory in the Garden of Eden?' In January, at the beginning of the millennium, Raymond and I drove down to Clare to take part in a demonstration. This was the first and last time either of us had spoken from the back of a lorry. Out of this commotion my 'Burren Prayer' was born:

> Gentians and lady's bedstraw embroider her frock.
> Her pockets are full of sloes and juniper berries.
>
> Quaking-grass panicles monitor her heartbeat.
> Her reflection blooms like mudwort in a puddle.
>
> Sea lavender and Irish eyebright at Poll Salach,
> On Black Head saxifrage and mountain-everlasting.
>
> *Our Lady of the Fertile Rocks, protect the Burren.*
> *Protect the Burren, Our Lady of the Fertile Rocks.*

The campaign was a success and work on the interpretative centre was abandoned. But our January protest had been met by angry counter-demonstrators. The construction of the centre would have generated short-term employment. Who were we and what business was it of ours? When we returned for some peaceable botanising, we were confronted with 'Keep Out' and 'Trespassers will be Prosecuted' signs. Our campaign had succeeded but at the cost of dividing the community and making visitors like ourselves unwelcome. Here again, we have the issue of who is entitled to speak about or for the West.

Damaged relations are gradually being repaired by the visionary work of Brendan Dunford and the Burrenbeo Trust. The Trust (of which I am a proud patron) aims to promote the self-sustaining conservation of the Burren. It recognises local farmers as the life-blood of the region and the best guardians of its heritage. The famous wild flowers are, after all, a by-product of sensitively balanced farming activity over many years.

Raymond Piper died in July 2007. At his funeral I began my eulogy with lines from Christopher Smart's exuberant *Jubilate Agno* – lines which encapsulate everything I'm trying to say. Raymond Piper might be speaking them:

> For flowers are good both for the living and the dead.
> For there is a language of flowers.
> For elegant phrases are nothing but flowers.
> For flowers are peculiarly the poetry of Christ.

In my elegy for Raymond I recall some of our orchid odysseys. On one of these he took me to the Saltee Islands to look for insular hybrids. We hired a small fishing smack called *Mystical Rose*. Here are the last two stanzas of 'Cloud Orchid':

> Undistracted in your greenhouse-
> Studio by caterpillar
> Droppings from the mimosa tree
> That twisted overhead, you

Gazed up through the branches and
The broken pane imagining
Your last flower portrait – 'for flowers
Are good both for the living
And the dead' – the minuscule
Cloud Orchid that grows in the rain
Forest's misty canopy.

The rusty fuse you brought home
From a specific hummock
In Carrigskeewaun – autumn
Lady's-tresses – yet to flower
Under your greenhouse's moony
Glass in Belfast – do you want
Me to move it from the sill
Onto the ground for moisture
Or re-pot it or hire, as once
We did, *Mystical Rose*
And chug out to the Saltees?

A cultural version of Alzheimer's Disease menaces what we now like
to call 'our heritage'. It could well be the end of our species. We shall
die if we let the wild flowers die. Some years ago I gave a reading at the
local secondary school in Louisburgh. If it hadn't been for the poems
and an RTÉ documentary Cabot and Viney had made about my Mayo
sojourns, many of the children wouldn't have believed that herons and
otters and stoats and falcons do indeed live just a few miles down the
road in Carrigskeewaun and Thallabaun. Very few of the children
had visited the area. On our own walks across the fields we hardly ever
meet anyone – no local children at play – an occasional shepherd

perhaps. So, last summer it was an intense pleasure to show my first grandson the wild flowers of Mayo. Our children now carry *their* children through the tidal channel to Carrigskeewaun. All five grandchildren have stayed in the cottage. And all five have inspired poems. 'The Fold' is for Catherine, the youngest:

> Why would the ewes and their lambs
> Assemble as though hypnotised
> Around the cottage? Do they sense
> A storm on its way? Or a fox?
> Darkness and quiet are folding
> All the sheep of Carrigskeewaun,
> Their fleeces lustrous, long wool
> For a baby's comfort-blanket,
> For Catherine asleep in her crib
> This midnight, our lambing-time.

In the cottage I often think of the first folk to live there, the O'Tooles who came from Inishdeigil, a tiny island at the mouth of the Killary. I can't imagine how they survived in such isolation. Mary O'Toole had eleven children on the island – without the aid of doctor or midwife. The state eventually provided the family with the cottage at Carrigskeewaun. In her new home Mary O'Toole would say: 'Now I can walk anywhere!' The thirteen O'Tooles were bilingual, played musical instruments, sang, and told stories. Their new home soon became famous as a ceilidh house. Folk came visiting from miles around. Some even rowed from Connemara in their currachs across the Killary for the music and a seat at the hearth. The Carrigskeewaun cottage is no longer a ceilidh house, alas. A poem by me will have to do instead! Here is the second half of 'Ceilidh':

The thirteen O'Tooles are singing about everything.
Their salty eggs are cherished for miles around.
There's a hazel copse near the lake without a name.
Dog violets, sorrel, wood spurge are growing there.
On Inishdeigil there's a well of the purest water.
Is that Arcturus or a faraway outhouse light?
The crescent moon's a coracle for Venus. Look
Through the tide and over the Owennadornaun
Are shouldered the coffins of the thirteen O'Tooles.

We can be so parochial in our sense of time and space. In the words of Tim Robinson 'the geographies over which we are so suicidally passionate are . . . fleeting expressions of the earth's face'. In the first poem in my forthcoming collection I describe David Cabot alone in Carrigskeewaun for the millennium:

My friend sits at the hearth keeping the cottage warm . . .
He has kept for this evening firewood that is very old.
Bog deal's five thousand years make the room too hot.

We are also being parochial when we ignore the great migrations taking place – in more senses than one – 'above our heads' – and the other heroic odysseys beneath the waves. In a poem called 'The Wren' I describe Carrigskeewaun as 'a townland whooper swans/ From the tundra remember, and the Saharan/ Wheatear'. Carrigskeewaun is not really a 'remote corner': it is a focal point, a nerve centre. When I walked with my friend the painter Jeffrey Morgan along Thallabaun Strand for the first time, we saw bottlenose dolphins in Clew Bay, then an otter capering out of the tide at Allaran Point. As we left for the cottage, five whooper swans circled above us on their way from Iceland to nearby Dooaghtry Lake.

During my years of visiting Carrigskeewaun, I have tried to 'sing about everything'. I have written poems there that touch on the Great War, the Holocaust, and the Troubles. The place has given me love poems, elegies, prayers, lullabies. I would like to end with the last poem in *A Hundred Doors*, 'Greenshank':

> When I've left Carrigskeewaun for the last time,
> I hope you discover something I've overlooked,
> Greenshanks, say, two or three, elegantly probing
> Where sand from the white strand and the burial mound
> Blows in. How long will Corragaun remain a lake?
> If I had to choose a bird call for reminding you,
> The greenshank's estuarial fluting would do.

Transcript of a lecture given in the John Hume Institute for Global Irish Studies, University College Dublin, on 1 February 2010

PART 6

THREE INTERVIEWS

THE LONGLEY TAPES

Interviewer: Robert Johnstone

Was yours a literary family?

No, I don't think I'd call my family literary. There was a very small bookcase, I remember. It had the same book-club books right the way through my childhood. When I started to buy books my mother used to say, 'Not another! Surely you've got enough!' On the other hand there was an artistic streak in the family. My sister Wendy, who's nine years older than I am, used to play the piano rather well, and one of my childhood memories is of lying in the bedroom above the living room and listening to her playing Chopin. Then my father, in the last years of his life, took to painting in oils. They were *awful* pictures, I suppose, but it's important to me now to realise that that need was there in him. My mother was, I think, a natural intellectual, but neither of my parents had what you'd call a full education, both leaving school at fourteen or fifteen. In third form at Inst, when I won a prize for English, the book I chose was the *Collected Poems of W. B. Yeats.* This really caused some alarm and consternation at home. So I think that there was an artistic streak in the family that never properly recognised itself.

You're actually a city boy, but a lot of your poetry's about birds and plants in the countryside. Did you spend a lot of time in the country as a boy, or do you now?

Where I grew up was part of the 1930s ribbon development and just opposite our house there was a field, and then further along the road it was suburban countryside. It's now all built up. Central things in my childhood were a big crab-apple tree, birds' nests, making tunnels in long grass, hearing the local riding-school horses clip-clopping along, Barnett's Park and the Lagan. Then gradually, when my father could afford a car, Donegal, County Down and Antrim. I love the Irish countryside. When I was putting together *Poems 1963-1983* and reading the proofs it occurred to me that I hadn't written enough about Belfast. I think that is a gap in the book. I don't know whether I can rectify it. Somehow, and I don't think I'm in any way unusual in this, I find I'm moved by trees in a way I'm not moved by lamp-posts and telegraph-poles, and I'm moved by birds in a way I'm not moved by aeroplanes and helicopters. Finally I write about what moves me. Before she died my mother told me that when I was a toddler I used to go obsessively into the garden and ask what the names of the plants were. Since the age of about five or six I've also been obsessively interested in birds, watching them and naming them.

You love music. Did you ever play an instrument?

No. My parents had spent money on Wendy, who I think could have been a good pianist, but when she failed to follow it through neither my twin Peter nor I were given piano lessons. At the age of about fifteen or sixteen I taught myself to memorise from sheet music a few pieces of Chopin. It would take me weeks and weeks to work out the notes – I couldn't read music – but I can still play some pieces that I taught myself . . . One has many regrets, but my major regret is that I can't make music, which means nearly as much to me as poetry, so I listen in a very vital way.

Poetry is musical.

The poetry I like always has to have melody or a musical element to it. One of the poets I admire the most, Derek Mahon, is master of the singing line.

Did you come to poetry through the Classics, or was it English?

In some ways I came to poetry despite the Classics. I'm very glad now I read Classics. There is the obvious, very early phase when, like all children, one's moved by rhymes, but I remember being moved by poetry in Form Two, in Billy Greer's class – the back row, about two rows from the window. I remember being bowled over by Keats's 'La Belle Dame' and Walter de la Mare's 'The Listeners'. I always enjoyed poetry – relished it musically. Before that, at primary school, I took pleasure in what the other pupils found a chore, learning by heart bits of the Old Testament, the Psalms, David and Jonathan, and so on.

But it was always poetry, never prose?

Yes, it was prose as well. Something must have happened in that Form Two. I was the only boy in the class who enjoyed *Travels with a Donkey* by R. L Stevenson. I got almost tactile pleasure out of that. I remember getting goose pimples when he ties up his donkey, gets into his sleeping bag and lights a cigarette – and feeling the same tactile pleasures reading *A Christmas Carol*. I remember reading that in bed over Christmas.

What you're describing there are specific situations, writing that evokes physical things. That's obviously something poetry does more than prose.

Good poetry and good prose have far more in common with each other than poetry has with verse. What you're suggesting is that my early reading – and it may still be so – took the lyrical moments out of prose works, which is probably what I still do with literature and music. I don't listen to a Beethoven string quartet with much architectonic intelligence. I think you absorb that. When you've listened to it for a hundred times you have an intuitive sense of its shape. But what I relish the first time and the hundredth time are the intense moments.

You must have scanned lines of verse. Did you enjoy that?

I think children do enjoy these exercises. As a teacher, I found pupils liked two things. They like the inspirational moments of teaching, but they also enjoy working out the mechanics. I remember as a schoolboy enjoying mastering theorems and algebraic equations, and I enjoyed scanning Latin lines. I was taught by a brilliant teacher, Dr Fay, and I wrote Latin and Greek verses – very bad ones. But it alerted me to certain things: the marvellous mixture of complexity and flow you can achieve in an inflected language. You know a word is the subject because of its ending, whereas in English you only know that by its position in the sentence. That lovely mixture still influences my fascination with what can be achieved through syntax, the arrangement of a sentence. Because I've been correcting the proofs of *Poems 1963–1983* I've realised that, even without trying, some poems are whole sentences. That's something that's dying out. The subordinate clause is in decline.

Nobody teaches you to write English verse. Personally, scanning Virgil was the only teaching in verse I ever had. The rest I had to learn from books on prosody or looking at other poets. Do you think the simple fact of counting the number of syllables in a Latin line made a difference in the way you write English?

No. I don't think it did. I think you're right, you can teach people to write verse. You can't teach them to write poetry, that's the big mystery. Then there's the difference between Latin and Greek verse and English. One's based on quantity and the other, English, is based on stress. The best thing that was ever said about English prosody was by Robert Frost, who said, 'There's strict iambic and loose iambic.' The rules are there to be broken. I remember at a WEA class talking about English metre, and it came down to that, strict iambic or loose iambic. It becomes poetry when you can't quite impose the rules. It goes on stress in English OK, but take something like 'To be or not to be, that is the question.' It's not 'to bé or nót to bé,' with equal stresses. It's 'To bé or nót (stronger) to bé, thát' (stronger again). I used to tell people in that WEA class that the iambic pentameter is the norm simply because there's a tendency in English to fall into iambic metre. Even in ordinary conversation we're often talking in iambs, and five of those empty your lungs and it's time to breathe in again. Prosody is born out of two things, the natural tendencies of the language, and our bodies, the capacity of our lungs.

Were there any classical poets you admired?

Didn't so much admire them at school. I was intimidated by them. But I remember getting just good enough to be able to plod through Homer and that was a revelation. He would still be a favourite poet – the sense of physical life that comes out of that story beneath its myth-ological/ historical overlay. And then I remember Fay had been to a summer course at Cambridge. I must have been sixteen or seventeen. Fay took us through the *Agamemnon*, especially the choruses, and passed on to us what he'd learnt – the deep, primitive rituals beneath the ornate structure. But, funny enough, it wasn't till I went to Trinity

College Dublin, and discovered the Latin love elegists, that I felt I'd come face to face with an ancient ghost. Catullus, but especially Propertius, whom I tried to translate when I was an undergraduate, and who's peculiarly modern in his sensibility. And just a few years ago I discovered Tibullus. I'm interested now in having a go at Ovid. Derek Mahon and Paul Muldoon are both interested as well, so I think I'd better get moving. At Trinity I did as little work as possible and called myself a lapsed classicist. I've forgotten most of my Latin and Greek but reading Sophocles, Aeschylus and the Latin love elegists was an important experience.

So, we've got to Trinity . . .

No, don't leave Inst yet.

What else can we say about Inst?

I'd like to talk about the music side. In a way, from the age of fourteen to seventeen I immersed myself in music just as deeply as I was later to immerse myself in poetry.

Was that jazz?

No, jazz didn't come until I was about twenty-five. I used to go to the Ulster Hall *every* Thursday to hear the old City of Belfast Orchestra. I can remember breaking into an almost sexual sweat when I heard Sibelius's second symphony. I spent *all* my pocket money on classical records; mostly romantic, Tchaikovsky, Rachmaninov, Sibelius, who's not really romantic. I've continued to buy records in a rather profligate fashion. I listen for at least one hour a day to Radio 3. An interesting thing happened the year I got married [1964]. I was twenty-five, and heard some jazz. It was Fats Waller. I went straight down to Solly Lipsitz's shop and bought two Fats Waller LPs. Later I was at a party in a crowded flat and there was one of those old-fashioned Dansette portable gramophones playing in the corner – Bessie Smith. I asked my host who was singing. It was one of the most majestic sounds I'd ever encountered. Now I suppose I would spend my money on jazz records because there's so much marvellous classical music on Radio 3. I've explored jazz and classical music as parallel obsessions.

You haven't mentioned Mozart or opera.

Working in the Arts Council there are some opera enthusiasts and they've interested me in opera. I'm an unabashed Verdi/ Puccini man. I have this theory that opera's really a realistic art form. What it puts on stage is how we feel, secret thoughts: 'Wouldn't it be lovely to make a pass at that girl across the room?' 'How am I going to restrain myself from punching that old fart on the nose?' There it all is in music. I got on to opera after I was forty. And Mozart of course. It was very foolish of me to omit him. I find that Mozart, Bach and Schubert are the constants. The other composers have their ups and downs.

Can we go to Trinity now?

No, I want to talk about sport.

Yes, it's something that's worried me about you, that you love rugby so much. I've never been able to understand it.

Well, the fact that so many awful people are interested in rugby doesn't have any bearing on the game. I played rugby at Inst with great enthusiasm. I was coached by Dr Fay in the under-14s and played for the

Medallion XV. One of the revelations of my life (what would Heaney call it? An 'epiphany'?) was the semi-final for the Medallion under-15 side against Methody [Methodist College], when I played my best game. I know I was never as good again, but it is important for me now to have had that experience. I was a second-row forward, a good defensive player. Then I played on the First XV and was dropped after January or February simply because I became bored by the maniacal devotion that was demanded. If you haven't done it, you can't quite appreciate the excitement before a match and the sense of fulfilment in doing something well. I try to get down to Lansdowne Road for the internationals. It's the only time I'm happy as a member of a crowd shouting the one thing, i.e. 'Ireland, Ireland, Ireland!' I remember about ten years ago taking Seamus Heaney to his first and only rugby match – Ireland against France. You had these awful Ballymena rednecks and Belfast solicitors and Kerry priests and Dublin Jackeens all together in the one big stadium. Seamus turned to me and, in a quite emotional way, said, 'Listen, they're all shouting for Ireland.'

Did you like the technical aspect of it, the formal part of rugby?

But that's the delight of sport. It's the shape a game takes and the shape a game makes.

Do you think poetry had got bogged down in technical aspects for a time? Just at the time you were writing your first book, there seemed to be no technique at all – free verse. A lot of people had been trying to develop new ways of measuring metre.

You mean William Carlos Williams's principle of breath, the stepped line?

Do you think that was all a dead end?

I like some of Williams a lot. I'm not too sure how it works. I'm inclined to agree with that old crosspatch Geoffrey Grigson, who says that America has produced 'poetry-less poetry'. In terms of what's happening now, I would be regarded as very conservative and traditionalist. I resent being called that. I do believe that poetry releases the tendencies of the language, and two of those tendencies are a drift towards pattern and rhyme. Rhyme is one of the attributes of language. I rhyme very little now, I don't know why that is. I don't think there are arguments for or against rhyme. It's a basic fact that it's one of the things that words do, and when I'm writing I like to embrace as many of the things that words do as possible. I am really unconvinced by what looks to me like pocket prose, prose chopped up into lines. Inasmuch as a lot of that is taken seriously, I think we're living in a kind of Dark Ages. My interest in form is a bit like the devotion of those monks in their cells illuminating manuscripts in the Dark Ages. But I'm not doctrinaire about these matters. The sort of poetry that fills me with wonder would include the marvellous stanzaic patterns of George Herbert, the hymn-like free verse of D. H. Lawrence's love poems, those beautiful free verse paragraphs in the *North American Sequence* of Theodore Roethke. I write in longhand. Muldoon for instance writes straight onto a typewriter: I could never do that. I seem to need the physical pleasure of using a soft pencil or one of those marvellous Japanese felt pens and paper. I cover the paper with a jumble of words. I'm going after a sound and rhythm. Eventually I go to the typewriter and I think, 'I've really loosened up, this is going to be much freer,' but when I type it out I see it's the same old oblongs and squares. That's what Auden said when someone asked him how he thought of his poems: 'As oblongs and squares.' It's almost as though this formal sense is now built-in. But if in order to express myself and my emotions and thoughts, which is what it's all about, I found myself writing free verse, say like those great animal poems of Lawrence, I'd be delighted. If I'm being true to myself by continuing to write in shapes, fair enough. So be it.

When you've written lines on the page, do you mark the stresses?

Never done that. I do it by ear. Sometimes I do a basic finger count. If the line sounds right and it seems long, or if it sounds and feels right and seems short, then OK. It's only out of curiosity that I'd do a count of stresses, not in order to change the line. I test the line in my mouth and in my ear, in a heightened state of excitement.

When you were first beginning to write poetry that you published, were there any contemporary poets that meant a lot to you?

I began in the dark really, writing when I was sixteen. That was as a result of falling madly in love with a girl called Pat. Most of what I wrote was an outpouring – verbal masturbation. I remember, though, working very hard on one poem, that was the breakthrough, when I was about sixteen or seventeen. It was about a night watchman and it ended: 'I can't desire what is not mine/ For things in reach are out of sight.' I worked very hard on that. It contained lots of clichéd images about red lamps being like rubies. But the knowledge grew that it wasn't just a question of pouring out onto the page, that one had to work at it. Then at about eighteen or nineteen I went to Trinity, where I more or less dropped classics and took up writing poetry and drinking Guinness in O'Neill's pub in Sussex Street. My first models had a disastrous effect. There was an enormous gap in my reading between Lucretius and W. H. Auden. The poets I liked were e. e. cummings, which meant that I went all lower-case and twee, and Wallace Stevens, which meant that I went all portentous. Then Derek Mahon arrived and we gutted the collected Louis MacNeice and the collected Graves together. I think they're still potent influences. The big discoveries of immediately contemporary poetry were three books: *For the Unfallen* by Geoffrey Hill, *The Less Deceived* by Philip Larkin, and *Lupercal* by Ted Hughes. It would be difficult to find their direct influence on the poems of my first book, but they're all so true – three astonishing books of poetry – that they cleared away a lot of my rubbishy, self-indulgent attitudes and approaches.

If you were suddenly transported to, say, England, would you feel you'd been cut off from your poetic roots – whatever they are?

Yes, whatever they might he. You can't quite talk about Belfast just as Belfast any more. All of us who've lived here for the past fifteen years have been through a unique, strange experience. The tragedy has its roots in our complex culture. We would be less aware of those complexities if it weren't for the Troubles. I find social intercourse outside of Ulster a shade two-dimensional, compared with the way we deport ourselves here. The North of Ireland is culturally exciting. One has to be tuned in all the time. One has to keep one's antennae in good repair. Ulster people are all radio hams sending out messages, little subtexts to each other. Conversation in literary London is bland by comparison. It is because of the confluence of cultures here, the Irish, the Scots, the English. It's all unresolved. I've said elsewhere, to use a geological metaphor, that English society – pre the miners' strike, that is – is sedimentary; Ireland, and especially Northern Ireland, is volcanic. Ulster/ Ireland is still working out what it wants to be and that's why it's a stimulating atmosphere.

In the sixties, to an outsider, there seemed to be a conscious alliance between you, Derek Mahon and Seamus Heaney. Was that the case, and, in any case, do you think you influenced each other?

There was no alliance at all. I'd met Derek at Trinity. He was a year or two below me and I'd just established myself as a 'college poet' (I always think that sounds like 'village idiot') and Mahon came along. He was so much more accomplished then than I was, and I suppose one of the brave things I did was to embrace the pain of recognising that he was a better poet than I was then. We became close friends. Then I came up here because of Edna's job at Queen's University, and met Seamus, whom I found enormously charming, beguiling and friendly, and open to the challenge and, if you like, the pain of coming to terms with me and Mahon, because for family reasons he'd worked hard to get a first-class degree and had come to poetry later than we had. So we were round a couple of bends in the road before he started. It was combative and no-holds-barred, and in no sense an alliance. Then I remember being in the Club Bar having a drink with Seamus and Jimmy walked in – Jimmy Simmons, just back from Africa. I don't think for a split second we thought in terms of Northern Irish poetry or Ulster poetry or being Ulster poets. We were struggling to write the stuff and struggling to get it published. If anyone thought in those terms, it was Philip Hobsbaum, who ran the 'Group'. We certainly didn't. There was no group, there was no school, there was no manifesto.

Was the Group a big help to any of you?

No. The Group was exciting in its way. I don't think it altered the way we developed. (Mahon was at the Group only once, incidentally.) What it did was introduce people and lend an air of seriousness and electricity to the notion of writing. I just missed Stewart Parker, who'd gone to live in the States. Hobsbaum had a nose for talent, there's no doubt about it. Anyone who was writing anything that was any good at all he seemed to know about and brought them to the Group, which was very rigorous and fierce – again, no holds barred. The Northern Irish literary scene owes Hobsbaum a lot, and it was his abilities as a ringmaster. Bringing people together, that was the important move. Things happen, there's competition in the air, and you feel less freak-ish trying to write.

So you didn't think of yourselves as Ulster writers? Presumably you didn't look at people like MacNeice and W. R. Rodgers in a conscious attempt to forge an Ulster . . .

No, no. I still don't think of myself as an Ulster writer. I think of myself as a writer who comes from Ulster, as an Ulsterman who writes. In the verse letter I wrote to Heaney I use the phrase 'Ulster poet, our Union title', which is meant to be critical of the idea of being an Ulster poet. When I was at school, mind you, it was exciting when an excellent English teacher, Joe Cowan, cyclostyled some poems by MacNeice and Rodgers, to know that men from this godforsaken place – and it really was a godforsaken place in those days – had written poems. When John Hewitt came back to live here [in 1972], that was a very important moment for the community, very important to me: an enormous endorsement . . . well, he endorsed the place with his life. I take pleasure in the works of MacNeice, Rodgers, Hewitt, but I don't think in terms of lineage or anything like that. They're part of the coin-cidence of talent.

So you wouldn't subscribe to an idea that may have become less fashionable in the visual arts – that the past really insists on the artist painting in a certain way

— he can't repeat what's already been done, or he must comment upon it, or react against it? Does this apply to poetry?

The extremes to which certain people in the visual arts go are not possible in poetry simply because the medium that poetry deals in is this everyday commodity which everybody shares, i.e. language. But there has been some pretty odd poetry, let's face it. I don't know what the poetic equivalent is of a completely black canvas with one pink dot in the left-hand corner. If a tradition has been exhausted there is a case for complete stylistic volte-face. But I don't think the tradition of the lyric poem in English has been exhausted. I disagreed in conversation with Craig Raine last week about the iambic measure being exhausted. If Shakespeare couldn't exhaust it, it must be inexhaustible! Modernism in English writing came about to some extent because two generations were decimated in the first and second world wars and certain American theorists, i.e. Eliot and Pound, moved in and filled a vacuum. And then a brilliant generation of poets in the thirties – mainly MacNeice and Auden – showed by their practice that the lyric tradition was not exhausted. They went back via Edward Thomas and Wilfred Owen, both of whom were killed in the trenches, to Hardy and Keats and Donne. I see myself as doing that in a humble way as well. Apart from that I think it's probably very bad for poets to think of themselves historically. Surely one writes simply because one has to . . . The lovely thing about poetry, as Auden said, is that there can never be an international style.

You said Northern Ireland was a godforsaken place in the old days. Did you feel, as poets, outsiders in society? Did you feel relieved of any guilt associated with being a member of that society?

I still feel an outsider in society. I can't speak for the other two. But part of being a self-absorbed twenty-three-year-old is automatically being an outsider. I was thinking of the days when CEMA [Committee for the Encouragement of Music and the Arts; later, Arts Council of Northern Ireland] refused to support Sam Thompson's play [about sectarianism in the shipyards] *Over the Bridge*. That Afrikaaner mentality which ruled the society until it eventually erupted in 1968 . . . let's face it, this place was godforsaken. But to be honest with you, I didn't feel any pang of guilt until 1968, when I attended the demonstration in Linenhall Street. That was because I might as well, as far as the curriculum at primary school and at Inst was concerned, have been living in Bolton or Southampton. There was no Irish literature, no Irish music, no Irish art. Nothing to remind us that we were living in Ireland, albeit a specialised part. Then when I went to Trinity there was the ban. It was a mortal sin, according to the dreadful Archbishop McQuaid, for Irish Catholics to go to this Protestant bastion. So apart from Brendan Kennelly, whose parish priest in Ballylongford was a bit of a rebel and insisted that he went to Trinity, I only had two Catholic friends: one was American, the other Rhodesian. I was living life very intensely – music, poetry, girls, drink – and it wasn't until I'd come back to Belfast and had met Seamus and Marie Heaney [in 1964] that the penny dropped and I realised that they were the first northern Irish Catholics who were close friends. I realised that there was an invisible apartheid in our community, and as far as I was concerned it had worked very well. Then from about 1968 to 1973 I was consumed with Protestant guilt. I've since decided that feeling guilty is a waste of time. Perhaps we moderate Protestants have said 'sorry' often enough?

I've written about you that you seemed conscious of the role of a poet. Do you know what I meant?

You're talking about the public role. The poet does have important responsibilities: to be as efficient and vigilant a custodian of the language as he can be, to be as true as possible to his own emotions and thoughts, and not to tell lies of any kind. That would apply to a poet like Emily Dickinson, who never left her house. With regard to their role in the community, it's important, especially in this post-modernist phase when poetry to a large extent has lost its audience, for poets, by the way they behave in public, to demystify poetry, and that involves a certain amount of innocent showing-off which, when I've had a few drinks, I quite enjoy. It's really like dressing up. I think showing-off's important. I encourage my three children to show off.

Pablo Neruda has a phrase, 'singing between joy and obligation' . . .

Joy obviously is one of the elements of art . . . But a poet's obligations – that's a big issue. I think the first obligation is to one's art, to the dictates of the imagination. Beyond that, a poet has the ordinary citizen's obligations. But it would be fatal for anyone sitting down to paint a picture or write a poem to think that they are contributing to society with a capital 'S'. I've always liked a Latin phrase, *'musarum sacerdos'*, priest of the Muses. This may go straight into 'Pseuds' Corner', but poetry, the effort to write it, reading it and living it, is, if you like, my religion. It gives me something akin to religious experience. Perhaps one of the things an artist should do is suggest the sacerdotal values of life – in a completely secular way, of course. Keep the churches out of it, please! 'Poet' comes from the Greek word, 'poetes', and then there's the Scots word, 'makar'. At one level a poet is someone who makes poems in the same way as a carpenter is someone who produces wooden artefacts. When I sit down I don't know what I'm going to write. There's some frisson, the nexus of an idea, a word, an emotion, a rhythm, and then the writing of the poem is an inner exploration that takes me to where I haven't been before, to unknown territory. Otherwise it would be just verse. I'm using the shapes, the forms of the poem as an explorer would use a compass. The exciting moment is when you make connections between two quite ordinary things. 'My love is like a red, red rose' – one of the most lovely connections in poetry. A moment of excitement for me was when I wrote that poem 'Thaw', about taking a shovelful of coal and snow out of the coal-house during the last heavy fall of snow – quite mundane. The following week I saw a blackbird on the lawn which obviously had an albino ancestor because it had one white feather. And the line just came: 'The thaw's a blackbird with one white feather.'

Do you write most of a poem in your head?

I have written one or two in my head because of circumstances. They were very short. I couldn't do a 'Tintern Abbey'. Didn't Wordsworth compose that when he was walking? I find I need a pencil and paper and the physical process of covering it. Which is a bit like when you're a child and waking up to find snow has fallen – the rush to be the first person to cover it with your footprints. I find I work very untidily on bits of paper and sometimes use different coloured inks – the invention of the Biro is a great thing – as a kind of stimulus. But given that, it's basically tested in my mouth and ears. It's an oral and aural thing, but I do need to write it out.

Do you do much rewriting? Do you go back after years and revise?

No. Most of my poems go through a lot of drafts. It seems like a swift process. Then when I discover the worksheets I realise just how hard I was working at it. The finished poem usually emerges after a great deal of effort. That doesn't mean to say there aren't poems that have come in one go. I might tinker with it here and there for a few months, but certainly I wouldn't change anything I'd written a couple of years ago, because I was a different person then. Most poets' revisions of earlier work are disastrous. Auden's, for instance. And I thoroughly dislike most of Derek Mahon's revisions of his early work. Yeats is an exception.

Many of your poems use special knowledge, for example about the natural world. While none of your poems are obscure, do you ever feel you'd like to be as accessible as Paul McCartney, for instance?

There's quite a lot of obscure reference in Paul McCartney, you know – *Sergeant Pepper* and things like that, with enclosed references to the drug scene. I write about the things that interest me. Among those interests would be botany, geology, natural history – areas which have beautiful words. I wouldn't use anything that couldn't be looked up in a fairly ordinary dictionary. All the time I strive towards clarity: it's dishonest not to try to be as clear as possible. That doesn't rule out the fact that sometimes one's moving in obscure emotional areas, and I have written occasionally an obscure poem but, given that it's obscure, it's still as clear as I can possibly make it. I know intuitively it has some truth although I couldn't paraphrase it.

All your books have dates as subtitles. Was that an indication that they were not conceived as entities?

The books weren't conceived as entities. I think it's very much a question of 'if you look after the pence the pounds will look after themselves'. There's an awful moment when you send off a book: you've had this nice fat folder and you send it off and all of a sudden you've

378

to start all over again. You don't know what you're going to do. The poems accumulate and you keep some and reject others and gradually you think you might have a book – a book rather than a miscellany of poems. If you're lucky you'll discern some pattern in it that your subconscious has been bringing about. I am a little suspicious of the programmatic approach. Heaney's *Station Island* and Craig Raine's *Rich* are recent examples, though there's much I admire in both collections. With regard to my dating, that's because I'm such an untidy person and the only thing I do with any precision is poetry. The dating is my gesture to anal tidiness! A bit pretentious, right enough, but I can't help doing it.

Did you ever feel the need to write a long, book-length poem, something like Patrick Kavanagh's The Great Hunger?

There's only one thing better than a good short poem, and that's a good long poem. Not *better* . . . I think I could, but somehow poems haven't presented themselves in that way. There's a lot of nonsense now being talked about bringing back narrative into poetry – poets resenting or envying the scope of the novel. I sympathise with that to some extent, but the novel set poetry free to do what it does best, i.e. intense lyrical expression. You know the way Graves translated the *Iliad*: into prose mostly, with the really important passages, the bits everybody knows, the intense flights, translated into poetry. But I'd love to be able to write something like *The Great Hunger*, which seems to me to be a great poem by a great poet. Or *Autumn Journal*, another great poem by a great poet. But there's something one-off about *Autumn Journal*, isn't there? I don't think it can be done again. Indeed MacNeice thought it could be done again with *Autumn Sequel*, which is a damp squib. I'm just very grateful for poems when they come along.

If they are four lines long, so be it. You need to have an awful lot to say to go beyond four lines. I also sense that with a lot of the great talents there's often an attendant prolixity. There's quite a lot of prolixity surrounding the birth of the things I write, I just choose not to publish it. When I teach those courses at the Arvon Foundation, by the end of the week the students mimic me: 'Cut it, cut it, cut it.' I believe that every word has to earn its place. It is amazing what you can say in four lines. I feel I've run the mile if I get to twenty-four lines.

You've said you haven't written much for three years. Why is that? Does it worry you?

Well, I don't know why it is. It does worry me. I've written very little since *The Echo Gate*, which was published in 1979, and practically nothing for the last three years. This may have something to do with being forty-five, the male menopause and all that. It may have something to do – and this is an intuitive, mysterious thing – with the feeling I had when I was putting the four books together, with a little coda of new poems: that I'd come full circle, that there's some kind of formal impasse and that I've got to break out of the circle that I've carefully, over twenty years, inscribed around myself. It might also have something to do with my job becoming more demanding. In a religious sense, I believe that my present silence is part of the impulse and sooner silence than forgery. I've enough technique now to be quite a good forger. So my attitude is to live as intensely and as honestly in other areas of life, in my job and as a husband, father and friend, and take it on trust that if I don't betray those areas, and if I don't betray my silence, the poems will come back again. It would be awful if they didn't.

Do you feel better after you've written a poem?

Oh, I feel great. It's like nothing else – a sense of achievement, the exhilaration of realising that, for an hour or two hours, one's been more intelligent, more emotionally precise and tuned up than one normally is. One's been living at a more intense level. It's also a kind of psychic release, the psychological equivalent of having an itch in the middle of your back: you can't get at it, you get out of bed and grab a ruler or a hairbrush – the release of that. It's a physical pleasure as well.

Many of your poems use Christian imagery. Are you a Christian?

No, I'm an atheist, but I'm a cultural Christian. My parents were lazy agnostics. I had a rush of blood to the head when I was sixteen and got myself confirmed, but I'm pleased to say that phase passed very quickly. I'm not one of those literary people who say 'I love the Old Testament as great literature' and ignore the New Testament. I do think the Old Testament is great literature, but I find the New Testament illuminating and enriching. I've been reading St Paul, for instance, especially his Letter to the Philippians. Paul begins like Ian Paisley and ends like Jesus. My socialism, if you like, is strengthened by reading the New Testament. I believe in Jesus as a historical fact, as a genius, as a poet and revolutionary: a *musarum sacerdos*, a man who produced the greatest, most simple, most earthly account of the sacerdotal values of life – the bread and the wine. I'm about as Christian as the Bishop of Durham [David Jenkins].

But you don't feel you have to talk in Christian terms because you live in Belfast, because everyone else does?

I haven't heard much Christian talk in Belfast, have you? The things that exercise theologians I find boring and irrelevant. The virgin birth and the resurrection, whether they're right or wrong doesn't engage my curiosity at all.

Some of the poems in your first book, No Continuing City, *are quite 'literary' in their language. I felt that as the books went on you became more colloquial and fluent. Looking back, how do you feel about the extremely formal style of a poem like, say, 'A Personal Statement'?*

I don't know what the word 'literary' means. It's odd that it always has a pejorative sense, like 'bookish'. That's the way I discovered how to write, by consciously setting myself formal challenges. 'A Personal Statement' came about partly because I discovered George Herbert at the late age of twenty-one or twenty-two, and was interested in patterns which used lines of varying lengths in a strict way. The usual development – I don't think I'm unusual – is towards increasing simplicity. In many ways the first book, and I think I *am* unusual in this, is one of my favourites, possibly my favourite. I'd rather like to get back to that kind of technical firework display. I don't think I'll ever be able to, but solving the problems I set myself in those poems was inspiring in itself. You know what Yeats said, when someone asked him where he got his ideas: 'Looking for the next rhyme.' You might find it hard to believe that 'A Personal Statement', as far as I can remember, came quite easily. That's the interesting thing, the way something that looks very formal and 'difficult' quite often comes more easily than a freer form. I suppose I would really like one day to write some distinguished free verse.

Do you ever say 'I would like to write a poem in a certain verse form'?

No, I don't work that way. 'A Personal Statement' came about really because a number of lines of those lengths occurred to me and I borrowed the stanzaic shape. But the lines came first. Mahon, for instance, has written some good villanelles, but for me the thought of sitting down to write a villanelle is quite foreign. *Poems 1963–1983* [published 1985] has three or four sonnets, but they didn't begin as sonnets, they ended up as sonnets. There is this mysterious moment you'll know about yourself, when you've got a number of lines and it's a bit like a mathematician with a segment of an arc: from that segment he can work out the size of the arc. You know at the back of your mind: 'Yes, this will probably be twenty-four lines' or 'This might be a sonnet'. You go on writing to find out if that intuition is correct and it often is. I find a lot of poems end up as twenty-four lines. It seems to be a magical number: six fours, eight threes, twelve twos.

Do you see any other movements or developments in the four books?

Do I see my poetry developing? Again subconsciously, one of the things I tried to do was advance on more than one front. In fact there are several tones of voice in the book. There might be a future development in exploring one of those, I don't know. I have some ideas for poems at the moment – I won't tell you what they are – I'm not sure whether they'll be developments. I'm not sure what 'development' is, I'm always hoping for a great big Whitmanesque splurge. But as I say, I start in a Whitmanesque, expansive mood, and write away, and the poems come out in shapely fashion.

I think it's true of many artists in any art form that once they've learned their craft there isn't necessarily any improvement or development. There may be a sudden change of direction, as when Louis MacNeice came up with The Burning Perch, *but from the first fully-achieved work it's all somehow there and just waiting to come out. Do you think that's true?*

It would seem to be true. The galley proofs of *Poems 1963–1983* have been very revealing: you see a number of poems on the same long page. The number of poems that are two stanzas of four, five or six lines – that seems to be a pattern which I wasn't aware of, that's the way they happened. On the other hand I would hope that I haven't been repeating myself. I hope that very much. We've talked about form a lot, but there's subject-matter. If there are developments, I'd hope they'd include me writing about things I haven't written enough about, for instance Belfast, certain aspects of my family's history, more 'political' poems, I don't know. Rather than talk about developments, I'd like to hope I haven't closed down any options. My formal preoccupations make me sympathise with, say, Mark Rothko, who painted for decades in blocks of paint: icons of pure colour, three bands of colour. Then his pictures became more and more sombre and he pushed this tendency to its logical conclusion and came up with an all-black canvas. Then he put a bullet through his head. I sympathise with his dilemma. On the other hand, if I were a painter I would like to be like Courbet, who painted flowers, naked women, seascapes, landscapes, skyscapes, portraits, animals, *everything*. I hope I've kept my pores open to such an extent that I'm potentially open to everything. Although of course life won't be long enough.

Obviously your poems arise from particular personal experiences, but because they're achieved they're never 'confessional'. How do you feel about autobiographical verse?

I dislike that fashion of confessional poetry. It's a journalistic notion.

384

The best poets who are thought of as confessional, Robert Lowell and Sylvia Plath, aren't really confessional at all. I do feel anxious about invading family privacies or about being private in public. When I write about my father I write about him because he's representative of a generation, the survivors of the trenches. My mother's more difficult. I've written a couple of elegies for her. I think bad poems in these areas are unforgiveable, in the same way that bad poems about the Troubles are unforgiveable, because they do damage with their clumsiness. But if the poem is an adequate artefact the artefact has a life of its own which protects the people depicted in it. If one was a painter, say, one should feel free, if one couldn't afford a model, to paint one's wife in the nude and then exhibit it. If it's a good painting people will forget about who's in the picture. So I would look to the symbolic import of the lives of those I've been involved with and isolate that. Of course a certain amount of personal, private pain unavoidably trails behind any poem.

Do you see Poems 1963–1983 *as a culmination?*

Well, I'm a bit nervous about it. I suppose it is a 'Collected Poems', but I've carefully avoided that name because it's the sort of thing that should happen when you're a good deal older than I am. Really I'm glad it's coming out because all four of my books are out of print and this is the most convenient way of reissuing them. But 'Collected Poems' sounds like a tombstone. I would have liked to have called it 'The First Four Books of Poems', but an American poet has already used that title. So let's just say it's a beginning.

The Honest Ulsterman 78 (Summer 1985)

'AU REVOIR, OEUVRE'

Interviewer: Peter McDonald

(This interview took place in Belfast on the night of the referendum about the Good Friday Agreement, 22 May 1998.)

You retired from your post in the Northern Ireland Arts Council in 1991, and have been prolific since then; is retirement, in whatever sense, something you find beneficial?

First of all, I didn't retire: I quit my job which I had done seriously for two decades. I now think that, apart from the privilege of working with artists, ninety per cent of the time I spent in the office was a waste of time, a waste of my life. I quit when I was fifty-one. I don't think I could write now in the way I do if I had a nine-to-five job. It's an interesting question. Mind you, I wouldn't call myself prolific exactly.

Retiring, or quitting, seems like a kind of youthful rebellion.

Middle-aged rebellion. Every Monday morning I try to remember to say 'Thank you, Lord. I'm not at the Senior Staff Meeting.' I do feel that a poem needs not just space, but, ideally, space around that space – space for meditation, reverie, subliminal link-ups. I sense that poetry happens at a level above or below intelligence. It doesn't come into being at a purely rational level. Of course, when a poem is being born, the reasoning part of the brain throbs away at full throttle, but all the other areas are overlapping and interacting as well, the emotional, intuitive, animal areas. For that interaction to blossom, space is required and freedom from silly distractions like committee work and agendas and review papers. For me, now, poems sometimes occur in clusters, in a way that they never used to. Thanks to having given up the job, there's a continuing sense of release. I feel like an ex-prisoner. If what I write now has any rigour, that rigour owes something to my having stuck it out in the crucible of a job and faced up to the difficulties. The job has left me with a healthy disregard for what you might call Public Life. I have no desire now to go to receptions, to be seen at gatherings of the great and the good, to stand and be bored to death by men in grey suits. Public Life is pretty rubbishy. I've had first-hand experience of all that. I retired when I was relatively young. I still feel young. I look forward to my next collection as though it were my first book. Partly because of the break, the big change in the pattern of my life, I feel in my late fifties like a young poet who is just beginning.

It's an age when writers sometimes give in to various kinds of flattery or blandishments. Do you think that many people at that stage want to feel like they're just beginning, or beginning again?

I suppose that as you grow older some sense of an accumulating *oeuvre* is unavoidable: but the very word sounds so pompous – you know, those people who talk about 'my work'. The funniest line I can think of comes from Robin Williams in a film I watched on a plane: he's an unsuccessful writer; he throws everything he's written into a wastepaper basket, and says '*Au revoir, oeuvre!*' There's always a danger of writers believing their own publicity. We live in a world of puff and solicited blurb, a world of favours and backscratching. In America, where you'd have thought the country's so huge it couldn't happen quite so cosily, everyone's giving his or her *imprimatur* to everyone else. You line up three or four well-known poets and a couple of eminent academics on the dust-jacket, and the rest of academe follow like sheep. That's death really, if you take pleasure in it. Mind you, the occasional puff's hard to resist, but you shouldn't inhale.

You've published a new Selected Poems *this year, the first since the more capacious* Poems 1963–1983 *thirteen years ago. Has your post-1985 output influenced the way you now look at your earlier poems?*

First of all, the 1963–83 book came into being simply because Tom Fenton, who produced such beautiful books under his Salamander imprint, reminded me that all of my four volumes were out of print, and he asked would I like to publish them together with some new work. That seemed like a good idea, but it was risky to bring out what amounted to a premature *Collected Poems*. I had been fairly severe on each of the books, so there wasn't a lot to excise (except from the third volume, *Man Lying on a Wall*, which I really did prune down). While putting my *Poems 1963-83* together I thought too long and hard about 'my work', my *oeuvre*; it made me self-conscious, and that was unhealthy. In every respect – from contents to binding and design – the book was exactly what I wanted. But with regard to form I seemed in some mysterious way to have come full circle. It was difficult to step outside that circle, to look beyond the book. I would advise against assembling a volume like that in your forties. In my first four books I had indulged a tendency to write short intense lyrics and then arrange them in sequences. Something different began to happen in *Gorse Fires* [1991] – some kind of involuntary denial of that urge to string poems together in rosaries. The book emerged like a big patchwork. I wanted any given poem to draw resonances from other poems ten or twenty pages in front or behind. I was aiming for a deeper cohesiveness. In more confident moments the book looks to me like one big poem, although each piece has its own title and independence. This process was taken further in *The Ghost Orchid* [1995]. As a result, there are fewer showpieces, anthology pieces, if I may be so bold. So it was harder to select poems from *Gorse Fires* and *The Ghost Orchid*. Both awoke in me affection for my very first collection, *No Continuing City*, the poems I wrote in my twenties. Perhaps I wouldn't have been able to control the later big splodgy pieces like 'The Butchers' if I hadn't set myself those formal challenges in my young days.

A lot of contemporary poetry is keen on size, often producing a kind of gigantism, but you seem as devoted as ever to the art of the miniature.

I've suggested somewhere else that miniature is not necessarily the same as minor. How many contemporary long poems have you actually finished, let alone enjoyed and re-read a few times? Why are we all so polite about the tedium and dead trees they cause? I suppose it's not unreasonable to want to take back from the novel narrative sweep and a cast of characters. The other side of the argument is that the novel has set poetry free to do what it does best, the intense lyric. I would love to write a long poem, something like the Intimations Ode, something spacious as well as concentrated. Gigantism is the word you used; I would use elephantiasis, which I gather is a medical condition. I'm not against ambition and reach, but if you can say it in four lines, why waste your time saying it in more? Challenge the world by all means, but it's bad for your poetry to take steroids.

I'm interested in what the formal discipline is that makes it possible to write a good four-line or two-line poem. You served your own apprenticeship to poets like George Herbert.

Well, I cogged some of his stanza patterns. I'd quite like to end my days exploring Herbertian shapes. It would be nice to return to writing poems like 'A Personal Statement' and 'The Hebrides' in my sixties and seventies. I don't know where the shape of a poem comes from. I certainly don't impose it. I write out of a jumble of emotions and vague notions and scraps of knowledge. At some stage a form or, rather, a shape mysteriously emerges. Was it Tennyson who said that a perfect lyric inscribes the shape of an S? That sense of a gesture, you know, the way you use your hand if you're bowing, if you're reaching out to shake somebody's hand, if you're going to stroke a cat, if you're holding a woman's hand to take her onto the dance-floor – all those gestures that are made in a couple of sweeps, the wave shaping up and then the wave collapsing, suggest two stanzas. Arranging the *Selected Poems*, I realised how many of my poems are two stanza jobs. Quite a few sonnets, for instance. The stanzas can be very long as in 'Wounds' or 'Company', but that's unusual. The single four-line poems and lone couplets are meant to be just as roomy in their own way. In my youth short poems tended to be longer poems cut down, the results of pruning. Now my short poems more or less happen like that. I know instinctively that they are complete. Capturing a moment of inspiration and just leaving it at that. The poem has to fill the page, even if it's only two lines long. Sometimes the brevity is a kind of tact, the only way I have of dealing with momentous subject matter without being offensive or impertinent – a touch and no more. For instance, my two-line poem, 'Terezín', was inspired by a photograph of a room in Terezín filled with hundreds of violins which had been confiscated from Jews and stored for handing out to young future Nazi Mozarts. I wanted my poem to approach the condition of silence:

No room has ever been as silent as the room
Where hundreds of violins are hung in unison.

My next collection [*The Weather in Japan*, 2000] will take its title from a two-line poem, a new form I've invented and am trying to impose on the world in the belief that the haiku is garrulous and overweight. Should I call it the low-ku? The title runs into the first line, and the couplet has to be as short as possible, and it has to rhyme: 'The Weather in Japan' (that's the title) 'Makes bead curtains of the rain,/ Of the mist a paper screen.' That's my near-silent way of suggesting what poetry might be. And in naming the book after such a brevity, I might be making a point about scale and importance.

The 'Terezín' poem's 'hung in unison' seems to relate to the hanging of the maid-servants later in Gorse Fires, *in 'The Butchers', the short poem prefiguring something in the longer one. Is this deliberate?*

No, I hadn't thought of that. I'm pleased though. One hopes that a book has such echoes and connections. But I wouldn't plant them deliberately. I'm not the kind of poet who arranges treasure-hunts to please the academics and keep them busy. Poetry should be surprising in deeper ways.

Your most extreme short poem is 'The Parting', where you compress the whole episode of Hector's farewell to Andromache into a couplet:

> He, 'Leave it to the big boys, Andromache.'
> 'Hector, my darling husband, och, och,' she.

There's something almost aggressive in that, almost violent in its relation to the original. How did you come to that point in your relation to Homer?

It's formally extreme, yes, but rather tender, I'd have thought. Did you notice that there's a six-syllable off-rhyme? My little Muldoonian moment. The good luck of that licensed the risk of sentimentality in 'och, och' – you know, the way we say that in Ulster with a sense of sorrow and impatience. So many tones: Och. I read Homer at school and was taught by W. B. Stanford, a great Homeric scholar, at Trinity. I didn't work very hard as a classicist. I spent more time exploring Dublin and James Joyce. I was inhaling *Ulysses* and got some early sense of Homer from him and from Bloom's wanderings. Years later various shocking things happened in my life: my mother's painful death in 1979, which reminded me of my father's death when I was young and unprepared – I'm still coming to terms with that – and then a sense of betrayal in my job, in my professional life, and all of the time for thirty years the poison of the Troubles. Somehow or other, in my late forties, re-acquaintance with the *Odyssey* allowed me to give expression to sorrows and toxins. Moments in the *Odyssey* chimed with emotions that I would have found almost impossible to deal with otherwise: heartbreak, paranoia, bitterness, hatred, fear. Homer gave me a new emotional and psychological vocabulary. The last poem in *Gorse Fires*, 'The Butchers', was a cleansing, a catharsis. I was purging feelings of distaste – distaste for Northern Ireland and its filthy sectarianism, for the professional career I'd pursued for twenty years, for Public Life and its poison.

Ovid joins Homer as a presence in The Ghost Orchid, *partly owing to the happenstance of your being approached to contribute to Michael Hofmann and James Lasdun's* After Ovid *anthology. Writing the Ovidian poems must have been a more deliberate process.*

The happenstance is rather alarming, isn't it, how much of what you write depends on chance? Hofmann and Lasdun asked me to do the Baucis and Philemon story which I took on initially in the spirit of a commission, but then I fell in love with it. And I was overwhelmed by other stories which I just had to try. There was nothing deliberate in the process. I was flailing around in the dark as I usually do. 'Spider-woman', the Arachne story, is half Ovid and half me (or David Attenborough in a toga). 'Ivory & Water' takes two of the stories, the woman changed into a fountain and the woman changed into ivory, the Arethusa and Pygmalion stories, and splices them to see if they might illuminate sexual neurosis. With 'Baucis & Philemon' I set myself a formal challenge – five-line stanzas, proper stanzas. I didn't see the point in simply dividing the flow into five-line units just for the look of it. I wanted each stanza to have some kind of internal logic. The formal restraint of the stanza or, say, something like Dryden's couplets, helps to control self-indulgence. So much contemporary translation is self-indulgent and reads like cut-up prose. For me the form, the stanzaic shape, is an endorsement, proof that I'm engaged with the Latin or Greek at an original level, that my versions are explorations.

The Ovidian material is obviously all about changes from one thing into another, about things failing to stand still. On the other hand, your poetry has often been attracted to stasis, or to leaving things poised, suspended – sometimes using lists, sometimes in a kind of rhythmic suspension. In that sense, aren't you a very conservative, rather than metamorphic poet?

God, you make me sound like a still life – and me thinking I was into nude studies and battle scenes. If I'm as immobile as you suggest, then Ovid turned up just in time. If things are poised or suspended – your words – then they're in danger of toppling, breaking, changing, aren't they? Perhaps I'm obsessed with the way things come and go, the way they fade, the way nothing lasts. There's a poem in *Gorse Fires* about the brief mark an otter's tail makes in wet sand. Those are the moments that move me. Poems give them a second chance. There's a danger of being paralysed imaginatively and emotionally, mesmerised by such fleeting mysteries. Therefore the invitation to the *Metamorphoses* party was good for me, it stopped some pores from closing, corrected certain mannerisms, and forced me to attempt again a young man's poetry. I got a kick out of the humour and surrealism, the high jinks. It was healthy to tousle the slightly Japanese, Chinese, feathery, leafy, butterfly-wingy side of my imagination.

You have recently brought out a chapbook of elegies, Broken Dishes.

Used to be pamphlets of love poems! 'Love poems, elegies: I am losing my place./ Elegies come between me and your face.' Those are the final (hidden) lines in *The Ghost Orchid*. It's a commonplace to suggest that elegies are love poems, love poems elegies. Love poems are full of the sadness of time passing. Elegies brim with the remembered liveliness of the dead. Elegies are a celebration as well as a lamentation. Weddings and funerals have so much in common (except that in Ireland funerals are more fun – better food, better drink): at both, our senses are sharpened and we register much more than usual – a striking face or hairdo, the wind's behaviour, a bird singing. And we're reminded that all of us have made the same double journey from our parents' naughty bits; that the journey continues in the general direction of decrepitude and death. Death and sex. What else is there to write about?

You aren't much given to revision of poems after they have been published.

No, I work hard to make the poems as good as they can be, and if they're not good enough I scrap them. I find it difficult after a gap of a few years to tinker – I'm more likely to destroy. A different person wrote them two years ago – certainly twenty years ago. Most poets' revisions are disastrous. They buckle and dent what was originally forged at a red-hot heat. In any case, you shouldn't be obsessed with your *oeuvre*, we agreed. When I'm assembling a book I concentrate as though I were writing a poem. A truly imagined arrangement will indicate gaps and generate new poems. I re-read the new poems in my folder in the hope that this might happen. I hardly ever look at my published books. *Au revoir, oeuvre*. I believe in letting your subconscious look after things. After my experience with *Poems 1963–83* I'm suspicious about being too self-aware. When I was last in the States I heard about a reading which was followed by a distinguished critic giving a lecture on that poet's work. Jesus. Even giving an interview . . . how many interviews did Beckett or Yeats give, or George Herbert? You live your life and you write your poems. If you do one dishonestly, the other will suffer.

This sense of honesty must relate somehow to your sense of how what you call Public Life actually impinges on your poetry. Despite all you say, do you still feel yourself in some way publicly accountable as a poet?

I wrote an elegy for an ice-cream man on the Lisburn Road who was murdered by the IRA. I read it on the radio, and I got a letter some time later from the murdered man's mother, a very beautiful letter. My poem ends with a list of twenty-one flowers – I'd never counted them – and it begins with a shorter list of ice-cream flavours. She said, I wouldn't have noticed, but there were twenty-one flower names in my poem and there were twenty-one ice-cream flavours in her son's shop. She signed herself The Ice-Cream Man's Mother. When I published my poem 'Ceasefire' in the *Irish Times* I got a letter from the father of Paul Maxwell, the sixteen-year-old boy who had been blown

up with Lord Mountbatten. Those letters matter more to me than any
amount of criticism I might receive in literary journals or attention in
the public world. I do mean that. I also believe in that wartime slogan,
'Careless talk costs lives'. To write carelessly and self-indulgently in a
place like Northern Ireland could have terrible consequences. I do
speak occasionally on radio and television in a measured way, mindful
of how much some fellow-citizens have suffered. If you look at the
work of the poets from this part of the world – Hewitt, Heaney, Mahon,
Carson, Muldoon, McGuckian, Ormsby – they have all behaved in
much the same way. Unavoidably, the poet's role here has been more
public than the role of a poet living in a more settled society. I don't
think that has made any of us feel self-important – the reverse probably. In its language the Good Friday Agreement depended on an
almost poetic precision and suggestiveness to get its complicated
message across. The good poetry that has emanated from here is like
that too, and for exactly the same reasons.

Thumbscrew 12 (Winter 1998–9)

'INTERVIEW: MICHAEL LONGLEY'

by Jody Allen Randolph

You are variously described as a nature poet, a love poet, a classical poet, a war poet, a political poet. Do any of these tags seem closer to home than others?

I don't care for pigeon-holing. I hope there are overlappings, the nature poetry fertilising the war poetry and so on. Advancing on a number of fronts at the same time looks like a good idea: if there's a freeze-up at points along the line, you can trickle forward somewhere else. Love poetry is at the core of the enterprise – the hub of the wheel from which the other preoccupations radiate like spokes. In my next collection *Snow Water* [2004] there will be eleven new love poems. I wouldn't mind being remembered as a love poet, a sexuagenarian love poet. I occasionally write poems about war – as a non-combatant. Only the soldier poets I revere such as Wilfred Owen and Keith Douglas produce what I would call proper war poetry. It's presumptuous to call oneself a poet. Anyone who begins a sentence 'As a poet, I' is probably not a poet. It's like calling yourself a saint. It's what I most want to be. Since I favour intensity of utterance and formal compression, you could say that I am trying to be a lyric poet.

Your parents were English, and you were born and raised in Belfast. Were there elements that particularly formed you as a poet?

I was brought up in Ireland by English parents. I lived my first eighteen years in a leafy Belfast suburb where there were big fields and old hedges beyond and even between the houses. From an early age I drifted between Englishness and Irishness, between town and country, between the Lisburn Road with its shops and cinemas and the river Lagan with its beech woods and meadows where I fell in love with wild birds and wild flowers. I am still drifting. Perhaps a certain indeterminacy keeps me impressionable. I would hate to be considered anything other than an Irish poet, but at the same time I remain true to my Britannic side. (Why be confined to just the one cultural allegiance?) Belfast is home, but I also feel at home in Romney Marsh, where my Kentish forbears hailed from – carpenters, blacksmiths, gamekeepers, farm labourers. My English parents introduced me to the western seaboard of Ireland when I was twelve. That changed my life. They too loved Donegal and Connemara.

Was there a particular point at which you knew you were going to be a poet, a moment when you crossed that bridge from writing poems to feeling you were a poet vocationally?

Like everyone else I desperately wanted as an adolescent to explore experiences and feelings and share them with others, especially girl-friends. But it wasn't until Trinity that the Muse moved centre stage. Being a poet is different from being a writer. Poetry can't be created to order. Yes, it's a vocation rather than a profession. Some poets are writers as well but they are usually protecting a core. I live from poem to poem, from hand to mouth. In 'Pascoli's Portrait' I say 'a poem's little more than a wing and a prayer'.

Your generation began to come together at Trinity. Each of you writes with great affection for those years. What was it about that environment and time that was so fertile for poetry?

Trinity was such a lovely place, an oasis in the middle of a capital city. We slummed it in our own rooms and played at being grown-ups. Terms were short. You could avoid hard work and make time for daydreaming. Among the small student population there was a healthy proportion of folk who would have been new to us provincials – English public-school toffs, an ex-GI or two, students from France, Sweden, colonial Africa, post-Farouk Egypt – very refreshing. We published our juvenilia in the undergraduate literary magazine *Icarus* and even stooped to writing some prose for the campus newspaper *Trinity News* (which Edna edited for a term, and in which she gave us our first reviews). Brendan Kennelly and Rudi Holzapfel were the best-known college poets. Of course Mahon and I wanted to be noticed. Mahon was the most accomplished. Eavan Boland swept in later, after we'd left Trinity, and took us by surprise. Exciting times, but I felt edgy and inadequate and not particularly happy. Perhaps the others felt that way too. Poetry obsessed us. We kept an eye on each other like sprinters at the start of a race.

You once described Alec Reid as a father figure, as the Philip Hobsbaum to young poets at Trinity. Can you talk a bit about the role he played?

Alec Reid was large and fat and untidy with a round head and white hair and pink face. He was an albino, nearly blind, with pebble-thick specs which he wore around his neck to catch food in as much as to peer through. One of the founder editors of *Icarus,* he was the literary genius loci. We craved the approval which he meted out sparingly. We felt anxious when we knew he was going to review *Icarus* in *Trinity News.* Derek told me, ahead of publication, that Alec had singled out for praise a poem of mine called 'Konzentrationslager'. My remembering all of that shows just how important he was for us. Literary exchanges were *ad hoc* compared to the Belfast Group under Philip

399

Hobsbaum. Alec did not proselytise. A very unorthodox academic, who reviewed theatre and was close to Samuel Beckett, he was not treated generously by Trinity. We suffered the slights on his behalf. We were devastated when his young son Michael died in America after undergoing open-heart surgery. Alec and Beatrice had scrimped and saved to take Michael across the Atlantic where the odds were supposed to be better. They were majestic in their sorrow. We all grew up a bit. Because I read Classics I saw less of Alec than the others who would have attended his inspirational lectures. I got to know him in the pubs and sat quietly while he monologued over his pint. His passions included Edward Thomas and Louis MacNeice. (Edna's and my subsequent work on those poets owes so much to him.) Alec Reid was a comic figure in some ways, but also princely, heroic. He left us in no doubt as to how important poetry is. We adored him.

Eavan Boland and Derek Mahon talk about poet Brendan Kennelly as another positive presence at Trinity during those years. Were there others?

I was overwhelmed and bewildered by Brendan Kennelly, a genius in his own way. But we never locked horns. I don't recall one 'poetry session' with him. Derek and Eavan were in the English/ Modern Languages orbit. I wasn't. They would have seen much more of Brendan than I did. The ethos of the Classics Department had a real impact on me, even though I was an idle scholar. It was probably the university's most distinguished humanities department. The Professor of Latin, Donald Wormell, read aloud from Propertius and Catullus as though they were living poets. I showed him my first Propertius translations and he was marvellously encouraging. I fell in love with the Latin love elegy, thanks to him. W. B. Stanford was a world figure, a great Homeric scholar. He summoned me to his rooms for missing lectures (which were compulsory in those days). He could have failed me my year. I was terrified. He scolded me, then smiled: 'I suppose you think that because you're a poet I'm going to let you off?' 'Of course not, sir.' 'Well, I am. I very much liked those recent poems in the magazine.' Many years later at his retirement dinner he came and sat beside me. 'If I had my life over again, I would choose to be a poet rather than a scholar.' In 1992 Trinity commissioned me to write a poem for their Quatercentenary commemorations. I devoted a section of 'River and Fountain' to Stanford '. . . teaching the *Poetics*, / He asked us for definitions, and accepted mine: / "Sir, if prose is a river, then poetry's a fountain".' I hope I have repaid both great men a little with my Homeric translations and my versions from Ovid's *Metamorphoses*. The seeds sown all those years ago by Stanford and Wormell did eventually germinate. Likewise, it took a long time for me to absorb the impact of Brendan Kennelly.

The years after you left Trinity and returned to Belfast were a very exciting time in Ireland – a time of great energy, with a real sense of possibility for poets. People, yourself included, were excited about Irish music and art. What was it like as a young poet during those years?

Edna got a lectureship at Queen's University. I followed her there, followed her home. The Trinity literary friendships had been a blessing. The next godsend was getting to know Seamus Heaney and his fiancée Marie Devlin. Because of the North's invisible apartheid and, in the south, the Church's Ban on Catholics attending Trinity, I didn't become friends with any Irish Catholics at school or university (with the possible exception of Brendan Kennelly, whom I didn't get to know all that well). I remember being shocked to realise that Seamus and Marie were my first Northern Irish Catholic friends. We met at a small party *chez* Hobsbaum. Seamus and I had seen each other's poems in the *Irish Times* and elsewhere. Seamus praised my 'Questionnaire for Walter Mitty' and 'Emily Dickinson', I his 'Advancement of Learning'. I was charmed, even when he started to sing for me. He has recently reminded me that I called him a stage Irishman. Bursting into song was not part of my cultural background. At school there wasn't a whiff of anything 'Irish', certainly not Irish songs. Marie sang beautifully. I remember her singing at their wedding. So I became aware of what I had been missing. I was all ears. The Heaneys warmed to my love of jazz and we sang Cole Porter songs on excursions in Seamus's Volkswagen. They showed real tenderness towards my stories of my father's Great War experiences. They loaned me a record of Joan Littlewood's *O What a Lovely War* which I think they'd seen in London on their honeymoon. Those songs from the trenches awakened filial emotions that had gone underground. Thanks to that interchange with the Heaneys, I wrote 'In Memoriam': the first of a life-long sequence of elegies for my father and the other boy-soldiers. There were many such reciprocities. The brilliant painter Colin Middleton became our friend, possibly the most technically proficient artist Ireland has yet produced. He was thirty years our senior. We loved to please him with new poems. At boozy sessions in his house we would stand up and recite by heart our latest efforts. I wrote my first piece of art criticism about Colin. Derek and Seamus and I all dedicated poems to him in our first volumes. A convection current seemed to be lifting us all upwards. We wanted to get better and better. We supported each other but only up to a point. We competed with each other more ferociously than perhaps we now remember.

It seems remarkable that your generation were all earnest Irish poets at the age of twenty to twenty-three, with a considerable amount of sustained thinking and talking about poetry. How did that evolve?

Derek Mahon and I had lived poetry very intensely at Trinity College Dublin, and then for a year in a slum in Merrion Square. Some of the poems in my first book respond to work by him. My 'No Continuing City' owes much to his 'Girls in their Seasons'. My 'Elegy for Fats Waller' is a response to his 'Death of a Film Star' (which in turn takes off from MacNeice's 'Death of an Actress'). Without his friendship my first book would have been much less ambitious. I travelled quickly, without taking a breath, from my rather wan juvenilia to the aspiring shapes of my first reasonable poems. I arrived back in Belfast feeling a bit shell-shocked – unable to tune in to another authentic new voice. At first I couldn't hear Seamus's lovely early poems, 'Churning Day', 'Death of a Naturalist'. There was anxiety and pain in the air as well as excitement. In 1964 Derek brought Eavan Boland to Belfast to meet Edna and me (she engaged hardly at all with the Heaneys). She scared the shit out of me. She could make me feel worthless. My brainwork goes into poems. In answer to her challenge, I wrote my formally most ambitious poem 'The Hebrides'.

There was a variety of influences in play in Irish poetry at the time that you were first publishing – the Irish lyric, the British 'Movement' poem, some of the American formalists and 'confessionals'. Could you talk a bit about poetry as you came to it and intersected with it at that time?

At Trinity I hopped all over the canon. As a classicist much of it was new to me. I read George Herbert as though he'd been published the previous week. (And I never had to answer an exam question on him!) I absorbed Philip Larkin, Ted Hughes and Geoffrey Hill – like-

403

wise, Richard Wilbur: a matchless virtuoso. I bruised my brain trying to write Wilburese. I never cared for what you call confessional poetry or for prissy anal-retentive formalism. Lowell's *Life Studies* is much too fine to be thought of as confessional, just as Wilbur soars above most of the other formalists. *Life Studies* lurks behind my 'In Memoriam', which was a break-through poem for me. I fell under the spell of e. e. cummings (I even encouraged Edna to write an essay on him for the college literary magazine, *Icarus*). Derek liked Ginsberg and the Beats more that I did. We read bits of 'Howl' aloud. We were interested in how to be rhetorical without sounding ridiculous. In my Trinity rooms we listened again and again to a recording of Wallace Stevens reading 'The Idea of Order at Key West'. We studied Lowell, Roethke, Crane – and, of course, Yeats and Hardy, Auden and MacNeice. Frost and Lawrence were there too. The Great War poets came a little later. A friend gave me Patrick Kavanagh's *Come Dance with Kitty Stobling* for my twenty-first birthday. There was no pattern to my reading. It was all hand-to-mouth.

One of the things that really strikes me about your generation of Irish poets is the strong 'we', even though you were a very diverse group of poets from different backgrounds. I have heard American poets speak of their poetic communities as primarily vertical, but your generation had a very strong horizontal dynamic. How important was that to your developing sense of yourself as a poet?

Belfast had been called 'the armpit of Europe,' 'a cultural Siberia': not somewhere you would expect to produce a flurry of poetry. Perhaps 'we' registers the relief of embattled aesthetes who have come through. 'We' also implies that imagination and creativity dissolve what is called here 'the sectarian divide.' 'We' embraces Catholic and Protestant. 'We' acknowledges friendly rivalry. But not for one moment did we think in terms of school or coterie. There were no manifestos. We never hunted in a pack. 'We' in my book now includes the astonishing next generation of Muldoon, Carson, McGuckian, Ormsby and brilliant younger poets such as Sinéad Morrissey and Leontia Flynn.

In the mid-sixties, you married and settled down in Belfast, teaching and writing, and your poetry began turning in different directions, away from rhyming couplets of your earlier work into the livelier, more relaxed work of An Exploded View. *This brings us to the early seventies – can you talk about the changes occurring in your work at that point?*

In 1966 I wrote some poems in rhyming couplets – 'Gathering Mushrooms,' 'Narcissus' and one of my best, 'Persephone'. I think of that kind of enclosed couplet as the ultimate stanza. My poems were getting tighter and tighter. Eventually I left myself no room. I wrote only one six-line poem in 1967, a couple in 1968 and hardly any in 1969. This was my first long silence, my first crisis. Was I trying too hard? I usually have problems with rhythm and form rather than subject matter. I needed to loosen up. I left my teaching job and for a while retired to snowy solitude in the Wicklow Hills. When you go on holiday the Muse does not necessarily accompany you. I couldn't write there and I had no alibis. Things got worse. The only bright spot was a surprise visit from Mahon who announced his arrival with a snowball launched through the half-door. The last poem I wrote for *No Continuing City* in the summer of 1968, 'Journey out of Essex,' explores John Clare's psychological crisis. Despite the theme, its relaxed movement suggested a way out of the woods. But I didn't take the hint and went on to produce more knotty wee poems which are placed towards the start of *An Exploded View*. So the thaw was glimpsed in the John Clare poem, but didn't get underway until later with 'Caravan' (at the very end of 1970).

'Caravan' was a breakthrough poem for you?

I wrote 'Caravan' in a happy trance, the words melting down the page, the quatrains and the rhymes easy-going. 1971 was a good year. I was composing in my head, on trains, on buses, out walking, at the office desk, at staff meetings, in the middle of conversations. I would scribble lines down higgledy-piggledy. When I typed them out to see what they looked like, the forms were already there. Problems had been solved at a subconscious level. I'm fond of those pieces and grateful for them. I remember each happy delivery, where I was and what I was doing. 'The Rope-makers' which came on the heels of 'Caravan'; 'Casualty' and 'Skara Brae' which flew onto my desk at the Arts Council of Northern Ireland; 'Options' which I completed in my head while a colleague enthused to me about theatrical matters. In the autumn of 1971 I wrote two verse letters in Marvellian octosyllabics to Heaney and Mahon, explorations of poetic sodality at a time of political crisis. These released into conversational cadences the rhyming couplets I had carved into marble in the sixties. The surge continued through 1972 and beyond. There was no sign of further trouble until 1979.

There was a gradual running down. In the seven years between 1979 and 1986 I wrote only a dozen or so poems – just one in 1982, one in 1984. I have no idea where poetry comes from and why it goes away. There may, though, be a number of reasons for my second crisis. Firstly, I was beginning to dislike my job in the Arts Council. I have the insights of a politician but not the temperament. Office politics corroded my soul – my own fault to some degree, but in retrospect I cannot regret speaking out and refusing to eat shit. Perhaps the poems that emerged later, after my retirement, were toughened in that crucible. Secondly, I was depressed and drinking too much – the male

menopause and all that. 'This middle stretch is bad for poets,' to quote
MacNeice. Thirdly, I published in 1985 *Poems 1963-1983*. I worked on that
collection obsessively. I got to know my own work and workings too
well. I became self-conscious, then anxious. That's when the juggler
drops his balls. Fourthly, my rhythms were faltering. I was writing
tight wee poems again. I took a sabbatical in 1986 and lived on my own
in the Mayo cottage at Carrigskeewaun for two long stretches in the
spring and the autumn. The harvest was nearly thirty new poems. I
returned to the office cleansed and clear-eyed. But almost immediately
I was sucked into a corrupt situation. I just had to fight. In so doing I
helped protect the sanity of a valued colleague and flush two scoun-
drels round the U-bend, but I produced only one poem that year, 'Jug
Band', an elegy for Philip Larkin. By the end of the eighties I was writing
again with some insouciance. I had grown utterly disenchanted with
arts bureaucracy. I applied for early retirement and got it. They were
glad to get rid of me. As I made my exit I was able to expose the direc-
tor-designate as a fraud. It was exhilarating to grab my freedom and
slay a dragon in one graceful movement. And I had produced in fits and
starts the poems for *Gorse Fires*, my first collection in twelve years. Its
publication coincided almost to the day with my escape.

*Looking back at those difficult years now, do you feel that the silent stretches were
detrimental to your work?*

If I hadn't been fighting battles on other fronts, I might have been
scribbling boring middle-aged verse – like MacNeice who twittered on
for a decade until the miraculous final poems. It seems that the Muse
favours the young and then, if you can weather the 'middle stretch',
the pensioners. Silence is part of the enterprise. Most poets write and
publish far too much. They forget the agricultural good sense of the

fallow period. The Muse despises whingers who bellyache about 'writer's block' and related ailments. One of the best things ever said to me about poetry was John Hewitt's off-hand remark: 'If you write poetry, it's your own fault.'

Going back to your years in the Arts Council, were there accomplishments you were particularly happy with?

I'm proud of quite a lot. I helped the finest general publisher in Ireland – the Blackstaff Press – to survive and kept a few magazines going against the odds. The poetry reading tours I organised featured some starry duets – Seamus Heaney and Derek Mahon, Paul Muldoon and James Simmons. 'The Planter and the Gael', with John Hewitt and John Montague, was called by the historian Roy Foster 'a landmark affirmation of creative cultural diversity'. With the tours, and by supporting the Queen's University English Society's programme of visiting writers, I wanted to bring to our benighted province what William Carlos Williams calls 'the news from poems'. I hoped that the interaction between artist and community would provide new sources of creative energy. I fought hard for more money for the individual artist. I was the first arts administrator in the entire archipelago to support traditional music, a programme that Ciaran Carson took over from me. I used to ask two simple questions. How much of our programme will posterity thank us for? How much of what we are doing differentiates us from Bolton or Wolverhampton? It was a huge privilege to work with the community's life-enhancers and help to deny the death-dealers.

You've always had friends who were painters, and over the years you have written frequently about painting. Have paintings, or the questions asked by painters, been important to your work?

I've already mentioned Colin Middleton. I wrote a review of a Gerard Dillon show for the *Irish Times*. I called him 'the poet of Irish painting'. Colin was quite miffed. Painters can be as touchy as poets. Gerry brought a lovely little painting of a Falls Road christening to the Arts Council as a gift for me. He didn't have Colin's technical facility, but his best work is, in my opinion, the best. I so admire that generation of northern artists – Middleton, Dillon, George Campbell, Dan O'Neill – autodidacts, free spirits, warriors. Today their paintings fetch huge sums. For most of their lives they didn't have the price of a pint. Gerry once offered me five large canvases for £100. (Alas, I didn't have £100.) He died in 1971 when he was only fifty-five. There's an elegy for him in *An Exploded View*. I've never met anyone funnier, subtler, more refined. I loved him dearly and think of him often. My next collection [*Snow Water*, 2004] contains a celebration of one of his masterpieces, *Yellow Bungalow*. I've had my portrait painted many times. I'm supposed to be a good sitter. I enjoy the sort of zen-like conversation that keeps a session going. Writing about painting is terribly difficult. I produce every couple of years a catalogue introduction for a fellow spirit. The challenge is to find metaphors and to avoid jargon. For me few places are more exciting than an artist's studio. I ask technical questions about the processes – also simple but difficult questions. 'Why's it that size? Why's it that shape?' My younger daughter Sarah is building up a reputation as an artist. The prospect of her next solo show excites me more than my forthcoming slim volume.

By 1975, the era in which you came of age as a poet had vanished into the complex reawakening and terrible convulsions of national issues. I am interested in the position of fierce independence as lyric poets your generation argued for in response to the political situation – a strong reinterpretation of vocation under

*pressure. Can you talk about your own transition as a poet during those years,
and how some of those pressures surfaced for you?*

I supported the civil rights movement. My English parents were
completely innocent of sectarianism. My education at Inst and Trinity
had been liberal Protestant, but very complacent. I had not attended
to the tawdry shortcomings of the Unionist government. So I began
by feeling guilty, embarrassed, apologetic, especially in the company
of my Catholic friends. When the Bogside erupted in 1969 and West
Belfast went up in flames, I was flabbergasted by the ferocity of it all.
Derek Mahon and I walked through the wreckage of the Falls Road. (I
describe that in my verse letter to him.) Part of me felt like an appalled
outsider: another part, the anti-Unionist, anti-establishment part, felt
exhilarated. The rest of me wanted to understand and explain what I
had hitherto ignored, the darkness and violence in my own community. Marie Heaney said to me: 'You're learning fast,' a double-edged
remark, a compliment and a rebuke. From journalists and broadcast-
ers there came echoes of the Second World War cry: 'Where are the
war poets?' and ivory-tower charges of fiddling while the Falls Road
burns. From the beginning, my friends and I resisted the temptation
to hitch a ride on yesterday's headlines, to write 'the poetry of the
latest atrocity'. (In *States of Ireland*, Conor Cruise O'Brien refers to the
dubious 'politics of the latest atrocity'.) We learned from each other
how complex the situation was, and how inadequate the political
certainties – Green Ireland, Orange Ulster. We knew there was no
point in versifying opinion and giving people what they wanted to
hear. We believed that poetry, the opposite of propaganda, should
encourage people to think and feel for themselves: it should appeal to
their 'generous instinct' (MacNeice's lovely phrase in *Modern Poetry*).
We hated what we now call 'Troubles trash'. We believed that, even

when generated by the best of intentions, bad poetry about the sufferings of fellow citizens would be impertinence: as part of an agenda it would be a blasphemy. We disliked the notion that civic unrest might be good for poetry, and poetry a solace for the bereaved and broken-hearted. We were none of us in the front line. So far as I can recall, we never discussed these dilemmas. We had no plans to face up to the crisis as a group, or to speak to the outside world about it. It was crucial to remain true to ourselves. We continued to write the poems that presented themselves, no doubt hoping that one day we might be able to produce something adequate about the Troubles. I have long sensed that it takes time for experience to settle to an imaginative depth where it can be transformed into art. We took our time. All of these judgements are in retrospect. I speak out of my own recollections and my reading of my friends' poems. I can't speak for them. I still find desperately moving the all-embracing tender-heartedness of such poems as Heaney's 'The Other Side' and Mahon's 'Afterlives'.

Did it make a difference that MacNeice and Kavanagh, and indeed most of an older generation of Irish poets (Rodgers, Colum, Clarke), died within a short time span, pushing your generation into more senior positions while still quite young? I know that Hewitt, Kinsella and Montague remained steady presences, but what effect, if any, did the absence of elders have?

I'm not really into this generational stuff. I find it all a bit authoritarian and patriarchal. I have never thought in Irish dynastic terms and don't see myself in some kind of Irish succession. I dislike the graveyard view of poetry, literary necrophilia, ancestor worship. I'm pretty sure MacNeice and Kavanagh would also disapprove. Mind you, Derek and Seamus and I drove to Kavanagh's funeral, and the three of us visited

Carrowdore Churchyard together to pay our respects to MacNeice's ashes. Their poetry is still with us. That's what matters.

With the painful eruption of national issues, came these early statements of young poets writing in a time of identity and change. 'Wounds' quickly became one of the central poems of this time, and remains so. Can you talk about the way you located yourself and your time through the theme of the father? Was your integration of those particular strands of your father's past into the poem partly a need to clarify your own identity in Irish poetry?

I remember standing in The Crown with John Hewitt watching the news soon after an IRA atrocity. A British Army officer was dismissing the perpetrators as subhuman animals. John, who was vehemently opposed to the IRA's campaign (as was I), turned to me and said: 'That young man is talking about *our* terrorists.' They were just as much products of our society as we were. They were not complete strangers. When I wrote the last two lines of 'Wounds' ('To the children, to a bewildered wife,/ I think "Sorry Missus" was what he said') I was empathising with the paramilitary killer. Marie Heaney told me the awful story. I had been wondering for some time what my father, an old soldier and an old fashioned patriot, would have had to say about the Troubles. Marie's story sparked off the poem and released my memories of my father's memories of the trenches. He appears in poems throughout my career, but mainly when I am contemplating the catastrophe of the Great War (though I see my Great War poems as oblique comments on the Troubles). I think 'The Linen Workers' is the only other poem where I enlist his aid explicitly in the context of our grim little civil war. He helps me to face into the horror of the Kingsmills massacre. There is plenty of room in Irish poetry for my English father. When I read that line in Seamus's 'The Toome Road'

('O charioteers, above your dormant guns'), I want to say – and perhaps one day in a poem I shall say – that in a time-warp one of those squaddies might be my father. Not everyone can boast an 'invisible, untoppled omphalos'. In 1972 Seamus and I drove to Newry to walk in the banned march in protest against Bloody Sunday. Army and police had blocked the main road and most of the side roads. It was a long nervy circuitous drive. We had plenty of time to talk. What would we say if we were stopped by paramilitaries and guns were pointed at us and we were asked 'What religion are you?' (Four years later the ten workmen murdered at Kingsmills were to give the wrong answer.) We agreed we would sink or swim by what we were – in our eyes not so much Catholic and Protestant as honest and brave.

Sometimes there is wistfulness in your writing about earlier years and relationships, before the Troubles brought such enormous changes. I am thinking here of your autobiographical essays in Tuppenny Stung. *Do you ever think you would have been different as a poet if those thirty years of violence hadn't intervened?*

No, I mourn the thousands who were killed.

Peter McDonald has written about love's challenge to the epic in your lyrics. Other critics have suggested that your nature poems counter the violence that surfaces in your political poems. Do you agree that these tensions exist in your work? Are your meticulous descriptions of the natural world counters to the long shadows of history that are your context as a poet?

In my love poems, I brush against the epic only in my borrowings from Homer and Ovid's great ragbag *Metamorphoses*. Inside epics such as the *Iliad* there are lots of little works of art waiting to be set free. I wade in against the narrative flow and freeze-frame telling moments to make what I hope are self-contained lyric poems. Painters do

413

the same thing. The most urgent political problems are ecological: how we share the planet with the plants and the other animals. My nature writing is my most political. In my Mayo poems I am not trying to escape from political violence. I want the light from Carrig-skeewaun to irradiate the northern darkness. Describing the world in a meticulous way is a consecration and a stay against damaging dogmatism.

I am also curious about the use of catalogues in your poems. In 'Laertes' you say 'the whole story is one catalogue and then another.' Is the catalogue an anti-narrative device in your work? Or something else entirely? How did cataloguing as a poetic strategy begin to interest you?

Since my early twenties some of my favourite lines have been Edward Thomas's 'If I should ever by chance grow rich/ I'll buy Codham, Cockridden, and Childerditch,/ Roses, Pyrgo and Lapwater,/ And let them all to my elder daughter.' Alec Reid first quoted them to me. Then there's the catalogue of the ships in the *Iliad*, all of the vast tragedy already implicated there. Poetry's origins are in ceremony. Poetry commemorates. At memorial services after 9/11 the heart of each ceremony was the recitation of victims' names. I've sensed this in Ireland too. Names are what we're left with. 'The whole story is one catalogue and then another.' In my elegies 'The Ice-cream Man' and 'The Fishing Party' I make long lists of flower names and the names of artificial flies and imply that each catalogue should go on forever.

By the late eighties, you were writing the poems that became Gorse Fires. *There was a lightness and flexibility that began to appear in these poems that wasn't always there in your earlier work. Part of this accomplishment seems to have come from experimenting with a longer, more flexible line. Can you talk about the changes you were making technically?*

The longer line helped – hexameters and alexandrines. From the beginning I have relished making poems out of single long sentences. Drawn-out syntax generates too many prepositions, conjunctions and present participles to fit comfortably into the pentameter where, even in Shakespeare, unimportant words like 'and' or 'of' often attract something very close to a stress to help the line along. These inconvenient syllables ripple out more peacefully in the longer line. And there's more room for strange sound effects – the sort of clashes and remote harmonies you get in Homer. Iambic pentameters can be too euphonious, especially if you've been composing them for most of your life. Although the process is mostly intuitive, I do occasionally ask myself: 'Why does the line end there?' If the whip is too long you can't crack it. If the shoelace is too short you can't tie it.

A form that appears frequently in your work is the poem consisting of a single long sentence. Can you talk about the form a bit more – your history with it, why it interests you, what it's good for, its properties or challenges?

The first poem of mine to survive, 'Epithalamion', I wrote in the summer of 1963. It contains two very long sentences weaving in and out of a knotty little stanza-shape of my own invention, for twenty-five lines and then for thirty – an attempt to generate energy by restricting the flow. For forty years I have regularly aimed for what Yeats calls 'a coincidence between period and stanza' or, more boldly, between period and poem – like splitting a log from top to bottom along the grain with a single axe-blow. So much contemporary verse lacks propulsion. It's a tedium of staccato stutters – oblivious to the complexities that can be created by angled clauses. In poetry a sentence can be made to do far more than in prose. A long sentence need not be a mere container. Rather, its facets and angles imply everything that cannot be contained. This is what fired Edward Thomas and Robert Frost – in their poems and in their brilliant correspondence about syntax and measure. The resplendent opening sentence of *Paradise Lost* should be inhaled regularly as an antidote to much contemporary practice. Yeats said: 'As I altered my syntax, I altered my intellect.'

In the single-sentence poem 'Horses' (from The Weather in Japan*), there is a kind of traffic between the human and nature – the horses weep hot tears for their killed charioteer. This happens in other poems as well. In an image from 'Two Skunks' (from* Snow Water*), 'A cardinal flusters at the bedroom window/ Like the soul of a little girl who hands over/ All of the red things her short life recalls'. In images like these, nature is used to tell a human story. What do you think the distance between the poet and nature is or should be?*

None. The poet is part of nature. Language is part of nature.

Irish nature poetry over the past century has been a series of dialogues with and revisions of the pastoral. It is tempting to read your work as part of that dialogue. The poems that attach specific birds or animals to humans I used to think of as a kind of magic pastoral. But when I read 'Heron', the elegy for Kenneth Koch from your forthcoming book Snow Water*, I thought maybe I had that wrong – that perhaps you weren't a nature poet in dialogue with the pastoral tradition so much as a poet of metamorphosis. 'You are so tall and skinny I shall conscript a heron . . . Tuck your head in like a heron and trail behind you / Your long legs, take to the air above a townland/ That encloses Carrigskeewaun and Central Park.' Looking back at earlier poems, like 'The Dry Cleaners' from* The Ghost Orchid*, I wonder has the concept of metamorphosis been important to your work?*

Irish nature poetry has only recently got under way – compared with the English tradition. We have mostly had the poetry of rural community: poetry with a more social or communitarian dimension. I don't see myself as a realist in that way. Perhaps I'm more of a symbolist? Poetry is metaphor and metamorphosis – 'All metaphor, Malachi, Stilts and all'. (I chose Yeats's 'High Talk' for my anthology, *20th-Century Irish Poems*.) There are several translations from the *Metamorphoses* in my collection *The Ghost Orchid*. That clearly makes it my most Ovidian book, but really all it did was emphasise a tendency that was always there. Ever since the cave-paintings, all art has involved human consciousness with the natural world.

In Snow Water *I see a different kind of lyric reach and daring. For instance, in 'A Norwegian Wedding' in sudden lines like 'How few friends anyone has. I'm glad we came' and 'Oh,/ His sore hands', referring to the crucifixion depicted by the narrow window above the wedding party. Something similar happens in the last stanza of your long poem 'Woodsmoke' with the lines 'Are there people here who are not your friends?/ A mother who doesn't understand, a sister?/ I am with you. From among the shadowy/ Mystifying voices I pick out yours./ We have to imagine one another/ Quickly, and then go home . . .'. Do you see differences between the work you were doing in* The Weather in Japan *and this new work?*

Not huge differences. New poems respond to old ones. As I grow older I think I probably become simpler and more insouciant. I'm interested in a lighter utterance that can somehow accommodate everything. I love the seemingly casual note in Frank O'Hara's *Lunch Poems*, the way he makes it the core of their meaning. Recently I've been greatly moved by the war poems of Apollinaire (in Robert Chandler's translations). He finds connections in a bombardment of distractions and manages to be all-embracing in a world that is being blown apart. He attempts love poetry in the shadow of death. I don't want to be thinking of myself as an older poet, and I don't want to be too conscious of my own processes. Wherever I'm going, I hope I'm still headed there, still travelling to Ithaca.

This is an abbreviated version of an interview, which appeared in *Colby Quarterly* (Maine, USA) 39, 3 (September 2003); and part of which appeared in *Poetry Ireland* 79 (2004).

INDEX

LIST OF SUBSCRIBERS

Mark Adair
Fleur Adcock
Maureen Alden
Kate Allen
Jonathan Allison
Bert Almon
Paul Assey
Janet and John Banville
Sebastian Barry
Colin Beer
Victor Blease
Stephen Boyce
Andrew Brewerton
Viscountess Bridgeman
Sally Brown
Adrian Byrne
David Cabot
Gerry J. Cambridge
Matthew Campbell
Mary Clayton and
   Niall MacMonagle
Wendy Clegg
Bob Collins
Paul Crosbie
Kevin Crossley-Holland
Patrick Crotty
Vanessa Davis
Clifford Davy
Gerald Dawe

Donnell Deeny
Greg Delanty
Francis J. Dempsey
Eamonn Dillon
Tom Durham
Olive Elliott
Richard Emeny
Ronald Ewart
Barbara FitzGerald
John Wilson Foster
Richard Furniss
George Gilliland and Judy Jordan
Robert Gilmore
David Gouldsborough
John Graby
Brendan Hackett
Adrian and Christine Hall
Carmel and Eamon Hanna
Claire Hanna
Patrick Harrington
Stephen Harrison
Hugh Haughton
Marie Heaney
Susan Hedigan
Richard Hutchings and
   Bryan Robinson
Kenneth Irvine
Bill and Maggie Jackson
Robert Johnstone

Fergal Keane
Liam Keaveney
Tim Kendall-Carpenter
Tony Kennedy
T. P. Kennedy
John Kerrigan
Paul Knolle
Nicholas Laird
Shane Lalor
Tessa Lang
George Larmour – The Ice
 Cream Man's Brother
Joep Leerssen
Jean Liddiard
Patricia Mallon
Barbara Mangles
Patricia McCarthy
Thomas McCarthy
Lucy McDiarmid
Frank McGuinness
Brian McLaughlin
Andrew McNeillie
Ruben Moi
Bel Mooney
Andrew Moorhouse
Jeffrey Morgan and Patricia Craig
Blake Morrison
Andrew Motion
Pat Moylan
Helen Mullarney

Alan Munton
Peter Murray
Sean O'Brien and Gerry Wardle
Bernard O'Donoghue
Jack O'Hare
Fintan O'Toole
David Oliver
Frank Ormsby
Nick Parfitt
James Peake
Shahed Power
Justin Quinn
Richard Russell
Lawrence Sail
Carole Satyamurti
David Schwartz
Roger Scott
Peter Spratt
Anne Tannahill
Oliver Taplin
David Taylor
D. G. Taylor
Paul Taylor
Roger Thorp
Anthony and Ann Thwaite
Denis Tuohy
Michael Viney
Ben Wagner
David Worthington